LOUISIANA FIDDLERS

LOUISIANA FIDDLERS

Ron Yule

With contributions from Bill Burge, Mary Evans,
Kevin S. Fontenot, Shawn Martin, and Billy McGee

UNIVERSITY PRESS OF MISSISSIPPI
JACKSON

www.upress.state.ms.us

The University Press of Mississippi is a member of
the Association of American University Presses.

Manufactured in the United States of America

First printing 2009
∞
Library of Congress Cataloging-in-Publication Data

Yule, Ron.
Louisiana fiddlers / Ron Yule, with contributions from Bill Burge ... [et al.].
p. cm. — (American made music series)
Includes bibliographical references and index.
ISBN 978-1-60473-295-5 (cloth : alk. paper) 1. Fiddlers—Louisiana—Biography.
I. Burge, Bill. II. Title.
ML398.Y83 2009
787.2092'2763—dc22
[B] 2009013372

British Library Cataloging-in-Publication Data available

CONTENTS

ACKNOWLEDGMENTS

No one ever accomplishes anything worthwhile without the help of those who have gone before, providing a documented foundation, and those who "dive in" on a venture and give their all with complete disregard for credit or adulation. They help to move the project forward because they believe in it and love it. It is a labor of love. Their work and thoughts are usually unheralded and unsung. With this in mind, I would like to acknowledge the persons who have made this project fly.

Thanks to the students of fiddle history who researched and established a foundation to tell the story of fiddlers and country musicians of old that could not presently be explored and told because of the passage of time. Thank you for interviewing and documenting these fiddlers while they were alive and studying them while research material was more readily available. And thanks for unselfishly sharing your materials for this project through publications, interviews, recordings, and archives.

The families of these fiddlers and musicians have been most gracious with the sharing of information, articles, interviews, pictures, and in many cases further research, all of which gave a merit of credibility to each article presented. This task would have been impossible without their assistance at every turn. The musicians themselves have unselfishly given of data and information, which provided color to the project and insight into the inner workings of the fiddling community of Louisiana.

Also included in these thanks are the libraries and archives, as well as their staffs: Allen Parish Library, Beauregard Parish Library, Bienville Parish Library, Calcasieu Parish Genealogical Library, Center for Louisiana Studies at Lafayette, Cajun French Music Association (CFMA) Hall of Fame (Eunice), CFMA Hall of Fame (Lake Charles Chapter), Desoto Parish Library, Grant

Parish Library, Jackson Parish Library, Louisiana Folklife Center at Northwestern State University, Louisiana State University at Shreveport Library, Louisiana Tech Library, McNeese State University Library, Newton County Library (Newton, Texas), Northwestern State University Library, Rapides Parish Library, Rapides Parish Genealogical Library, Red River Parish Library, Sabine Parish Library, Shreve Library, Tyrell Library (Beaumont, Texas), Vernon Parish Library, and Winn Parish Library.

Then there are the peripheral people who proofread, criticized, reviewed, suggested, repaired equipment, and created new ideas by being a part of the scene at all phases.

Thanks to all of you: Lisa Abney, Ph.D., and the Louisiana Folklife Center staff, Jeanette Aguillard, Johnnie Allen, Vorance Barzas, Fred Beavers, Katherine Beavers, Richard Bertrand, Mastern and June Brack, Ryan Brasseaux, Clyde Brewer, Elton Brindley, Gordon Broussard, Carrol Broussard, Andrew Brown, Bill Burge, Domenica Carriere, Clay Carter, Hadley Castille, Bornice Colvin Chellette, Fonda and Vernon Cogdill, Jimmy Coke, Carlton and Connie Cole, Steve Conn, George Conner, Mitchell Conner, Jennifer Cooper, Shelby Clark, Bill Clark, Louella and John Crochet, Luderin Darbone, Troy and Edwina DeRamus, Ed Dettenheim, Michael Doucet, Mary Evans, Lillian Fallin, Jeanne Farque, Lyle Ferbrache, Elsie Ferguson, Kevin S. Fontenot, Patricia Foreman, Tillman Franks, Eddie Friday, Bernella Frugé, Shamus Fuller, Charles Gardner, Wilson and Ron Granger, David Greely, Mary Grimsley, Oran Guidry Jr., Bob Hardin, Jean Harkness, Lester and Pearl Hood, James Jeter, Jan and Jewel Johnson, Patricia Johnson, Peter Jones, Lynn Kay, Eugene Kendrick, Bill Kenney, Tim Knight, Hermon and Marion Lasyone, Rick Lagneaux, Bill Landrum, Joe LeBlanc, Bobby Leger, Ervin Lejeune, Arthur Leger, John Leleux, Creola Lasyone Linzay, Mike Luster, Dot Manuel, Shawn Martin, Edy Mathews, Matt Mathews, Nicole Mathews, Billy McGee, Chuck Nation, Jim Nation, Cliff Newman, Maida Owens, Brenda Perkins, Thomas Philyaw, Tina Pilione, Letha Rogers, Elbert Richardson, Ralph Richardson, Murray Richardson, Susan Roach, Ph.D., and the staff at the North Louisiana Regional Folklife Program, Buzz and Winston Salard, Eric Salmon, Marc Savoy, Tim Savoy, Ken Smith, A. B. Sonnier, Delmar Sonnier, Beverly Spell, Joe Spence, Eloise Stack, Jean Strickland, Beecher Stuckey, Sharon Sweeters, Luke Thompson, Lynn Thompson, Curtis Thompson, Milton Vanicor, Jane Vidrine, Crawford Vincent, Paul Woodard, Emily Young, and Georgia Yule.

Thanks to the contributors of photos and images for this project: Arhoolie Records and Chris Strachwitz, Delores Barber, Fred Beavers, Troy Beavers

Family, David Minor Bennett, Ray Brandin, Clyde Brewer, Elton Brindley, Carrol Broussard, Andrew Brown, Bill Burge, Hadley Castille, Center for Louisiana Studies, CFMA Hall of Fame, Mary Evans, Elsie Ferguson, Pete Hardin Family, Jean Harkness, Bronice Colvin Chellette, Bill Clark, Jimmy Coke, Steve Conn and Molly Conn Wiley, Mitchell Conner, Fonda Cogdill, Luderin Darbone, Michael Doucet, Ivy Dugas, Lillian Fallin, Eddie Friday Family, Lyle Ferbrache, Dave Freeman, Bernella Frugé, Jerome Hammons, Jewel Johnson, Doug Kershaw, Richard Langley, Floyd LeBlanc Family, Arthur Leger, Ervin Lejeune, John Leleux, Louisiana Department of Tourism, Louisiana Folklife Center, Louisiana Pecan Festival, Creola Linzay, Ann Graham, Wilson Granger Family, Mary Grimsley, Oran Guidry Jr., Peter Jones, Jack Kay Family, Bill Landrum, Hermon and Marion Lasyone, Shawn Martin, Brenda Perkins, Billy McGee, J. J. Minion, Chuck Nation, Jim Nation, Tom Philyaw, Tina Pilione, Ralph Richardson, Susan Roach, Letha Rogers, H. P. and Winston Salard, Dave Simpson, Smithsonian Folkways Records, Delmar Sonnier, Joe Spence, Eloise Stack, Jean Strickland, Joe Suchanek, Tony Thibodeaux, Harry Todd, Luke Thompson, Judy Tyler, Pee Wee Whitewing, and Paul Woodard.

Thanks to everyone!

FIDDLERS' SELECTION

This book represents what could be termed the beginnings of a Louisiana Fiddlers Hall of Fame. The fiddlers profiled in this publication were the most influential to other Louisiana fiddlers, and affected the Louisiana music scene as a whole—in my opinion Louisiana's most notable during the twentieth century, whether their role and impact was as sideman, performing artist, recording artist, teacher, performer/luthier, or promoter/performer.

There was no formal selection committee to cite these fiddlers, but rather a constant review and request for input from knowledgeable musicians, music historians, fiddlers, and fiddle buffs throughout Louisiana. Had there been a formal committee, it would have included Fred Beavers, Clifford Blackmon, Mastern Brack, Andrew Brown, Richard and Anya Burgess, Hadley Castille, Michael Doucet, Jimmy Edwards, Mary Evans, Lyle Ferbrache, Kevin S. Fontenot, Eddie Friday, David Greely, Mary Grimsley, Bill Kirkpatrick, Hermon Lasyone, Mike Luster, Murray Richardson, Susan Roach, Buzz and Winston Salard, Tina Pilione, Ken and Buford Smith, Jane Vidrine, and Paul Woodard. These musicians and historians were instrumental in the selection process, fielding questions and volunteering input. In general, I made the final decision about inclusion in this book.

The criteria for selection encompassed a continual review of varied aspects including a fiddler's impact on other fiddlers as well as the listening public. All aspects of each artist's influence on fiddling in Louisiana were weighed, including stylistic differences between the fiddlers, which presented some concern: How do you compare a swing fiddler with a hoedown fiddler with a Cajun fiddler? A judge at a Louisiana fiddle contest might face the same problem. Although these fiddlers from different styles intermingled, very few learned the unique appointments of the other's style. After much pondering, the primary questions finally became: What impact did these fiddlers have on other fiddlers and the listening public, and what was their status within their own style(s)? What effect did they have on the fiddling tradition in Louisiana?

After years of research in the libraries and private collections of fiddlers, contact with family and researchers from California to Florida, countless hours of listening to and interviewing fiddlers and friends, I began to wonder why there is no Louisiana Fiddler's Hall of Fame. I reckon this may be a close facsimile. Here it is: a book that could probably be titled *Ron Yule's Louisiana Fiddlers Hall of Fame*.

A FEW NOTES

Over the course of review, many readers presented questions about terms used in the book and various interpretations. Hopefully this will clarify my meaning and position on these issues.

First the term *old time* or *old timey* addresses the fiddling tradition of the past in Louisiana and no other state. No attempt has been made to equate this term with the meaning it has come to hold in the last few years—namely, a music tradition steeped in mountain music, clawhammer banjos, and fiddling associated with the eastern United States. Although many of the fiddlers in this book and their families had roots in the eastern style, their own style developed as they migrated to Louisiana, basically a two-part fiddle tune form.

The term *pineywood fiddler* is used throughout the book, a self-descriptive term used by many Louisiana fiddlers who claimed they were just "pinewoods fiddlers."

A common term used in fiddle circles by Cajun musicians is *bassing*, which involves the playing of chords and rhythm behind the accordion or another fiddle. The technique is found in many different forms of fiddle music. It is usually termed second fiddle or called *seconding* when played in most fiddle music.

In the profiles of several north Louisiana fiddlers, the Old Fiddlers Club of Shreveport is mentioned. This famous group of fiddlers was also known at various times as the Old Fiddlers Club of North Louisiana or simply the Old Fiddlers Club. These terms are used interchangeably throughout the book.

No matter what style they played, the fiddlers profiled in this book are basically rural country fiddlers. The licks, bowings, and noting from one style can easily be adapted to another, and most have demonstrated this. Although many like to categorize fiddlers into various slots for convenience, in this book they will all be considered country fiddlers with a preference for one or more styles of playing throughout their careers. Nearly all started their careers in a rural setting.

This book addresses country fiddlers who learned the traditional way, "by ear"—although one fiddler in this lot quit "violining" and began fiddling late in life, becoming a respected fiddler among his peers.

A description of the sound produced by a particular fiddler, or my interpretation thereof, is seldom addressed in this book. Comments from others have been used, however. I feel this is a matter of personal taste and would not want to hinder the interpretation of anyone who listened to a recording of one of these fine fiddlers. It is probably a topic best left to discussion in another setting.

INTRODUCTION

By the beginning of the twentieth century Louisiana already had a rich fiddling tradition among its rural population. Musicians who had roots from all over the nation and world brought their fiddle traditions with them to the Bayou State. As noted in *My Fiddlin' Grounds*, this tradition was not unique to any one area but had followed the same general migratory flow that has been noted by Joyce Cauthen in *With Fiddle and Well-Rosined Bow: A History of Old-Time Fiddling in Alabama*, Earl Spielman in *Traditional North America Fiddling: A Methodology for the Historical and Comparative Analytical Style Study of Instrumental Music Tradition*, and Phillip Martin in *Farmhouse Fiddlers: Music and Dance Traditions in the Midwest.*

The Louisiana rural country music we know today had its roots in this tradition. At the turn of the century rural country music was mainly associated with the country dances, serenades, traveling troupes, and campfire and front porch pickings found throughout the farmland, logging camps, oil boom camps, and small towns of Louisiana. This music of the Louisiana country folk included both rural old time fiddling as well as Cajun music. The format was usually the same: a fiddle or fiddlers and possibly several accompanying rhythm instruments. Tunes and dances associated with the "old country" included reels, waltzes, schottisches, hornpipes, slides, jigs, mazurkas, and two-steps, many which did not survive the twentieth century. Not only would many disappear, but the fiddlers of the twentieth century soon began to play styles and tunes that a nineteenth-century fiddler could never have visualized.

Many fiddlers are believed to have migrated directly into the state from Europe at ports along the Gulf Coast. Fiddlers have been counted among the slaves on plantations throughout Louisiana, providing entertainment not only for themselves in their quarters but also for the plantation owners when important events occurred in the community. Several have noted that many plantation owners and workers taught slaves to play the fiddle. Acadians who migrated to Louisiana after expulsion from Nova Scotia in the mid-1700s were known to count the fiddle among their musical instruments by the late 1700s. During the 1800s the fiddle was a main music provider for country gatherings, country dances, and *bals de maison* among the Cajun community.

As the expanding population migrated to Louisiana overland from the East Coast and Midwest of the United States and territories of Texas, fiddle was the instrument of choice for several reasons. First, the fiddle was compact and could be stowed very easily among the family's meager possessions for transport to a new family home. Second, it provided a connection to the musical sounds of home and a memorable heritage, whether the British Isles or some other remembered European homeland. And third, fiddle music could be both melodic and rhythmic, especially when combined with many common household items such as spoons, straws, broom handles, and tubs that provided rhythm for the fiddle.

The major portion of studies into modern country music history in the United States usually begins with the advent of recorded rural country music in the early 1920s. These studies parallel the numerous major trend-setting changes in the sounds and presentation of rural country music to the listening public. The same trend is noted for Cajun music, or any music that has involved the rural country fiddler. The external forces that affected the rural country fiddler are the same that were observed during the growth of modern country music during the twentieth century.

Around the turn of the century, changes that began to occur at an accelerated rate eventually altered the position of the fiddle in rural country and Cajun music. Increased availability of accompanying musical instruments, availability of electricity and the unique lifestyle-changing devices that went with it, and increasing mobility provided by the automobile are examples noted by several authors. Pre–World War II influences by media conglomerates and increasing media attention to commercial appeal after the war had major ramifications on the state of fiddling throughout the nation.

Banjo, guitar, mandolin, and bass fiddle, all instruments of the string band, became readily available (especially through mail-order houses and mercantile outlets). This gave the fiddler a new rhythm section to accompany his tunes and altered the face of local country dances and eventually the dancehalls. In addition to being louder, the fusion of these sounds complemented the melody line, yielding a fuller sound for the listener than the previously heard sound of a lone fiddle.

With the availability of electricity and its expansion to the rural community came the radio, the record player, and eventually television that could be used in the home, reducing the need for Saturday night country house dances. With country recordings whose production began in the early 1920s, came the availability of "near instant" music which could be called on at any time, changing not only the entertainment choices of rural folk, but also changing the tune learning methods of fiddlers. Many new-style electrically amplified musical instruments found their way to the previously acoustic string band. Sound amplification via PA systems provided a means of presenting live music to the public in larger venues and formats. Changes continue today with newly created technologies.

Phillip Martin, in *Farmhouse Fiddlers,* cites the advent of the automobile as a major factor in the decline of home-based rural dance and fiddle music. The car provided the means of attending larger dances and the excitement of meeting more dancers at dances a farther distance away, ultimately diminishing the importance and impact of local house dances. By 1950 country house dances were essentially gone from the landscape throughout Louisiana.

With these changes came the introduction of new musical sounds to fiddlers who had been content to play traditional fiddle tunes in a simple setting. These influences brought new ideas in the form of Tin Pan Alley, swing, jazz, and blues as well as pop tunes of the time. Beginning in the mid-1920s and increasing after World War II, a boom in the commercial presentation of country music on recordings, radio and television, and live performances resulted in a major focus on the financial bottom line. The acoustic stringed instruments that had been major parts of early country music—namely the mandolin and fiddle—almost disappeared from the commercial scene by the late 1950s.

These changes occurred in every area of the United States, and Louisiana was no exception. Louisiana country music was affected not only by the normal changes but also by diverse populations that immigrated to the area. The influence of swing from southeast Texas and the Dallas/Fort Worth area was evident in the western corridor from Lake Charles to Shreveport. Blues, prevalent from Shreveport to New Orleans, became more prevalent in country music and altered both playing and listening styles. Coupled with the jazz influence rolling out of New Orleans, this created an even more diversified sound. Moreover, transplanted Acadians in the southern end of the state had their own unique style and musical base born of their French ancestry, and it was also changing.

Combinations of these changes further altered the sounds being heard by dancers and listeners. The introduction of the diatonic accordion by the Germans at the turn of the century completely changed the sound and presentation of rural French music. By the 1930s, these bands added other stringed instruments, introduced swing and eventually country music to their repertories, and began to perform in more formal dancehall settings. These forms are still a part of the Cajun music we hear today.

The old time fiddlers who inhabited the northern and western regions of Louisiana went through the same multiple changes, altering their approach and style with the introduction of new musical ideas. These changes can be noted in the early part of the century with string bands that added accompanying instruments such as guitar, mandolin, bass fiddle, and banjo. In the 1930s, with the presence of electricity and larger dancehalls came the introduction of electrically amplified instruments and a new music, western swing. Shreveport radio that had previously aired string band music from the Old Fiddlers Club, the Taylor-Grigg Melodymakers, and the Pelican Wildcats gave way to the sounds of country music influenced by blues and swing. Finally, postwar popular country and western music eventually melded into the sounds of pop music and rock and roll.

By the 1960s, old-time and Louisiana country fiddlers who had lost their central role in the newer styles of country music during the late forties and early fifties found a haven in the form of bluegrass music and the popular fiddle contests that emerged throughout Louisiana. With depopularization of the fiddle in mainstream country music came a decrease in the fiddle sound heard on recordings. Although not well researched, this one fact could possibly be directly responsible for the current loss of the fiddle tradition and the decrease in the number of fiddlers learning today.

The fiddlers presented in *Louisiana Fiddlers* have been major players in this explosion of changes in the country music sound and in many cases have had to adapt in order to continue their role in the country music of the period. In each era and area of Louisiana, the fiddler has taken his place in country music as a musical force, creator, and influence on the sound the public hears. Profiled in this publication are the fiddlers who were best at bringing country music to realization throughout its many changes, torchbearers who gave their unique contributions to the music and passed it on to succeeding generations. Some seemed to breeze through the changes and adaptations required to play, especially commercially; others held on to the old ways and continued to play music steeped in their ancestry. Each of these fiddlers has made his own special contribution to the country music of the twentieth century.

These profiles have been compiled over the last few years in the course of informally gathering data for the archives of several centers of music history study in Louisiana: Louisiana Folklife Center, Northwestern State University, Natchitoches; McNeese State University Archives, Lake Charles; The Center for Louisiana Studies, University of Louisiana at Lafayette; North Louisiana Regional Folklife Center at Louisiana Tech, Ruston; and the Cajun French Music Association, Lake Charles Chapter. Profiles include most of Louisiana's finest fiddlers and represent the first biographical data presented in print about many of these influential musicians and the effect they had on both the stabilization and movement within the changing country music circles of twentieth-century Louisiana. As country music moved from a rural to an urban setting and a local to a regional, national, and finally global setting, these fiddlers made their mark within these changes.

Many, such as 1920s fiddlers Cecil Burge (Singer) and Hiter Colvin (Dubach), traveled the circuit playing on early radio stations, on the streets, and in small clubs throughout northern and western Louisiana. They were some of the first professional Louisiana fiddlers.

Other early fiddlers John W. Daniel (Pineville), S. R. Patterson (Shreveport), Dr. J. E. Richardson (Shreveport), Henry Welch (Dodson), W. E. Caston (Red Oak), and Fleecy Philyaw (Red Oak) were old-time fiddlers who promoted square dancing and were instrumental in the success of early-twentieth-century fiddle contests in northern Louisiana. Most played on early Shreveport radio and were instrumental in the success of commercial country music beginning in the mid-1920s.

Early old-time fiddlers Varise Conner (Lake Arthur) and Aud Lewing (Many) played at country dances and performed throughout their local community, opting not to play professionally. Their influence on future fiddlers in the latter part of the century created a lasting legacy for these local fiddlers.

With the 1930s country music was affected by changes in recording, transportation, and communication. The careers of fiddlers "Lonnie" Hall (Shreveport), "Preacher" Harkness (Vivian), Eddie Friday (Pleasant Hill), "Peanut" Conn (Pineville), and Luderin Darbone (Hackberry) were directly involved with country music during this period. Several of these fiddlers reached their stature playing with some of the most recorded and noted bands of the era.

The period following the end of World War II brought major changes to Louisiana country music; fiddlers Jack Kay (Leesville), Bob Henderson (Gonzales), Eddie Raxsdale (Alexandria), "Dobber" Johnson (Shreveport), "Tex" Grimsley (Shreveport), Bill Kirkpatrick (Shreveport), Hank Strickland (Many), Ralph Richardson (Choupique), Abe Manuel (Lake Charles), and Pete Hardin (Haynesville) were a major part of that movement. Each was instrumental in one way or another with the success of country music, country music shows, dancehalls, and local radio stations, continuing the fiddler's newfound position as a band sideman.

Following these great fiddlers in the fifties and sixties were more pioneers: Warren Ferrier (Montgomery), Paul Woodard (Arcadia), Elton Brindley (Starks), Mastern Brack (Evans), Troy Beavers (Homer), Fred Beavers (Simsboro), and Ray Beebe (Lena) carried the fiddle sound into the modern era as it was being quieted on many country music fronts.

Traditional Cajun music in south Louisiana was carried on by the efforts of fiddlers who played the Cajun tunes and rejected the influence of swing and country. The "Dean of Cajun Music," Dennis McGee (Eunice), as well as Wade Frugé (Eunice), held on to the old ways and eventually influenced countless younger players in the latter part of the century who were interested in the Cajun fiddling of the 1800s.

J. B. Fuselier (Oberlin), Wilson Granger (Durald), Lionel Leleux (Leleux), Dewey Balfa (Gran Louis) and Robert Bertrand (Hathaway) shared the stage with many Cajun/swing/country fiddlers although their styles remain basically in the earlier traditions of Cajun music.

Other Cajun-style fiddlers—Harry Choates (Cow Bayou), Hadley Castille (Opelousas), Leo Soileau (Ville Platte), Rufus Thibodeaux (Ridge), Tony Thibodeaux (Scott), Merlin Fontenot (Eunice), "Cheese" Read (Mamou), "Doc" Guidry (Scott), Doug Kershaw (Lake Arthur), and Floyd LeBlanc (Mermentau)—with careers beginning in the thirties, 'forties, and fifties were deeply influenced by the more modern sounds of swing and country although they continued to play Cajun music. Many who were influenced by sounds outside their native Cajun land had lengthy careers playing music on a regional and national scale as well as throughout Louisiana.

Two modern Cajun fiddlers, Michael Doucet (Scott) and David Greely (Denham Springs), studied the earlier master Cajun fiddlers with rare passion, although they were influenced by other styles. They continue playing for worldwide audiences and influencing today's fiddlers.

Bluegrass fiddlers Al Jordan (Calhoun), Jewel Lasyone (Dry Prong), Chuck Nation (Denham Springs), Kennie Lamb (Baton Rouge), Buzz Salard (Natchitoches), and Winston Salard (Baton Rouge) were all pioneers in this budding style of mountain music beginning in the fifties and sixties.

By the 1970s, the modern era of the fiddle contest became the stage for many. Ken Smith (Kinder), Curry Perkins (Reeves), and Mary Grimsley (Shreveport) were instrumental in the success of the contests, both as competitors and as teachers. Also sharing the stage with these rural country and Cajun fiddlers of the twentieth century are Creole/zydeco fiddler Canray Fontenot (Welsh) and blues fiddler "Gatemouth" Brown (Vinton).

Each of these pioneering fiddlers affected and influenced country music in Louisiana. These players were the Fiddler's Fiddlers—the ones sought out, studied, and listened to by other fiddlers. Louisiana rural, country, and Cajun music would not be the same without their contributions.

RON YULE

LOUISIANA FIDDLERS

Photo courtesy of Louisiana Department of Tourism/Susan Roach.

DEWEY BALFA

(1927–1993) Grand Louis

Born on March 20, 1927, Dewey Balfa first started learning the fiddle around the age of nine from hearing his father, Charles, play Cajun music not only on fiddle but other instruments as well. Dewey was a part of the fourth generation of known Cajun musicians in the Balfa family. His first efforts on the fiddle were noted in his July 18, 1980, interview with Tim Knight:

> *There was no lessons given for you to learn to play an instrument. You picked it up and you did the best you can if you could. . . . I can remember the time when I was about 12 or 13 years old. Back then, they'd thresh rice, they'd have a big haystack. A lot of times my old mama would say, 'Turn loose of that cat, get out the house, I can't stand it anymore." . . . 'cause I'as trying to learn the fiddle back then. I'd go to the south part of the haystack and play my fiddle (because it was warmer in the winter months).*

Balfa's instructional LP, 1977. Courtesy of Smithsonian Folkways Records.

Dewey soon started playing house dances around the community with his brothers: Will also on fiddle, Rodney on guitar, Burkeman on triangle, and friend Hadley Fontenot on accordion. They called themselves the Musical Brothers, sometimes playing as a string band without the accordion. He was also influenced by other fiddle giants including J. B. Fuselier, Leo Soileau, Bob Wills, and Harry Choates.

At the age of 16, toward the end of World War II, Dewey left Grand Louis to work in the Consolidated Ship Yard in Port Arthur, Texas. Soon after, he joined the merchant marine, spending three and a half years at sea before returning to Louisiana and the music and culture he loved. After being away from Cajun music and playing other styles of music during his tenure in the merchant marine, he made one trip home on vacation and heard a Cajun dance band. This rekindled his interest in the Cajun style of music and he left the "sea," returning home to play music.

Balfa rejoined his band of brothers, including Harry, who performed occasionally on guitar. They sometimes played as many as eight dances a week and still held down their full-time jobs. The Balfa Brothers worked a circuit across Evangeline, St. Landry, Jeff Davis, and Acadia Parishes, mainly playing dancehalls and clubs. This lasted about a year before they laid music aside.

In 1948, Dewey married Hilda Frugé and returned to the farm, curtailing his musical adventures as much as possible. By 1952, he started selling insurance for Automotive Life, a job he kept until he retired. To make ends meet he eventually drove an Evangeline Parish school bus and owned a discount furniture store in Mamou.

Arhoolie LP/CD 312. Courtesy of Arhoolie Records.

Dewey played with other groups beside the Balfa Brothers and began recording for the Khoury label in the early 1950s. Tunes recorded in these early years included "La Valse de Bon Baurche," "Le Two Step de Ville Platte," "La Valse de Courage," and "La Valse de Temper Tate" with Elise Deshotel; "LSU French Waltz," "Carolina Blues," "La Valse de Holly Beach," and "Shamrock Waltz" with Nathan Abshire. Nathan and Dewey worked the Lake Charles scene in the early 1950s. Milton Vanicor recalls that, while he was playing with Iry Lejeune, many times Nathan Abshire and Dewey, after playing at Jones Bar north of Lake Charles, would come to the Shamrock Club in north Lake Charles and play until 1:00 a.m. The two groups would join in a jam session everyone enjoyed. Along with his brothers, Dewey played some with J. Y. Sebastian from Grand Prairie and the Louisiana Rhythmaires. Vorance Barzas recalls Dewey riding to their home on horseback to play at jam sessions.

This playing with various groups continued until 1964 when Ralph Rinzler came to Louisiana looking for traditional grassroots music for performances at the Newport Folk Festival in Rhode Island. Paul Tate Sr. met with Rinzler, and they made a tour of south Louisiana looking for performers of authentic Cajun culture and music. Together they chose musicians to travel to the festival and represent south Louisiana.

The first band included Gladius Thibodeaux, Louis "Vinesse" Lejeune (a cousin of Iry Lejeune) and Revon Reed on triangle, as well as Dewey. Nick Pittman describes the scene on this first historic occasion in the *Times of Acadiana*, April 18, 2006.

> *When the guitarist couldn't make it, Dewey Balfa volunteered as a last-minute replacement. It would be the largest crowd any of them had ever played for as their careers were spent playing to audiences numbering in the hundreds at house dances, family gatherings and nightclubs. When the band stepped out on stage it was before 17,000 music fans all searching for something new and fresh in an untouched form of American music. Many in the crowd had never heard Cajun music or knew little about it. Others who had heard it called it chanky-chank (a derogatory term at the time) and were certain it would be laughed off the stage.*
>
> *The band opened with "Grand Mamou" and quickly received a standing ovation from the crowd of newly converted Cajun music fans that would not let them off the stage. Not long after, Balfa would pen the "Newport Waltz," a song recounting the experience; first recorded on their debut full length album for Swallow Records in 1965. Three years later, Balfa returned with brothers Rodney and Will, Hadley Fontenot and his daughter Nelda. For him, the trips to Newport were eye-opening experiences that would shape the rest of his life.*

Dewey began to travel throughout the United States, Canada, and Europe playing Cajun music for audiences hungry for their brand of music. These mid-1960s journeys sparked an avid interest in Cajun culture that has continued until today, opening the door for other acts from the area that soon followed. The Mamou Cajun Band performed at Newport in 1965 and featured Adam Landreneau on fiddle, Cyprien Landreneau on accordion, and Revon Reed on triangle. Creole musicians Bois Sec Ardoin and Canray Fontenot performed there in 1966. The Musical Brothers were invited to Newport in 1967 and continued playing throughout the country for concerts and festivals like the 1969 Festival of American Folklife in Washington, D.C., as well as throughout Europe.

Their first professional recording was on the Swallow label, "Le Valse de Bambocheurs"/"Indian on a Stump." Swallow followed with two LPs, including *Balfa Brothers Play Traditional Cajun Music*. In 1972 the Balfas appeared in the Les Blank documentary *Spend It All,* introducing a new generation to the lively Cajun sound. Several more recordings included *The Cajuns* on Sonet and *The Good Times Are Killing Me* on Swallow. The latter included the soundtrack for the documentary of the same name and featured a group comprised of Dewey, Rodney, accordion player Nathan Menard, fiddler Dick Richard, J. W. Pelsia on steel guitar, Austin Broussard on drums, and Rodney's son Tony on bass guitar playing some of the more nontraditional sounds of modern Cajun music.

Hadley Castille, Harold Fontenot, unidentified, Elrige Aguillard, and Dewey Balfa. Photo courtesy of Hadley Castille.

Nathan Abshire, who had worked with Dewey off and on throughout southwest Louisiana, toured and worked with the brothers. Ray Abshire, Nathan's cousin, also worked with the group from 1969 to 1975, alternating with Marc Savoy. They toured extensively throughout the United States and internationally from Leone and Bordeaux, France, to the Olympics in Mexico City, where they played the Olympics Festival in 1968.

The family that had entertained so many was struck with tragedy when, in 1978, Rodney and Will died in an accident while driving to Avoyelles Parish, near Bunkie, to visit family members. The next year, Dewey's wife, Hilda, died as a result of trichinosis. Despite these setbacks, Dewey continued performing, using Cajun musicians such as Dick Richard, Tony Balfa, Marc Savoy, and Ally Young.

Numerous recordings were produced by various combinations of musicians, and albums and singles were released on Swallow and Folkways. The trio of Marc Savoy, D. L. Menard, and Balfa recorded *Underneath the Green Oak Tree* on Arhoolie. In 1976 Dewey joined forces with noted folk performer

Tracy Schwarz and made two instructional Cajun fiddle albums, the first of their kind. Ten years later they rejoined to record another album.

There are numerous documentaries featuring Dewey, his Musical Brothers, and the French culture. They also did the soundtrack for *Southern Comfort*, a movie set in the swamps of the Atchafalaya Basin.

After his trip to Newport in 1964, Dewey became known as the "cultural ambassador" for Cajun French culture. His untiring efforts continued until his death on June 17, 1993. Besides his workshops and instructional records, he fielded a number of now-famous fiddlers as his disciples, including David Greely, Michael Doucet, Steve Riley, Peter Schwarz, Courtney Granger, Dirk Powell, Kevin Wimmer, and countless others.

Via the "folk artists in the schools," countless workshops at festivals throughout the country, and other projects through grants from the National Endowment for the Arts, his influence has been felt by throngs of Cajun music lovers. In 1988, Balfa was named adjunct professor of Cajun music at the University of Southwestern Louisiana.

Besides his induction into the Cajun French Music Association Halls of Fame in Eunice and Lake Charles, Dewey was awarded a National Heritage Fellowship by the National Endowment for the Arts. Numerous other awards have followed.

At the turn of the century, Dewey's daughter, Christine, began to follow in her father's footsteps. She carried the torch by helping start the Dewey Balfa Cajun and Creole Heritage Week, a weeklong camp of studies into Cajun history, culture, and musicianship held annually at Chicot State Park, north of Ville Platte. Dewey's wishes for his Cajun musical heritage continue to unfold.

Interviews by Ron Yule: Vorance Barzas (7-15-2007) and Milton Vanicor (3-12-2006).
Interview by Tim Knight: Dewey Balfa (7-18-1980) at Port Neches, Texas.

References

Ancelet, Barry. "Dewey Balfa: A Cultural Ambassador." *Accordions, Fiddles, Two-Step, and Swing,* Ryan A. Brasseaux and Kevin S. Fontenot, editors. Center for Louisiana Studies, Lafayette, 2006.

Pittman, Nick. "Remembering The Balfas." *Times of Acadiana*, Lafayette, Louisiana, April 18, 2006.

Savoy, Ann. *Cajun Music: A Reflection of a People*. Bluebird Press, Eunice, Louisiana, 1984.

Schwarz, Tracy. Liner notes. *Cajun Legend Dewey Balfa and Friends.* Swallow Records, 1986.

Yule, Ron, et al. *Cajun French Music Association Hall of Fame, Lake Charles Chapter.* Fiddle Country Publishing, DeRidder, Louisiana, 2004.

Photo courtesy of Susan Roach.

FRED BEAVERS

(1932–) Simsboro

Fred Beavers is mostly noted for his fine contest fiddling, but has played many fiddle styles of country music from bluegrass to country to swing. Born in 1932 at Homer, he began playing the guitar at the age of ten on a Gene Autry guitar. He struggled to learn, and a conflict over the guitar with his father led to his quitting. At the age of 13, he decided to take up the fiddle and began by learning "Deep in the Heart of Texas." His family had fiddlers on both sides, being one of the more respected fiddling families in north Louisiana. Many fiddlers remember their first contact with the instrument as hearing the Beavers from Claiborne Parish and learning from this association.

Fred struggled with the fiddle and finally began to learn tunes like "Soldier's Joy" and "Arkansas Traveler" from his maternal grandfather, Tom Owens. Before his last year in high school, he spent the summer playing with his

Grey Eagles: Sam Raborn, Les Tucker, Leslie Raborn, and Fred Beavers. Rebel State Park. Photo courtesy of Louisiana Folklife Center, NSU.

cousin, Troy Beavers, in his band called the Southern Swing Boys. They played around Homer and as far west as Bossier City and had a weekly Saturday radio show on KVMA in Magnolia, Arkansas. Fred recalled that Pete Hardin, one of his fiddling heroes, would sit in with them when they played around Bossier City. After high school he played with a few groups around Homer, but when he married he played very little for the next ten years.

In 1962 Fred moved to Ruston and met Paul Woodard, a noted north Louisiana fiddler who not only learned the traditional style of fiddling from his family, but expanded his knowledge of the instrument by becoming a trained violinist at Louisiana Tech. Paul convinced Fred to take up the fiddle again, and they began to play on the Homer Hayride, a weekly show featuring country and western music.

Two other fiddlers who commanded Fred's attention during this period were Lonnie Hall and Preacher Harkness. Both had played with Bob and Joe Shelton and the Sunshine Boys and had appeared on many recordings, radio stations, and shows around Dallas and Shreveport.

Paul also introduced him to the fiddling contest world by taking him to the Gilmer, Texas, contest in the fall of 1963. Fred immediately became enamored with this style and the playing of Texas fiddle champions Benny Thomasson, Norman and Vernon Solomon, Louis and Major Franklin, Dick Barrett, and

Fred and Ben Robinson in Fred's fiddle shop. Photo courtesy of Susan Roach.

Texas Shorty. For the next ten years this became an annual trek, and he ardently studied these Texas masters as well as he could from afar. He entered the contest each year and eventually won seventh place in 1971—a major accomplishment against this competition. He attended every contest he could in Texas, including those at Crockett and Athens. During this period he also traveled and played with Lonnie Hall, who attended these contests.

The contest scene in Louisiana was meager compared to that in Texas, but began to increase by the early 1970s. At that time it consisted of a few parish fairs and a few festivals. The Louisiana State Fair had even dropped its contest, which had been a tradition from 1912 to the beginning of World War II.

Southern Swing Boys, 1949. Photo courtesy of Troy Beavers family.

Traditionally, Louisiana fiddlers played in the typical style of two-part tunes in a simple country/hoedown fashion, many being influenced by recordings featuring Nashville fiddlers on square dance records. Fred began to introduce the Texas style of fiddling to contests in Louisiana by learning tunes like "Sally Goodin" and "Grey Eagle" with their many ornate, nonrepetitious variations. Although he still retained some of the old style in his playing and did not learn the style exactly the way the Texas fiddlers played it, his focus was on the Texas style of presentation and arrangement. By 1970, when fiddle contests began to take bloom in Louisiana, Fred had a good hold on the style and everyone took notice of his playing. He set Louisiana contest fiddling on a new path and it was here to stay.

In 1964 he and his family moved to Choudrant, and Fred joined the staff band at the Twin Cities Jamboree in Monroe. The band included Lamon Godwin (steel), Elic Myatt (bass and guitar), Jack Hollingsworth (rhythm guitar and vocals), and Fred (fiddle). At this show Fred met the Bluegrass Riders, who were legends in north Louisiana bluegrass circles. Members included Pappy Booth, Al Jordan, George Mercer, Ralph Tucker, and Calvin Free. Also during this period Doc Savage, a noted local instrument maker and picker, was playing the rodeo circuit and Fred joined him when he could. Fred was becoming a versatile fiddler, learning all styles of fiddle necessary to play in this northern Louisiana region.

After the building that held the Twin Cities Jamboree was destroyed in 1969, Fred continued to play in fiddle contests and around the area at jam sessions. By the mid-1970s bluegrass festivals were going strong and he attended and played in many of the famous all-night jam sessions with Pappy Booth, Al Jordan, Bobby Tucker, Joe Spence, and Mickey Davis. He was learning the bluegrass style of fiddling popularized at that time by Kenny Baker, Blaine Sprouse, Bobby Hicks, and Vassar Clements. He attended festivals at Pollock, Natchitoches, Coushatta, and Bossier City when his work schedule permitted.

In the late 1970s Howdy Edwards, a local swing fiddler, moved and left a void in a new band Jack Hollingsworth had started. They were a part of the Over 50 Club and played for senior citizens at the Civic Center in Monroe, as well as the Senior Citizen Centers in Monroe, Rayville, and Benoit. Fred joined them and also played with The Twin City Jamboree Boys until 1989, when his mother's health problems heightened.

By the mid-1980s, Fred was wanting to return to his real love, string band music and Texas fiddle tunes, so he formed the Grey Eagles Stringband, which included, over the years, Paul Woodard, Brandy Beavers (his granddaughter), Leslie and Sam Raborn, Ben Robinson, and Les Tucker. They appeared at workshops, local shows, nursing homes, the New Orleans Jazz and Heritage Festival, the Dixie Jamboree, the NSU/Natchitoches Folklife Festival, and the Louisiana Folklife Festival.

Fred is also a master violinmaker and repairman, and has kept fiddles repaired for north Louisiana fiddlers over the last thirty years. Not only has he been a major force in the preservation of fiddle music by performing, but he has given much time to demonstrating his folkcraft at folklife workshops. Sometimes he appeared with Lionel Leleux, the noted Cajun fiddle maker and repairman whose work Fred respected. In 2001, he received a grant from the Louisiana Division of Arts to teach fiddle making to Ben Robinson, an up-and-coming Louisiana fiddler.

Fred has been honored with several awards including being crowned the Louisiana State Fiddle Champion in 1991 and 2003. He was the Senior Division champion on six different occasions. In 2002 he was inducted into the Hall of Master Folk Artists at Northwestern State University. His greatest legacy has been his introduction of the Texas style of contest fiddling to north Louisiana fiddlers and his preservation, teaching, and performance of this music within the Louisiana fiddle tradition.

Interviews by Ron Yule: Fred Beavers (2-13-2004 and 6-5-2005).

Photo courtesy of Troy Beavers family.

TROY BEAVERS

(1921–1980) Homer

The Beavers family is central to the fiddle tradition of north Louisiana. As far back as anyone can recall, there has been a fiddler in the family, and Troy Beavers, one of the premier members of this clan, was one of the most noted. As a youngster, he fell in love with the sound of the instrument from hearing his uncles, John and Louis Beavers, and father, Jeff, play around the house, in Homer. Fred Beavers, a cousin, notes that Jeff was a good hoedown fiddler with good timing and rhythm. Troy's wife, Katherine, recalls hearing tales that Troy would "run his mother crazy" playing and practicing around the house.

Until his twenties, his playing was confined to front-porch picking and playing with his family. He then became enamored with the sounds of the country and swing fiddle, loving the twin fiddle sounds of the country and swing bands he heard on the radio. This is the basic playing style he developed, instead of the old-timey hoedown fiddling of his ancestors. Fred notes that he played some hoedowns like "Soldier's Joy" and "Arkansas Traveler," but usually played pop and swing tunes like "What About You."

In the early 1940s Troy was drafted into the air force, and was a photographer on a bomber taking pictures of bombing raids. When he returned to Homer, he took up the fiddle again and pursued playing in a band. Sometime in the mid-to-late 1940s he joined the Louisiana Swing Boys, a band headed by nonmusician Horace "Rusty" Gilbert. Besides other local bookings, they appeared on the Ruston Hardware Jamboree, a weekly show on KRUS, Ruston. Band members included Frank Corbin, Minden (bass); John O. Wright, Minden (guitar); "Rusty" Gilbert (announcer); Billie Reeves, Minden (guitar and vocals); Troy (fiddle); W. L. "Dub" Thomas, Homer (vocals and guitar), and Tommy Tomlinson, Minden (lead guitar).

That band was short-lived, and in 1949 Troy formed the Southern Swing Boys, a group that played in clubs around the Minden/Bossier City/Shreveport area. Some of their favorite places to play were the clubs on the Bossier Strip. For a while, they played on the radio at KVMA in Magnolia, Arkansas, and KTBS in Shreveport. Troy was noted for being a good harmony player and utilized the twin fiddle sounds he heard when Haynesville fiddler Pete Hardin was in the band. Over the years Troy used different musicians, including Pete Hardin (twin fiddle), Cotton Quarles (steel), Dale Kelly (lap steel), Eugene Kendrick (upright bass), Jerry Kennedy (guitar), and Fred Beavers (rhythm guitar). Fred recalls the band playing tunes like "Back Up and Push" and "Draggin' the Bow," but most of the numbers were pop, country, or swing. Their repertoire mainly included the country songs popularized by Hank Williams, Ernest Tubb, Red Foley, and other country and radio stars.

By 1952 the group had disbanded. Fred quit playing for a while, and Tommy Tomlinson began playing lead guitar with the legendary Johnny Horton and Tillman Franks on the Louisiana Hayride and on the road. Tommy stayed with Horton until they were in the eastern Texas car accident that cost Horton his life and Tomlinson his leg.

Troy began working for the Claiborne Butane Company, Homer Electric Plant, and eventually went into the air conditioner business. He mainly played at numerous jam sessions and get-togethers with his friends. Katherine recalls they had pickers at their home all the time. She says, "They'd gather up and here they'd go. They always had a good time. I was always envious because I couldn't play something and join in with them."

Ed Dettenheim, who had played guitar on the Louisiana Hayride, recalls the many jams they had at the "Y" (in the woods), at Corney Lake, the Homer

Louisiana Swing Boys, 1948: Frank Corbin, John Wright, Rusty Gilbert, Jim ____ (KRUS announcer), Billie Reeves, Troy Beavers, Dub Thomas, and Gerald Tomlinson. Photo courtesy of the Troy Beavers family.

Electric Plant, and at Troy's and Eugene Kendrick's homes. Pickers included Eugene Kendrick, Jim Kendrick, "Dub" Thomas, Tommy Gore, Fred Beavers, and Paul Woodard. The focus of their playing continued to be swing and pop tunes like "Royal Hawaiian Hotel," "When They Baptized Sister Lucy Lee," and "Texas Bluebonnet Girl" and other western tunes. Ed notes that Troy loved it when Paul Woodard came by because he played tenor on his fiddle to create the twin fiddle sound. Ed describes Troy's fiddling: "He had as smooth of a touch and a perfect ear as any I ever heard."

In the 1960s Troy began attending fiddle contests with Fred. They attended and placed in contests in Gilmer, Texas, and all over northern Louisiana at Shongaloo, the Poke Salad Festival in Blanchard, Monroe, and Hammell Park. Fred recounts that Troy was a good waltz player and played "The Waltz You Saved for Me" and "Goodnight Waltz" as well as Howdy Forrester's "Cathy with the Raven Black Hair." Mary Grimsley, of Shreveport, competed against him on numerous occasions and notes his "Morning Glory Waltz " was second to none. She said, "He was a good fiddler, but he did not play contest style."

In the mid-1960s Troy joined Fred Beavers, Paul Woodard, Dub Thomas, and Ed Dettenheim on the stage of the Homer Hayride, a weekly country music show. This lasted a couple of years.

Troy's two sons have carried on the musical legacy of their father, but on a smaller scale. Johnny plays guitar and joins in regular jam sessions around Minden; Tommy learned the bass and guitar but seldom plays anymore.

In 1980 Troy passed away, as a result of a traffic accident. Troy was a local legend and is still known around this north Louisiana community as the "King of Smooth."

Interviews by Ron Yule: Fred Beavers (6-19-2006), Katherine Beavers (10-18-2004), Ed Dettenheim (10-18-2004), Eugene Kendrick (10-21-2004), and Bill Kirkpatrick (6-20-2008).

Reference

Franks, Tillman. *I Was There When It Happened.* Sweet Dreams Publishing, Many, Louisiana, 2000.

Photo courtesy of Susan Roach.

RAY BEEBE

(1915–1980) Lena

Ray Beebe was a fiddler extraordinaire. He not only played in the style common to the hill country around Lena, but he sang many of the old tunes while he was playing, a feat in itself. He was famous for his love of the instrument and showmanship while performing in any venue, whether it was a stage show or a dance.

The Beebe family attended all the old country dances around Lena and Ray became interested in the fiddle and its lively sound. At the age of six, he made a cigar-box fiddle and began sawing around on it. He was learning to play a little when, as luck would have it, a ruckus at one of the dances produced his first real fiddle. Dave Rachal held a dance at his home and during the dance a fight broke out. During the melee one fiddler hit another over the head with his fiddle, and rendered it unplayable. Dave had remembered Ray's intense interest and gave the fiddle to him. Ray painstakingly restored it and began to

Vernon Cogdill and Ray Beebe, 1940s. Photo courtesy of Fonda Cogdill.

play on it. His brother, Percy said, "He would go anywhere he heard of a fiddler so he could learn more tunes. Even if he only knew a couple of tunes." His main sources for learning were Lena fiddler Charlie Guin, who was in his seventies at the time, and Carl Watson from nearby Janie. Both were well-known country dance fiddlers from the Rapides and Natchitoches Parishes region of central Louisiana.

By his teens, Ray had learned enough tunes and was ready to get his feet wet playing country dances with his brother Percy seconding on the guitar. Others who played with him were Aubrey Watson and Hermon Lasyone. Percy recalls that they would sometimes walk four or five miles to dances around Lena, Sharp, and Flatwoods. He said, "They'd pass the hat and we'd get a bunch of pennies and nickels."

Ray joined the military in 1942, serving in the navy. He was involved in the invasion at Normandy and also served in the Pacific campaign. He was known to play with other musicians on the ship, his fiddle never far away. Percy recalls that, when the Big Three (Franklin Roosevelt, Josef Stalin, and Winston Churchill) met on the battleship where he was stationed, Ray played the fiddle

North Louisiana Stringband, 1980: Don Mayo, Herbert Meche, Troy DeRamus, and Ray Beebe. Photo courtesy of Susan Roach.

for them along with some fellow servicemen. This was one of the highlights of his musical career. After World War II he remained in the National Guard for eighteen years.

Troy DeRamus recalls Ray's love for the fiddle in *Louisiana I Love*, an unpublished account he wrote for one of his books:

> *In October of 1945, service men and women were being discharged from different branches of the services by the multiplied thousands, all scampering to get home and to mama's home cooking. Little Ray Beebe, a navy man, had made his separation from the service in New Orleans and was aboard a bus docked in the Baton Rouge terminal waiting to depart north through Alexandria, Lena Station, and on to Shreveport. The bus was loaded with service men and college students all making their way home; the students for a holiday and the discharged veterans for "good."*
>
> *A student from Loyola University of New Orleans, Andrew Fowler, was headed to LeCompte and a much-earned rest from his studies. I sat spellbound one day when he was telling a tale about a fiddle player, who had returned to this bus after a pit stop in Baton Rouge, with a fiddle case under his arm. He said his name was Beebe and he handled the case as if it were worth its weight in gold. I myself had just met Ray Beebe in Aunt Lucy's Café, in Pineville, a short time back, and he had*

that fiddle case under his right arm, holding it as if it were an heirloom from his grandfather.

Fowler said, "There were as many standing as there were seated. I was lucky I found a seat, but Beebe had to stand. He took from the case a fiddle with rosin covering the top, as if it had been played night and day for ten years. Beebe tightened his bow hair and that fiddle came alive with 'Down Yonder,' then 'Sally Goodin,' 'Take Me Back to Tulsa,' fiddling while he sang and did a little dance." Fowler said, "He was still going strong when he pulled the cord stopping the bus at the Laumori Road that led to his home North of LeCompte."

After returning home, Ray played with Al Robinson at shows and on KALB. Al was a songwriter and penned "Alexandria Gal," which they promoted when they went to Nashville to try to get on the Grand Ole Opry. He joined Jelly Elliott and the Singing Cowboys and Clyde Baum and the Happy Hillbillies for a while, playing mainly on radio and at school shows around central Louisiana. In the late 1940s he began playing square dances with Canadian-born caller Mel Hinkley at Camp Polk, Myles Park, Camp Beauregard, and other places around central Louisiana. This live square dance troupe included Eddie Friday, Louis Peck, Lammie Gaspard, Eddie Raxsdale, and Hermon Lasyone.

In the early 1950s he joined the staff of the Old Barn Dance and played on Saturday at the square dances and on KSYL. Anywhere anybody needed him he would go. He played everywhere from the Bridges Club in Cloutierville to Dubé Hall in Alexandria. During the 1950s he played with Cliff Carnahan and Doug Lee and the Blues Chasers at the Catholic Hall in Cloutierville. In 1960 he worked at the 112 Club for Leon Melder, when Leon cut his hand and could not play the fiddle. He continued to play at the Moose Lodge and other clubs after the closure of the Old Barn Dance and on KALB television with different groups.

During the years following World War II, Ray had a television repair shop in Ball, as well as being in the National Guard. He even worked as a Pentecostal preacher (in Texas) and in the postal service for a while.

In the late 1960s Ray entered numerous contests in the central Louisiana area, winning at the Pecan Festival at Colfax, Natchitoches Christmas Festival, Fish Creek Campground, and Jena. In 1970 he won the inaugural Louisiana State Championship at Boyce. He continued to enter and place in contests until the late 1970s.

The last years of his life were spent playing at a Saturday night show in the Lena area and at the Old Barn in Boyce with Troy DeRamus and the Big D

Band and eventually the North Louisiana Stringband. This acoustic ensemble included Herman White, Don Mayo, and Herbert Meche, as well as Ray and Troy. They played at the Old Barn, local festivals, and the Natchitoches Folklife Festival. In 1980 the group recorded an LP, *The North Louisiana Stringband*, under the direction of the Louisiana Folklife Center at Natchitoches. Besides Ray and the North Louisiana Stringband, it also featured Tex Grimsley, Eddie Raxsdale, and Dennis Elliott, three of Louisiana's best fiddlers. The CD is still available from the Louisiana Folklife Center, Northwestern State University, Box 3663, Natchitoches, Louisiana, 71457-9980.

To hear Ray play was a throwback to the fiddlers of yesteryear. He was a real showman and sang and played many of the old fiddle tunes. Some of his favorites were "Whoa Mule Whoa," "Ida Red," and "Boil Them Cabbage Down," which he sang while playing the fiddle. One of his favorite tunes was "Ragtime Annie," which Troy DeRamus said he played when he won the championship in 1970. He could adapt to and learn any style, as Ken Smith, the five-time Louisiana state champion, noted in a recent interview. He could play several tunes, including "New Broom," in the Texas style. He was the last of a certain breed of Louisiana pineywoods fiddlers.

Ray passed away from cancer in 1980.

Interviews by Ron Yule: Percy Beebe (2-17-2004), Troy DeRamus (6-17-2003), Ken Smith (3-22-2003), and Velma Spikes (2-17-2004).

References

DeRamus, Troy. *Louisiana I Love*. Unpublished account in possession of author, 2004.

Roach, Susan. Liner notes. *The North Louisiana Stringband*. LP 37882. Louisiana Folklife Center, Northwestern University, Natchitoches, Louisiana, 1981.

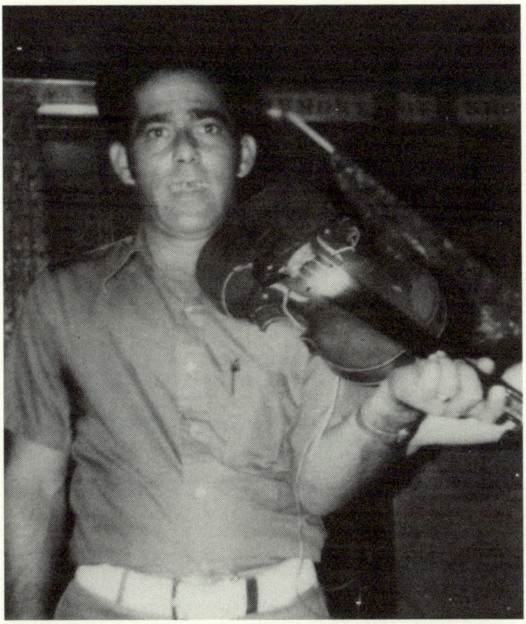

Photo courtesy of CFMA Hall of Fame Collection, Lake Charles.

ROBERT BERTRAND

(1938–1974) Lake Charles

Robert Bertrand was born July 27, 1938, and lived around Hathaway until his family moved to Lake Charles around 1950. Although his career was brief, he played music with many local Cajun musicians, recording an unknown number of Cajun and Cajun-country songs on several local labels. His father, Jake, was a Cajun fiddler, and had played at country dances before their move to Lake Charles. As a youngster, Robert followed in his father's footsteps and began learning all the instruments of the Cajun band, specializing mainly on the fiddle. They were playing at dancehalls near Eunice as early as 1950, when Robert was twelve.

Although Robert played several musical instruments, the fiddle would be the one, besides his voice, for which he would be remembered. His fiddling hero was Harry Choates, whom he probably heard as a small child on radio and record and possibly at performances. Several have noted that he had captured a lot of the sound of Will Kegley, a Jennings fiddler who was popular on KPLC at the time and was the originator of the legendary Pine Grove Boys. Another respected fiddler Robert studied was Tony Thibodeaux, who played in Robert's band for a while in the 1960s.

In 1949, Bobby Leger moved to Lake Charles from his childhood home near Church Point and settled on Warren Street. In 1952 the Bertrand family moved and was living several houses down on Warren Street. In the evenings, Bobby would take his accordion out and play the tunes he had played at dances and house parties around his boyhood Church Point home. Jake Bertrand, who lived down the street, heard the music one evening and followed it to the Leger home, eventually telling Bobby that his son, Robert, played the drums and hinted to Bobby that they could start a band. As a group they soon began to play in the evenings, and neighborhood families would come and sit on the sidewalk or in the front yard to listen to them play. Harry, Bobby's son, recalls as a youngster people coming from all over the block to listen and dance, both in the yard and in the street.

This led to the eventual formation of a band that consisted of Bobby on accordion, Jake on fiddle, Robert on drums, and Hilrae Mott of Lake Charles on rhythm guitar. Bobby was working offshore at the time, one week in and one week out. Martin "Bull" Leger, who had a Cajun band, The Little Bulls, replaced Bobby on the weekends while he was working offshore, provided he was not booked at another club.

Leroy, Bobby's son, began learning drums, being coached by Robert who wanted to get off the drums and play fiddle or guitar. Robert began playing guitar and would fill in on fiddle when Jake was unable to play. Robert, who was considered a natural at Cajun vocals, provided the vocals in the group.

Unnamed at first, the band soon began to play at clubs throughout southwest Louisiana. The name was born one night when they played at Newman's Country Club in Evangeline. The owner suggested they call themselves the Lake Charles Playboys, a name Bobby would use until he retired from music in the early 1990s.

From 1955 to 1957, Robert cut several songs with the Lake Charles Playboys. "Caroline, Caroline" was cut in J. D. Miller's Studio in Crowley. Robert and Bobby had a conflict over the singing of the song, so Bobby sang the song, the only vocal he ever recorded. Although Robert did not attend the original session, he did overdub fiddle at a later date. Robert played on other recordings on the Fais Do Do and Cajun Classics labels. Recorded tunes included "Trop Tard," "Drunkard's Blues" ("Le Bon Vieux Whiskie"), "Lost Love

Louisiana Ramblers: Atlas Frugé, Robert Bertrand, Garland Domingue, Ervin Lejeune, Junior Benoit. Etley's Lounge, Eunice, early 1970s. Photo courtesy of Ervin Lejeune.

Waltz," "Drunkard's Two-Step," "It's Too Late," "Chere Te Mon," "Memphis," "Mother's Day Waltz," and "Prison Waltz." Personnel included Robert, Bobby, Leroy Leger, and Louis Fournerat, who played steel guitar. Louis, who eventually landed in the Houston music scene, also played with the Kershaws, the Musical Aces, and Iry Lejeune during his career.

Robert played off and on with the Lake Charles Playboys, but played with other groups as well. In fact, until he passed away in 1974, his career was working as a sideman playing with nearly every major band and Cajun musician in the area while working with his own band, the Louisiana Ramblers. A versatile musician, he played bass and accordion as well as fiddle, drums, or guitar with any band that called on him.

Robert is remembered by many for playing drums with the legendary Iry Lejeune. Around 1954 he played for a short while with a band composed of Iry, fiddler Wilson Granger, and another neighbor, Alfred "Duckhead" Cormier. They played from China, in southeast Texas, to Breaux Bridge, east of Lafayette. Most sources note that Robert did not record with Iry because no one can find drums on these early recordings. Recordings during this period were recorded at Iry's Lacassine home with the tape recorder sitting on the kitchen table. Wilson Granger recalled that Robert did not play on these sessions that featured a combination of the accordion, fiddle, and guitar.

Although Robert did not record with Iry on any original sessions, it is noted that he did appear on some of Iry's records playing the fiddle, bass, and guitar. In the late 1960s, with a need for more instrumentation on Iry's recordings, Eddie Shuler hired Robert to overdub instruments onto previous arrangements. Ervin Lejeune, Iry's son, recalls that most fiddle recordings by Robert Bertrand in the late 1960s and early 1970s period were recorded with Iry Lejeune's "Amati" fiddle. Robert liked the sound and playability of it, especially when tuned in GDAE, and borrowed it when he could for these sessions.

With constant movement from band to band, Robert played in the late 1950s with Nathan Abshire as well as Bobby Leger, until Bobby's move to Midland, Texas, with the Mobil Oil Company. Except for occasional appearances with the Lake Charles Playboys when Bobby needed a fill-in, Robert did not play with him in the 1960s.

In the late 1950s and early 1960s, Robert played the guitar and sang with Sidney Brown and the Traveler Playboys, and it has been recalled by some that he recorded with them during this period. During the 1960s he continued this trend with many other groups, playing fiddle, drums, or guitar. He played and recorded with Cajun French Music Association Hall of Famers Nathan Abshire, Phil Menard and the Louisiana Travelers, Blackie Forrestier and the Cajun Aces, Geno Thibodeaux and the Musical Aces, and John Oliver. When Floyd LeBlanc left Joe Bonsall and the Orange Playboys, in the mid-1960s, Robert came in and played a while, recording "Hack a Moreau" on one of their sessions.

He continued to play under the band name Louisiana Ramblers, utilizing numerous musicians including Carrol Broussard, Ronnie Anderson, Marc Savoy, Ray Abshire, Tony Thibodeaux, Johnny Comeaux, Ed Gary, and Hilrae Mott.

Around 1965 Jo-El Sonnier moved to Lake Charles from his Acadia Parish home and played with Robert and the Louisiana Ramblers. They played the Shamrock Club, the hotspot at the time, as well as other local clubs. They cut four sides for the Goldband label: "Pas Revenir A La Maison" (Didn't Come Home), "Nous Passe Votre Porte" (We Passed Your Door), "Mon Senx Ont Sou" (My 50 Cents), and "Bottom Apartment." Jo-El continued to record with Goldband and eventually moved to California.

By 1967 Robert had become the main vocalist for Phil Menard and his Louisiana Travelers, recording "Phil's Blues," "The Other Love," "Dougas Day

Special," "My Papa and Mama," "Grande Texanna," and "La Sha Chere." This band included Garland Domingue, Wallace Derouen, and Nelson Bergeron or Mervin Faul.

Mervin Faul recalls that, during the period before Robert's death, Robert played under the Louisiana Ramblers name using the same basic personnel and a different accordion player. Accordion players included Geno Thibodeaux, Nolan Cormier, Ervin Lejeune, and John Oliver. He recorded "Te Mamou Blues," "Te Maurice," "All Through the Night," "Four Corners Waltz," "Mowata Blues," and "Te Galow" with John Oliver; "Poagy Boat Special" and "Louisiana Rambler Waltz" with Nolan Cormier; and "No Salt in the Beans" and "Seagram, Here We Go" with Geno Thibodeaux. Additional recording personnel for these sessions included Mervin Faul, Garland Domingue, Wallace Derouen, and Ferran Faul.

Two 45s with Ervin Lejeune on accordion included "Daylight Waltz," "I Don't Care What You Do," "Lawtell Two-Step," and "Love Bridge Waltz." "Daylight Waltz" and "I Don't Care What You Do" featured Ed Gary on his initial vocal recordings.

By 1970 Robert's versatility allowed him to become a session musician at Eddie Shuler's Goldband Studio in Lake Charles. Eddie used him to overdub on previously recorded material as well as performing on live sessions on an unknown number of recordings.

In the early 1970s Robert, along with Mervin Faul, Garland Domingue, and Wallace Derouen, made an eight-track tape that featured fiddle and steel guitar with no accordion. Tunes included: "I'll Take You Home," "Tee Maurice," "Don't Get Married," "My Papa," "Country Gentleman," "You All Come," "Corrina, Corrina," "Drunkard's Waltz," and "Buggy Tracks."

Robert died on February 8, 1974, of a heart attack, but his recorded music lives on and Cajun bands still play his music to this day. He has influenced many of the younger fiddlers with his smooth, bluesy approach to Cajun music. Several accordion players have acknowledged that he was one of the best to "bass" (play chords and rhythm) behind the accordion.

After years of absence from the record shelves, his music was finally showcased in the 1990s on a CD on the Goldband label. These songs were reissued from Goldband's collection and include many of Robert's most requested tunes.

Robert has posthumously received several awards from the Cajun music community. In 1990 he was inducted into the Cajun French Music Association

Hall of Fame, in Lake Charles, and a few years later received their Heritage Award. In 2003 he was inducted into the Cajun French Music Association Hall of Fame, in Eunice.

Interviews by Ron Yule: Richard Bertrand (4-22-2003), Andrew Brown (9-21-2008), Mervin Faul (1-19-2006, 1-28-2006), Ed Fournerat (7-15-2004), Wilson Granger (5-25-2005, 6-2-2005), Bobby and Harry Leger (12-10-2005), Leroy Leger (1-15-2006), Ervin Lejeune (1-28-2006), Phil Menard (11-9-2005), Cliff Newman (1-19-2006), and Tim Savoy (5-8-2003).

References

Lake Charles American Press. Robert Bertrand obituary, February 9, 1974.

Yule, Ron. *Iry Lejeune: Wailin' the Blues Cajun Style.* Fiddle Country Publishing, DeRidder, Louisiana, 2006.

———. "Robert Bertrand, Louisiana Rambler." Unpublished article and Discography.

Yule, Ron, et al. *Cajun French Music Association Hall of Fame, Lake Charles Chapter.* Fiddle Country Publishing, DeRidder, Louisiana, 2004.

Photo courtesy of Shawn Martin.

MASTERN BRACK

(1932–) Evans

Like many of the fiddlers of yesteryear, Mastern Brack comes from a long family tradition of fiddling. As far back as the 1840s, the Brack family has had a house full of fiddlers. Uncle Henderson Brack (1839–1924) was a famous fiddling figure in the Newton County, Texas area, having lost his right arm in the Civil War battle at Pleasant Hill, Louisiana, on April 9, 1864, and continuing to play with one arm. The Bracks were noted regional and local entertainers who played at country dances, front-porch pickings, and family reunions as far back as anyone can remember, a tradition they continue today.

The Bracks migrated from Tennessee to Natchitoches Parish in the early 1800s. They eventually moved to the upper Imperial Calcasieu Parish region of western Louisiana and finally landed in upper Newton County, Texas, near Burkeville. Adrian S. Brack, Mastern's father, was originally from Newton County but moved the family to Evans, Vernon Parish, in 1945. They settled on a farm, Adrian S. farmed and raised cattle and other farm animals to support the family. Like all farm life, times were touch and go, but they always found time for a little music. He described the old country dances of the early 1900s to Mastern, noting that some would last all night until the sun came up the next morning. Besides playing at country dances, Adrian S. taught the family to play several musical instruments. Adrian L., the oldest son, had learned to fiddle long before their move to Evans, and eventually became very accomplished on mandolin. The Bracks were a full family band with Ruth on guitar, Faye on piano and steel, Adeline on piano, and Adrian L. and Mastern on fiddles and mandolin. They were the typical country family band, playing and singing country gospel with three- and four-part harmony at family gatherings and especially at church.

By 1945, when the Bracks moved to Vernon Parish, Mastern had been playing fiddle for three years. Most fiddlers in the area played in a short bowing style, sawing the notes individually. Mastern's maternal grandfather, Lee Peters, played in this style, and this was the style that brother Adrian L. tended to use on most of his hoedowns. Mastern used the longbow style of playing, a style his father had played and taught him. Mastern describes his style as being "very smooth and he pulled a long bow." This style involves slurring and playing multiple notes per bow stroke. Mastern has mastered this longbow style of playing to a T.

By the late 1940s, Mastern began venturing away from the family group and playing with bands in clubs around Leesville. He says, "They'd have to slip me in the back door because of my age." He also entered a few fiddle contests and remembers entering the Vernon Parish Fair fiddle contest on several occasions in the late 1940s and early fifties. He cannot recall where he placed.

By the 1950s he was playing every kind of country music he could. He played with Woodrow Smith (guitar), Wayne Parker (guitar), and Murtis Speights (fiddle) at the Welcome Club and Nut Club around Leesville. Besides the weekend club dates, they played on KLLA, Leesville, for a while then moved to KDLA, DeRidder, appearing on the Saturday afternoon Hillbilly Jamboree, where country groups were featured all afternoon. Groups such as The Rhythm Rascals (Hesters), Bailey Boys, Red Andrews, Troy Weldon and the Dixie Rhythm Ramblers, Spencer and Matt Hinson, Julian Campbell, and Roy Burks and the Horsebranch Ramblers performed weekly. Regular sessions were held at the Beauregard Parish Airport Hangar, and Mastern was a part of these sessions. Entertaining musicians included his brother-in-law, Frank Strange, and Cecil and Billy Burge.

Buck Tyler and the Musicmasters, 1973: David Calhoun, Frank Strange, Buck Tyler, Mastern Brack, Huey Gill, and Huey Strange. Photo courtesy of Judy Tyler.

Mastern has always been a good breakdown and waltz player, but is noted especially for his improvisational talent playing backup behind a singer or country band. During the 1950s and sixties, he honed his skills by listening to many recordings of the popular country stars at the time and attending and playing on numerous country shows in the local area. The stars of the Louisiana Hayride would tour the area performing at school shows and Mastern was always in demand to play. He heard fiddlers like Curly Fox, Kenny Baker, Chubby Wise, Mac McGaha, and Rufus Thibodeaux, and introduced their licks into his repertoire. Besides being influenced by Evans fiddler Murtis Speights' Cliff Bruner–style fiddle, he played with Jack Kay, who played with Webb Pierce in the 1950s. Jack would come to the local clubs where Mastern was playing and sit in with the band, as well as attending the many family reunions and music sessions in western Vernon Parish.

Mastern also notes that recordings of these masters greatly influenced his playing. Frank Strange once recalled that Mastern could hear a Ray Price tune one time and copy the fiddle break. His harmony playing is spontaneous and unique, like the graceful noting of his lead lines.

In 1964 Mastern married and began to raise a family. His music was never very far away on the back burner, and he began to play with Frank Strange in his Country Playboy Band. They played at local shows on the same bill as country stars Porter Wagoner and Jimmy C. Newman. The band consisted of

Mastern Brack Fiddlin' Family. Back: Kathy Bonner, Jenae Riley, Mastern Brack, Isaac Riley, Eden Bonner, and Becky Riley. Front: Levi Bonner. Photo courtesy of Brack family/J. J. Minion.

Bobby Burks (guitar), Buddy Brooks (bass guitar), Buck Tyler (lead guitar), Frank Strange (rhythm guitar), and Mastern.

By the 1970s, Buck Tyler had taken over the vocal and lead guitar work and formed his own group, Buck Tyler and the Musicmasters. Mastern joined them and, by 1974, they not only had become local celebrities but were noticed by promoters at the upstart Hayride USA, in Bossier City, Louisiana. They appeared three times in 1975 on the show, which eventually would bear the name Louisiana Hayride. On one occasion they were the featured group.

During the late 1970s, Mastern worked in southeast Texas and jammed with Ralph Richardson and many of the swing players in the Golden Triangle area around Orange and Port Arthur. He had always been a fan of Johnny Gimble's fiddling, and these sessions gave him an opportunity to hone and practice those skills.

During the period from 1962 to 1976, Mastern entered and won numerous fiddle contests. He won the Beauregard Parish Fair contest seven years in a row, a feat accomplished by only two other fiddlers, Theodosia Iles and Cecil Burge. He placed high in all the other contests and in 1975 came in second at the Louisiana State Championship in Boyce.

The musical talent of the Brack family continues to provide beautiful string music throughout west central Louisiana. Mastern's daughters, Kathy and Becky, and their children continue the string tradition, first learning classical string technique from Dr. Karen Gordy in Leesville and supplementing that with traditional learning techniques from Mastern. They play at churches, nursing homes, concerts, and events around the area.

By the 1980s Mastern began to focus on playing gospel music in church and playing benefits, nursing homes, and occasional jam sessions at reunions, parks, and family gatherings. He had come full circle and was now playing in the same setting as when he started, in a family type of setting. He has played at the Congregational Methodist Church in Evans for the past fifty-five years and continues today. He has earned the well-deserved respect of his peers, the fiddlers, who all love and appreciate his creative and emotion-filled touch on the fiddle. When you hear him play, you know the fiddle is in the hands of a master.

Interview by Ron Yule: Mastern Brack (3-29-2008 and many informal conversations over the years).

References

DeRidder Enterprise. "Old Folks Day Winners Named." October 10, 1962.

———. "Winners Announced." October 12, 1968.

Southwest Louisiana Fiddle and Bluegrass Club Newsletter. Ron and Georgia Yule, editors. DeRidder, Louisiana, 1974–76.

Photo courtesy of Joe Suchanek.

ELTON BRINDLEY

(1932–) Starks

Elton Brindley (b. 1932) started playing fiddle at age ten, after seeing the fiddle player with Bruce Broussard's band at a Starks Elementary School concert. Since his family had little money, he improvised and made a one-string fiddle from a board, stretching baling wire over a Pet milk can for sound. He played his first tune, "Ida Red," on this instrument. He cannot recall any ancestors who played the fiddle, but his daddy did play the harmonica.

Elton learned to play alongside Huey Buxton, a friend of about the same age. They finally progressed enough to begin playing country dances around the Starks area. Elton describes the country dances around Starks: "You mean the kind at someone's house where they'd push the furniture back and put the fiddler wherever they could? That was when nobody had electricity. I can remember one night when they played 'Sally Goodin' for nearly twenty minutes and still didn't wear all the dancers out."

Elton Brindley, Ellis Windham, and Eric Brindley. Sabine River Opry, Fields, ca. 1970. Photo courtesy of Elton Brindley.

Over the years, he has played with his friends from around Starks (Nathan Hyatt, Huey Buxton, Richard Langley, Norman Gibson, and Joe Suchanek) and all the Windhams (Clayton, Ellis, George, and Enoch). Being a sought-after country band fiddler, Elton has played at many clubs in southwest Louisiana and in east Texas, including the Club 87, Buster's Lounge, and Louann's Club. During his early years he also worked out of the Musician's Union Hall in Beaumont, Texas. For many years, he played with the pickers from the Sabine River bottom at George Windham's Sabine River Opry, below Fields. It was a hotspot for forties- and fifties-style country music and fiddling. People came from Texas and southwest Louisiana to listen to and play music every Saturday night in the seventies and early eighties.

Professionally, he has played with Paul Howard and the Arkansas Cotton Pickers, Hawkshaw Hawkins, George Jones (one night), and Andrew Cormier and the Rambling Aces. In the late 1940s, while hanging around some of the local clubs, he met Harry Choates and recalls playing on his fiddle.

Although he has not played in clubs for years, Elton continues playing at local shows like the Lone Pine Park in Ragley, Southeast Texas Bluegrass Music

Nathan Hyatt, Huey Buxton, Richard Langley, and Elton Brindley. Unknown club in east Texas, early 1950s. Photo courtesy of Richard Langley.

Club Show in Sour Lake, Texas, and Triple Creek Music Park at Woodville, Texas. For a while in the eighties and nineties he played a weekly show at Tuffy's Restaurant in Mauriceville, Texas, with Carroll Benoit and the Bayou Country Grass. He currently plays with his brother-in-law, Nathan Hyatt, the Not Brothers, and the Sabine Bluegrass Band.

Although Elton does not copy anyone, he plays in a style much like his fiddling hero, Dale Potter, and the country fiddlers of the 1950s. Referred to by many as "Mr. Double Stop," he eloquently plays a continual flow of chords and is one of the best backup fiddlers in the area. As a country sideman, his playing is a throwback to the beautiful double-stop cushion as heard on many 1940s and 1950s country records by the likes of Dale Potter, Jack Kay, or Shorty Lavender. Elton is a very versatile fiddler. At any given show he may play country with one group and follow that by backing up a bluegrass band and playing a few fiddle tunes and waltzes. Due to his unique style of Cajun fiddling, he has become noted for his renditions of "Jole Blon" and "Port Arthur Waltz," favorites at any country show where he plays. He has also given numerous workshops on Cajun and country fiddling to aspiring fiddlers.

Elton's brother, Eric, is also an accomplished fiddler. With Elton's ability to play double stops and harmony on the fiddle, the brother duet laid their claim to fame in the seventies with several twin-fiddle contest wins in southwest Louisiana. They can twin fiddle in many styles, from a Kenny Baker/Joe Greene "High Country" to Tommy Jackson's "Twin Fiddle Polka" to a beautiful western swing version of "Maiden's Prayer"/ "Faded Love."

Elton has also penned three tunes, which have been featured on several LPs and cassettes. He has written "The Mom Brindley Waltz" and "Chucklehead Stomp" and co-wrote "Twilight Waltz" with his brother, Eric. Their fiddling and these tunes are featured on Ellis Windham's 1977 production, *Hey Diddle Diddle, the Cat and the Fiddle*, which also features Ellis, Clayton Windham, and Dave Odegar. Elton has also recorded on numerous solo studio projects including several 45s in the forties and fifties, and cut a tape with Carroll Benoit and Bayou Country Grass while they were playing at Tuffy's Restaurant in the early 1990s.

Elton is like fine wine. He is in his seventies and plays better than ever.

Interviews by Ron Yule: Elton Brindley (2-13-2008) and Ellis Windham (2-12-2008).

References

Southwest Louisiana Fiddle and Bluegrass Club Newsletters. Ron and Georgia Yule, editors. DeRidder, Louisiana, 1974–76.

Windham, Ellis. Liner notes. *Hey Diddle Diddle, the Cat and the Fiddle,* 1977.

Photo courtesy of Susan Roach.

CLARENCE "GATEMOUTH" BROWN
(1924–2005) Slidell

Clarence "Gatemouth" Brown does not fit the mold of the normal country fiddler playing what has been described as a fusion of blues, R&B, country, swing, bebop, and Cajun. Although he is known for his guitar work on his many albums and shows, the fiddle took a special place in his music. To the many who appreciated his fiddle playing, he was known to bring the house down playing his unique combination of swing, big band, and blues.

Gatemouth was born into a musical family in 1924 near the Louisiana border at Vinton, Louisiana, and raised in Orange, Texas, a hop, skip and jump across the Sabine River. After life in Texas and even Nashville, he settled in Slidell, Louisiana, where he resided until Hurricane Katrina forced him to evacuate to Orange. He passed away shortly after that on September 10, 2005.

Brown played guitar, fiddle, viola, drums, mandolin, and harmonica, to name a few instruments; he learned to love music from his father, a railroad worker who sang and played fiddle in a Cajun band. Brown always named his father as his greatest musical influence. In an interview with Gus Weill on the *Louisiana Legends* series on PBS television in 2000, he noted:

> *But I have to start back in the beginning—my father. He's the reason for what I'm doing today. And I will always give him credit for my success.... When did I know I was going to be a musician? Before I was born. My dad would play, and my mom said I'd do this [taps on stomach] and try to break out. So when I was born—at the age of five that I can remember, I picked up an old guitar and played behind my daddy. I didn't know what I was doing, but I remember making some kind of noise. Then when I took it out, I'd try to make the sound like he'd sound and I went from there.*

Brown also started playing fiddle by age five. In an interview with Candace Corrigan on *The Nashville Nobody Knows*, he stated:

> *I first got involved by listening and watching, trying to work along with my father, when I was five years old. My father, and my uncles, and all these guys, on the weekends, they would play music at each other's houses. And that was fun, they didn't have no nightclub, I couldn't go to no nightclub, no way. But I used to set up all night and listen to my dad play, and after I got to be a teenager, me and some white guys used to get together and play at their houses, and when we got tired we'd all scatter on the floor, all of us, and sleep and get up the next morning and go on our way.*

Numerous articles have been written about Gatemouth, but few have focused on his fiddling and fiddle style. Like the guitar, he used the fiddle beautifully to punctuate what he felt at the time in his music. He felt equally at home on an old breakdown like "Up Jumped the Devil," Cajun numbers, two-steps, or an up-tempo country song. All were played with creativity and feel, but his improvisational fiddle skills came to the forefront on blues numbers, where he would use everything from long slides to torrid bowing to a quick series of cascading chorded fifths to get the "just right" effect. Gatemouth's shows mainly featured the more bluesy style of fiddle or viola, but on any occasion he might tear into a Cajun tune like "Diggy Liggy Lo," "Jole Blon," "Big Mamou," or "Jambalaya." Pianist Steve Conn recalls him playing "San Antonio Rose" on the shows he played with Gatemouth in 1976, and also noted that he always played "Jambalaya." Gatemouth had a unique ability to "make his fiddle talk," appearing to say words using controlled left-hand movements.

Gatemouth Brown ca. 1950. Photo courtesy of Andrew Brown.

Pianist Rick Lagneaux, who played with Brown at Poet's Inn in Lafayette, noted that, besides Cajun tunes, he played several swing numbers on fiddle. "He didn't play the fiddle much, but what he played fit and was impressive." He felt the fiddle was a secondary instrument for Brown, used to work the crowd and show a different side of his music to his audience.

By the age of ten, Gatemouth had learned guitar, playing a thumb/finger picking style he used all his life, always trying to make his guitar sound like his fiddle.

In his teens Brown toured as a drummer with swing bands and was nicknamed "Gatemouth" for his deep voice. After a brief stint in the army, he returned in 1945 to Texas, where he was inspired by blues guitarist T-Bone Walker.

In 1946 he was in San Antonio, playing drums and singing at Don Albert's Keyhole with an all-Caucasian band called the Hoyt Hughes Orchestra. Don Robey met him and told him to stop by his place, the Bronze Peacock in Houston, if he ever made it to Houston. A year later he hitchhiked from San Antonio to Houston, following up on the invitation.

Brown's career took off in 1947 when Walker came down with a stomach ailment and had to leave the stage at the Peacock. After an invitation to sing, Brown grabbed Walker's guitar and wowed the crowd by picking and singing a song he invented on the spot, "Gatemouth Boogie." The crowd of 650 responded by giving him $615 in tips.

From there his career took off, with numerous albums and tours throughout the world. He eventually landed in Nashville in the 1970s and did several projects with Roy Clark, played on *Hee Haw*, and recorded the country comedy tune "May the Bird of Paradise Fly Up Your Nose." His no-musical-boundaries approach even had him recording Hank Williams's "Jambalaya" with Cajun accordionist Jo-El Sonnier.

Touching on many styles of music, Gatemouth won eight W. C. Handy Awards and was nominated for seven Grammys, winning once. He was also a recipient of the Rhythm & Blues Foundation's prestigious Pioneer Award, the National Academy of Recording Arts and Sciences Heroes, and, a few months before his death, the 2005 Louisiana Governor's Arts Award for Lifetime Achievement.

Gatemouth's love for the fiddle, which could be a throwback to the days of his youth listening to his daddy play, is best noted by the fact that his CB handle was "Fast Fiddler."

Interviews by Ron Yule: Hadley Castille (3-15-2007), Steve Conn (3-16-2007), and Rick Lagneaux (3-15-2007).

References

Corrigan, Candace. Taped interview with Gatemouth Brown on *The Nashville Nobody Knows*. June 12, 2005.

Weill, Gus. Taped interview with Gatemouth Brown on *Louisiana Legends*. PBS, 2000.

Photo courtesy of Bill Burge.

CECIL BURGE

(1906–1986) Singer

Singer, Louisiana is a blink in the eye to the modern passerby. Who would think that this one-store town might be the birthplace of Beauregard Parish's most noted fiddler? The main industry today is logging, just as it was at the turn of the century; only the equipment is different. This was the occupation of the Burges, who lived at the edge of the Louisiana pineywoods forests just before it turns into the wetlands and the bayous of southwest Louisiana. Cecil Burge was born there in 1906 and would become the most famous Beauregard fiddler of the century, playing for governors, generals, and the common man.

Barn dances were a way of life and a relief from the toils of the woods. Nearly everyone attended these Saturday night parties. It was at these dances that Cecil first heard the strains of one of the smoothest fiddlers in the country, Ed Pruitt. By the age of five he was learning from Pruitt, and soon began playing the barn dances, eventually forming a band of his own. This band

Edgar Pruitt, Cecil Burge, and Ted Burge, ca. 1930. Photo courtesy of Bill Burge.

included his brothers Gordon, Ted, and Charlie Burge; Edgar Pruitt, a cousin of Ed; and a friend, Buddy Canney, from nearby Longville. They would ride horses or go by horse-drawn wagon to these sometimes all-night dances as far away as five miles. Sometimes they were not the safest place to be. Bill, Cecil's son, remembers his dad talking about the rough times one could experience at these country shindigs.

By 1922 Cecil had honed his skills on fiddle and was ready to leave home, to make his fortune somewhere besides behind a mule in the Beauregard piney-woods. Sometime in the early 1920s, he arrived in Beaumont, Texas, and began to play for the Kansas City Railroad as a member of their booster band. They had a baseball team and a group of musicians who traveled the country and played as entertainment to help promote the KC Railroad at each stop along the line. The baseball team would play the local team in the afternoon and the musicians would entertain at shows and dances at night. They rode the rail and stopped in towns all over east Texas, western Louisiana, and sometimes as far north as Kansas City, Missouri.

By 1924 KFDM in Beaumont was broadcasting, and they began appearing on a regularly scheduled program playing pop tunes, old waltzes, and fiddle tunes of yesteryear. During this time, Cecil wrote their theme song, "KFDM Rag," which he adapted from an old fiddle tune. Cecil would commute from home with his open rail pass, giving him access to moving about with ease, and he wound up spending a lot of time at different radio stations around the country. By the late 1920s he was using his rail pass to get to Shreveport to play with the numerous musicians in the north Louisiana city. KWKH, KWEA, and KRMD had opened their airwaves to fiddlers and begun programming local country musicians as well as string bands like the Taylor-Grigg Melodymakers and the Pelican Wildcats.

Jimmie Davis was also appearing on KWKH, singing in the bluesy style of many country singers at the time. In the late 1920s Cecil met Davis and played with him off and on until 1943, especially when both were in the northwest and central Louisiana areas. Besides singing on the streets of Shreveport, they began to tour the area and play at schools and clubs.

Wherever they went they played the music of the region. In central Louisiana towns like Cheneyville, Marksville, Jonesville, Winnfield, and Mansura, the listeners liked their music with a more Cajun and country sound; in Shreveport, Longview, Texas, and Kilgore, Texas, they played local favorites, even one that played on the weather conditions in east Texas towns: "Is It Muddy in Kilgore When It Rains?" Davis continued this trend throughout his career, learning Cajun tunes such as "Colinda" to appeal to that audience.

The dates are not known, but Cecil began to play on Huey Long's campaigns. Bill notes that his father was paid a hundred dollars per week, an unheard-of sum for that time. He also notes that the early thirties brought appearances on programs at WBAP in Fort Worth, Texas, for the Burris Mill Flour Company, the sponsor of the Light Crust Doughboys. Cecil began learning the swing tunes of the Texas musicians and included them in his repertoire long after he left the road.

In his final phase with Davis, they ventured back into California where Jimmie appeared in two of the Charles Starrett/Durango Kid movies. Cecil appeared as an extra.

In 1943 the music business was gearing down because of the war effort, and Cecil left the band to return to Louisiana and raise his family in DeRidder. Jimmie Davis helped him get work as a fireman at Camp Polk near Leesville, a job he kept until Camp Polk closed at the end of the war. He went into law enforcement for the next few years, as a policeman for the city of DeRidder and then as a deputy for the Beauregard Parish Sheriff Department. In the late 1950s he regained his job as a fireman at the newly opened Fort Polk, and retired there in 1970.

Although he played professionally on the road, local musicians mainly recall his prowess at contest fiddling. From the 1920s until 1985, he was a feared

Cecil Burge in his last contest at the Beauregard Parish Fair, 1985. Photo courtesy of Bill Burge.

contestant at fiddle contests, winning the Beauregard Parish Fair Fiddle Contest more times than any other fiddler in the area.

He never was far from the fiddle from 1944 until his death in 1986. His large 5/4 fiddle (probably a viola strung with violin strings) was always sitting on top of his upright piano, ready for a tune at any moment. Known as a good vocalist, he might sit down at the piano and play and sing in an impromptu performance. During the 1950s, weekly jam sessions at the Beauregard Airport Hangar brought musicians from all over the area, including Billy Burge, John Bailey, Mastern Brack, Frank Strange, Elvin Lambert, and Newman Morgan. He played at parties, the airport hangar, and house parties; neighbors talk of him playing on the front porch and in the backyard of his Wilson Street home in DeRidder. In the 1970s, house parties with friends John Bailey, Don Bellah, Jack and Myrtle Arledge, Bud and George Wilcox, Ron Yule, and Orville Johnson were a weekly event. Cecil would fill the air with his most requested tunes: "Rubber Dolly," "Annie Laurie," "Whispering Hope," "Waltz You Saved for Me," and "Memphis Strut."

It is not known whether he recorded professionally, but home recordings of his playing in the late sixties and seventies exist.

Interviews by Ron Yule: Bill Burge (6-21-2002 and 8-3-2005).

A FEW CECIL BURGE/JIMMIE DAVIS STORIES

by Bill Burge

The following stories recalled by Bill were heard when Cecil, Jimmie Davis, and Guy Allen would get together in DeRidder and visit. Guy Allen, who had played the bass fiddle with Clark's Merrymakers in the late 1930s, joined Davis's band until he entered the Baptist ministry in the early 1940s. He was the pastor at the Texas Avenue Baptist Church in DeRidder during this period.

THE PAWNBROKER AND THE ITALIAN FIDDLE

The band was working out of a small town in north Louisiana, and could not pay their room and board at the local hotel. They had been working for the door [that is, their income was solely from paid admissions] and were not getting much pay from their efforts. They got their heads together and decided to work a number on the local pawnbroker. Cecil carried his fiddle, an old Strad copy, to the pawnshop and told the broker he had fallen on hard times and needed to pawn his fiddle for a few days. He told the broker he had inherited it from his grandpa, who brought it from Italy. Cecil pawned the fiddle for five dollars with the agreement that he would be back and pick it up for fifteen dollars on Friday.

Jimmie Davis waited two days until Wednesday and, dressed to the hilt, walked into the pawnshop and announced that he was from Camille Antique Company in New York. He said he was passing through and was looking for items to buy for an upcoming auction and sale. After browsing for a while, he asked to see the fiddle hanging on the wall. He held it and mulled over it for a while, eventually offering fifty dollars for the old beat-up instrument. The pawnbroker replied, "I'd like to, but I can't sell the fiddle, the big man who pawned it would kill me if I sold it. It belonged to his grandfather who brought it over from Italy." Jimmie, looking into the fiddle through the f-holes, noted, " I see that on the label. It's an Antonius Stradivarius, made in Italy." He made him another offer; "I'll give you a hundred fifty for it right now." The pawnbroker refused, stating again that he had to hold it until Friday. Jimmie said, "Here's my phone number in New York, scribbling down a fictitious number. This is my last offer. If you get the fiddle, call me and I'll give you three hundred dollars for it."

On Friday Cecil showed up to claim the now-famous Italian violin. The broker offered him fifty dollars for it. After a bit of dickering, they agreed on seventy dollars; Cecil took the money. The band paid their bills, loaded up the touring car, stopped in the next town, and bought another fiddle for five dollars.

THE TOURING CAR

Jimmie and the Rainbow Ramblers would travel from one town to the next in a touring car pulling a trailer, which carried their grip and instruments. The car was a three-seater. On one trip to a small north Louisiana town near Coushatta, they played their show under the light of kerosene lanterns. There was no electricity and it was pitch black when they loaded their instruments in the trailer to leave. As was the case with many musicians, the band had been imbibing too much spirits, so the "designated driver" role fell to Jimmie. They all piled into the car with Jimmie driving, cranked the engine, put it in gear, and the car went nowhere. He changed gears and revved the motor up again. They went nowhere. Jimmie said, "Cecil, get that light and see what's wrong." Even though he was a little tipsy and did not feel like it, he grabbed the light, and stepped out of the car to see what was the matter. Someone had jacked up the car and trailer, blocked them up, and stolen all the wheels. They were going nowhere.

It was three days before wheels and tires could be sent from Alexandria and they could be on their way.

THE BUCKET OF BLOOD

The Ramblers were playing somewhere around Glenmora on one of their many central Louisiana tours, at a joint the locals termed the "Bucket of Blood." It had not gotten its name because the place served Bloody Marys or was a blood donation site. This place was rough. The nightly fight and bloodbath broke out about 11 o'clock, and before long the whole place was filled with a frenzy of wild fighting, swinging drunks, and crazed dancers. The band finally got in on the act (they had been drinking, too). During the melee, some guy ran in and tried to hit Cecil with his fist. Like a scripted movie scene, Cecil whopped him over the head with his fiddle and down the man went. He did not stay on the floor very long. He came flying up with a drawn knife and hit Cecil in the throat. Guy Allen, the tenor guitar and bass player, grabbed Cecil when he saw him go down and held him. Before long, he felt something warm on his leg and in his boot. It was Cecil's blood. They rushed him to the hospital and Guy recalled, "I could feel his blood sloshing in my boot as I walked."

Guy would later become a Baptist minister and serve congregations in Pineville and DeRidder.

©2003 Rick Lagneaux.

HADLEY J. CASTILLE

(1933–) Opelousas

With ancestors and family members who played music, Hadley J. Castille was destined to play, and he chose the fiddle to express himself musically. His father, François, played the accordion, and his Uncle Cyprien played the fiddle left-handed. Although they both played dances, they seldom played together. For reasons unknown to Hadley, Cyprien played with other fiddlers at the dances he attended, while Francois played with his own fiddler friends.

Hadley was born in Leonville on March 3, 1933, and took an interest in the fiddle around age nine after his brother, Donadieu, began learning. On days when it was too hot for little Hadley to help with the farming, he would stay in the house. He had been listening to his brother play and decided to try it, so he would take the fiddle off the armoire and start trying to learn. When his brother would hear him trying to play, he'd come in and take it from him and "whip him good." Hadley recalls Cyprien, who lived with the family by then,

Three Generations of Castilles: Blake Castille, Sarah Jayde Williams, and Hadley Castille. Photo by author.

showing them the bowing. Hadley says, "I can remember from way back then how important bowing was in Cajun fiddling—the very core of it, because of the rhythm for the dancers. I think that's the reason they played it that way. . . . It gave the Cajun dancers a feeling for the rhythm." Hadley once described it as a "sort of chugging style." He also notes that Cyprien did not play "over the bass" but reversed the strings to play as a mirror image of a right-handed fiddler. Hadley notes that on occasion Cyprien would reverse the strings so they could play, but by the time the strings finally were reversed, they would forget what he had shown them. He recalls they also listened to the Grand Ole Opry, trying to pick up songs and licks.

Hadley recounts that François was a farmer and the family moved quite often during his youth, so Hadley was exposed to many scenarios of music and the Cajun culture. After a brief move near the bayou, he remembers playing "round games" during Lent, when no one played music. He notes they did a lot of singing. Around 1945 they moved back to Pecaniere, where more people were playing music. On one of their trips, he heard Harry Choates playing "Jole Blon" on the jukebox at the local grocery store/barroom, the Silver Slipper. "The first time I heard that it blew my mind—I was a kid—I must have been about eleven or twelve then—I was playing pretty good, but when I heard that, it changed my playing altogether—completely. I got away from what my old uncle had taught me. I never forgot it, but I got away. I wanted to do what Harry was doing." He notes that all the young fiddlers around Pecaniere were trying to learn the Choates style of fiddling.

His brothers Donadieu and Deiudone had joined a band after the war and were playing country-style music at the Courtableau in Port Barre. They played with one fiddle and three guitars. The owner, a man named Belazaire, would come and get them and take them to the dance and then bring them home after the dance. Hadley says he went a few times but was only thirteen at the time, so his father would not let him go very often.

They then moved back near the bayou and close to the Silver Slipper dance-hall, a place where the Landry Boys and Doc Guidry and Happy Fats often played. They heard more music and attended more dances.

After another move near Port Barre around 1950, he formed a band with some of his friends in high school: Nolan Robin, Felton Hargroder, and Eaves Guidroz. They acquired a PA system and played their first job at Roy's Bar in Port Barre, following it by playing near Courtableau and at house parties. They also played on Saturday morning on KSLO Amateur Hour, playing with Happy Fats and Doc Guidry as well as the Rayne Playboys featuring a young Rufus Thibodeaux on fiddle. Hadley recalls it was a very popular show and says, "It was there I got to meet Rufus and really appreciate his talent."

In this band, Hadley had his first experience with an electrified violin using a DeArmond pickup. He recalls one mishap he will never forget:

> *We were in the middle of this room. In order to plug in the amps, I had to get on a chair and unscrew the light fixture and screw in an adapter with some plug-ins on the side. So I put my fiddle on the floor—I had bought that fiddle from a cousin of mine for fourteen dollars, I believe. And I really loved my fiddle. I put that fiddle on the floor and climbed on that chair. When I climbed off that chair I stepped on my fiddle. That was the end of that production. . . . That's the most sickening feeling I can remember.*

After working a year on the farm after graduation, Hadley headed to New Orleans to play in a country band. He played for four or five months at a couple of clubs in Westwego, and moved back, eventually enlisting in the U.S. Army. The Korean War ended soon after he arrived at Fort Hood, Texas, and he spent his whole tour of duty in Killeen. Throughout Hadley's service time he played in the band a fellow soldier, Dave Edge, formed. They played on base, in Temple, Waco, Killen, College Station, and around central Texas. One especially enjoyable event he remembers was hearing Hank Thompson and the Brazos Valley Boys and getting to meet the legendary steel guitarist, Pee Wee Whitewing, who is playing on Hadley's new CD project.

After his discharge, he returned to the area and played with the Veteran Playboys while he went to plumbing school. He soon met his wife, Earline, and although he did not give up the fiddle completely, he concentrated on his new plumbing business and his family. Playing was sporadic until he met Harold Fontenot in the 1960s; by the 1970s, they were playing at different events around St. Landry Parish with Merlin Fontenot, Jody Smith, and Felton Hargroder.

Hadley began concentrating on playing Cajun music, and around 1980 his music career took off when he was invited to go to Canada and perform. On his first trip to the Saskatchewan festival, a Canadian family band backed him and the response was tremendous. Even though the Canadians spoke French, they had never heard French Cajun music. This trip and the response of the Canadian people to his music gave his fiddling new life. After returning home, he began to relearn many of the old Cajun tunes and to sharpen his skills on his bowing. He soon returned to Saskatchewan to play on a television show, and for the next eighteen years he played the Canadian festival. The doors were now open and Hadley and his band, along with some Cajun chefs, began to appear at festivals in British Columbia, Thunder Bay, Montreal, and Quebec. On successive trips his son, Blake, who had previously played rock music, accompanied him and the varying band of Sharecroppers who played in his groups. This past year the circle was completed; his granddaughter, fiddler Sarah Jayde Williams, accompanied the gang to Canada for the first time.

Numerous recordings have been produced by Hadley and his Sharecropper Band. Starting with a need for something to sell to the Canadian fans, as well as fans in the United States and especially south Louisiana who were hungry to hear Hadley's music, they recorded numerous projects. Recently he returned to his musical roots in Leonville, with *Quarante Acres et Deux Mulés*. His most recent effort is *Refait* on the Swallow label. A recent DVD, *Cajun Swamp Fiddler, Hadley J. Castille: A Lesson in Cajun Fiddle Music* for Mel Bay Productions, has sold well and is a must for students of Hadley's fiddle style.

Hadley continues to entertain, playing at festivals, restaurants, and shows throughout North America with the Sharecropper Band. He is in demand at many workshops and is constantly giving back to the public, showing his gratitude for their response to his music. After years of fielding a large band with many instruments, he occasionally scales down to utilize the talents of his own family. Basically a threesome billed as the 3 Generations of Castilles with Blake and Jayde, his schedule is as full as ever. New projects are in the works for the Castille Family.

The family circle is still alive with more than five generations of Castilles who have now played music. From their roots in Leonville to their crowd-pleasing stage performances, they have been a credit to their heritage.

Interviews by Ron Yule: Hadley Castille (3-20-2007 and 8-1-2008).

Photo courtesy of the Thomas Philyaw Collection/Ron Yule.

W. E. "WILLIE" CASTON

(1862–1928) Red Oak

W. E. "Willie" Caston was born in 1862, in Jackson, Mississippi, of Irish descendants, and migrated to the community of Red Oak, about five miles north of Coushatta toward Ringgold. He had moved to Red Oak in 1878, and was a farmer, woodworker, and blacksmith. He was very talented and his woodworking skills were so good he built at least one fiddle, which is still in the family. Although it is not known when and how he learned the fiddle, it is thought that his talent on the fiddle was passed down from his ancestors.

Besides being a respected country fiddler, Willie was a teacher. Thomas Philyaw, his grandson, notes that of Willie's thirteen children, ten played a musical instrument of some kind. He taught them how to play bass fiddle, fiddle, mandolin, drums, and piano. Murray Richardson recalls his brother, Bill, a fiddle champion at the Louisiana State Fair, traveling to Coushatta in the mid-1920s to learn old fiddle tunes from Mr. Caston. Murray says Bill was a classically trained violinist and could write the music down while Mr. Caston played the tunes. All efforts to retrieve some of these transcriptions have proved fruitless. Willie was noted in fiddling circles around the northwest part of Louisiana, especially in Shreveport for his attendance at fiddle contests and square dances.

Like other country groups from that era, Willie and the children played at country dances and socials around Coushatta and Red Oak. Ancestors recall the many hoedowns on the weekends in Coushatta and Shreveport. With children who played all the stringed instruments, they had an in-house string band. Fleecy was the most noted fiddler of the children, apparently inheriting her father's great talent for the instrument. She was an award-winning contest fiddler and played with the Old Fiddlers Club of North Louisiana and with a band formed with her husband, Thomas Philyaw, in the 1930s and early 1940s. She also played guitar and mandolin. Daughter Willie played guitar, mandolin, and fiddle, although she was not as talented on fiddle as Fleecy. Van played bass fiddle and played a little on the fiddle. Ed played guitar, and Thomas Philyaw Jr. recalls Perry playing an instrument, but cannot recall which one.

Both Murray Richardson and *The Haynesville News* note that Willie played many times with the members of the Old Fiddlers Club of North Louisiana. They played at get-togethers at the home of Dr. J. E. Richardson; at the Majestic Building in downtown Shreveport, where Dr. Richardson had his office; on Shreveport radio stations; and at square dances organized by Dr. Richardson. This group of musicians was a Who's Who of fiddlers in the northwest part of the state in the early part of the twentieth century. Included were noted fiddlers John W. Daniel, Sanford R. Patterson, Bill Richardson, and H. C. Wilkerson, as well as Caston's daughter, Fleecy.

Dr. Richardson, who had started the Old Fiddlers Club of North Louisiana, encouraged all the fiddlers to form clubs in their hometowns. A club was formed in Coushatta and Willie was probably a member. This probably accounts for his knowledge of and participation in the many contests in the region.

It has been noted that, in the early part of the 1900s, numerous contests were held in northern Louisiana. Willie continually was a top prizewinner in these contests. One year after the Louisiana State Fair initiated its highly regarded contest in 1912, Willie took the top prize. He continued to enter and placed second in 1915, 1917, 1924, 1926, and 1927, and third in 1914. In 1925 he reached the second level of competition, but was forced to withdraw because of illness. At Shreveport he competed against some of the area's most noted fiddlers,

J. F. Page, H. C. Wilkerson, Willie Caston, and John W. Daniel. Louisiana State Fair Fiddle Contest, 1926. Photo courtesy of the Thomas Philyaw Collection/Ron Yule.

including John W. Daniel (Pineville), H. C. Wilkerson (Shreveport), Dave Page (Center, Texas), Bob Garrett (Timpson, Texas), Jim Pate (Nacogdoches, Texas), and Sanford R. Patterson (Shreveport).

When the Central Louisiana Fair, at Alexandria, began its fiddle contest, Caston was one of its first entrants. At the Alexandria contest, he won first in 1924 and 1927, second in 1925, and third in 1922. Articles in the *Alexandria Town Talk* indicate his contest repertoire included "Forked Deer," "Leatherbreeches," "Sally with the Pancakes," "Natchez Under the Hill," "Natchez Over the Hill," and "Thump the Devil."

He was also known to enter and win at a contest in New Orleans, sometime before 1926.

Several of Caston's children continued the tradition of contest fiddling. His daughter Fleecy Caston Philyaw was a formidable foe at fiddle contests, like her father before her. She won many contests throughout the area, placing second in Haynesville (1928), second at the Louisiana State Fair (1941), first at the Louisiana State Fair (1942), and first at the Claiborne Parish Fair (1948). Van, who lived in Haynesville, played the bass and helped to run the contest at the Claiborne Parish Fair after World War II. Modern-day fiddler Fred Beavers recalls Van playing the fiddle at the Claiborne Parish Fair.

A pioneering early-twentieth-century fiddler, teacher, and promoter, Willie Caston was one of the most respected fiddlers in the northwest area.

Interviews by Ron Yule: Fred Beavers (10-21-04) and Thomas Philyaw Jr. (4-17-2005).

References

Alexandria Town Talk. "Old Fiddlers in Big Contest." October 14, 1922.

———. "Old Fiddlers Draw Crowd." October 25, 1924.

———. "Old Fiddlers Play at Fair." October 24, 1925.

———. "Fiddlers and Better Babies Contest Hold Interest at Big Fair." October 22, 1927.

Haynesville News. "Van Caston's Father Dies In a Shreveport Hospital Friday." September 20, 1928.

Shreveport Journal. "Old Fiddlers' Contest won By Arcadia Fiddler." November 9, 1914.

———. "Hughes Spur Man Wins Old Fiddlers' Contest." November 2, 1917.

———. "Homemade Violins and One Picked Up From Battlefield Figure in Contest. J. W. Daniel Judged Best 'Old Fiddler.'" November 4, 1920.

———. "Jim Pate Wins First Place in Old Fiddlers' Contest at Fair." November 3, 1921.

———. "Old Fiddlers and Boy Scouts Given the Right of Way." October 26, 1922.

———. "Dave Page King of Old Fiddlers At La State Fair." October 25, 1923.

———. "32 Enter the Old Fiddlers' Contest." November 4, 1924.

———. "Dave Page Wins First Place in Old Fiddlers' Contest." November 6, 1924.

———. "Thirty-Seven Old Fiddlers Enter Annual Contest at La. State Fair." November 4 1925.

———. "J. W. Daniels of Shreveport Wins Fiddlers' Contest." November 5, 1925.

———. "Shreveport Man Wins Fiddlers' Contest at Fair." November 4, 1926.

———. "37 Old Fiddlers Stage Fine Show at the 1926 Fair." November 5, 1926.

———. "Winners in Old Fiddlers' Contest at State Fair." November 5, 1926.

———. "Patterson Wins '27 Old Fiddlers' Contest at Fair." November 4, 1927.

Shreveport Times. "Old Fiddlers Competition." November 12, 1913.

———. "Old Fiddlers Have Good Time." November 10, 1914.

———. "Prizes for All Entered in Old Fiddlers' Contest." November 5, 1915.

———. "Brothers Fiddle For Honors at State Fair." November 3, 1916.

———. "Old Fiddlers Match." October 24, 1919.

———. "Old Fiddlers Draw Big." November 4, 1921.

———. "Biggest Day of State Fair." October 27, 1922.

———. "Old Fiddlers in Action / Old Fiddlers in Fine Trim." October 27, 1923.

———. "Center Texas Man Wins Old Fiddlers' Contest For Second Time." November 7, 1924.

———. "Old Fiddlers to Play Today." November 5, 1925.

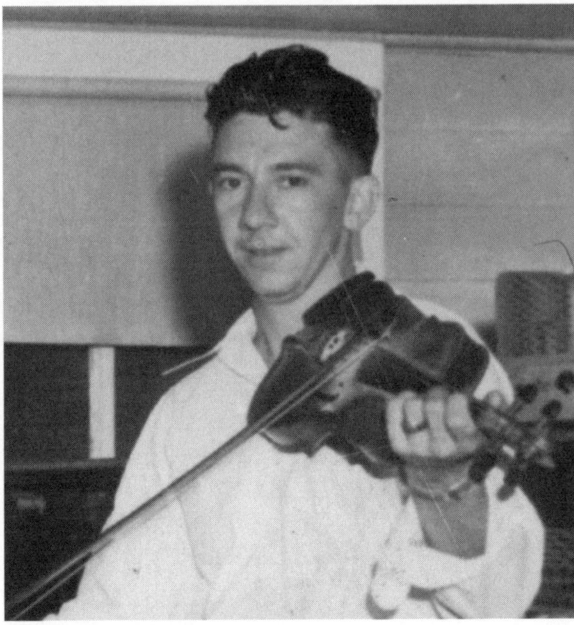

Photo courtesy of Delmar Sonnier.

HARRY CHOATES

(1922–1951) Cow Bayou

Harry Choates was born December 26, 1922, in a rural area in Vermillion Parish. He was a belated Christmas present for his parents Clarence and Edolia, as well as a gift to swing and Cajun music and especially fiddlers everywhere. He was the undisputed "King of Cajun Swing Fiddle," revered by country, swing, and Cajun fiddlers alike. Tim Knight, a Choates biographer, considers him "a special American genius." Karen Smith Lancon in her tribute to Harry on his tombstone terms him the "Godfather of Cajun Music." Crawford Vincent, a noted sideman who played with Choates, says, "He put Cajun on the map." He had a touch on the fiddle that was second to none. It is as if he was "born to play the fiddle."

Not much is known about his upbringing and formal education, but sometime in his youth he took steps to become very proficient on fiddle and guitar. He was known to also play mandolin and piano.

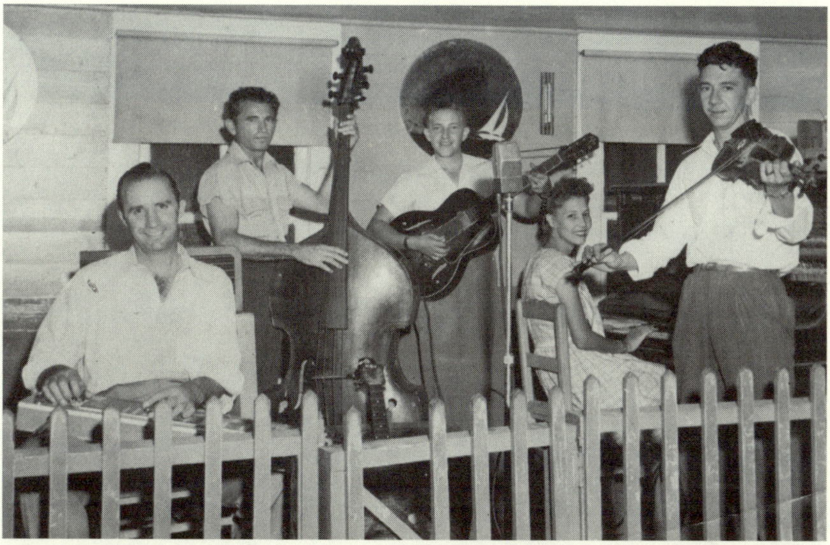

Red Fabacher, B. D. Williams, Joe Manuel, Johnnie Manuel, and Harry Choates. Unknown location, 1947. Photo courtesy of Delmar Sonnier.

Tim Knight notes in his liner notes to *Harry Choates: The Fiddle King of Cajun Swing*:

> *With his borrowed fiddle he and a friend who played guitar would visit barber shops, sit on the floor and play for the enjoyment of the shop's customers. Milton Bellot, a Port Arthur barber, had vivid recollections of the 12-year-old Harry Choates playing in his own very special style. When Harry would hit the high notes he would rise to his toes much to the delight of his listeners who would pitch nickels, dimes, and quarters to this budding musical genius.*

Crawford Vincent notes that Harry learned a lot from Cliff Bruner, a western swing fiddler who moved into the Houston/Beaumont area in 1937. Vincent believes Bruner was a main influence on him. In 1939 Choates joined Happy Fats and the Rayne-Bo Ramblers, playing on KVOL and at clubs in the area. They played western swing and very little French music. Although his stay with the Rayne-Bo Ramblers was short, it produced his first recording session. He played both electric guitar and fiddle and his reputation with the guitar was outweighing his talent on the fiddle.

Harry drifted from band to band and finally joined Leo Soileau, playing guitar, in the early 1940s. It was in this band that he met and played with some of his future band members, learned to really play Cajun fiddle and sing in

Hadley Castille and Tim Knight at Harry Choates's gravesite, 2005. Photo by author.

French, and learned the "Eh-Ha-Ha" which would be a trademark on many of his recordings. As before, he drifted from one band to the next while playing with Soileau. World War II brought induction into the Army. Following his service, he rejoined Leo Soileau and drifted again in and out of the band before leaving for good.

On March 31, 1946, Choates recorded his famous "Jole Blon" at Quinn Studios in Houston. It was done in an up-tempo waltz rhythm, which was probably an influence from his swing days. It reached an unheard-of #4 on *Billboard*'s country chart. Side B was "Basile Waltz," sung by Joe Manuel. This "Jole Blon" has influenced more fiddlers in the western corridor of Louisiana than any one recording. Fiddlers of all styles many times reply, "Harry Choates's 'Jole Blon'" when asked, "What's your favorite tune?" Old timers from Mamou to Lake Charles have recalled dances with Harry and said they were exciting and he would pack the house. One old-timer recalled "Jole Blon" being played over and over in a bar in Oberlin, and no one ever tired of hearing it.

Playing as Harry Choates and the Melody Boys (soon renamed the Jole Blon Boys), Harry played from the Avalon Club in Basile to Speedy's Broken Mirror in Sulphur to the Lighthouse in Port Arthur, Texas. They also began playing on radio station KPLC in Lake Charles.

Following the success of "Jole Blon" many other songs were recorded, including "Allons a Lafayette," "Cajun Hop," "Port Arthur Waltz," "Port Arthur Blues," "Poor Hobo," "Draggin' the Bow," "Louisiana Waltz," "Rubber Dolly," "Honky Tonk Boogie," and "Wrong Keyhole," a list of tunes that are still studied by Cajun, country, and swing fiddlers to this day. All the available Gold Star recordings plus those made with Happy Fats are available on Bear Family Records 16355 (2-CD set). The accompanying booklet *Devil in the Bayou*, by Andrew Brown, is the most extensive biographical work done to date on Harry Choates. This revealing book alone is worth the price of the package.

Harry never realized the nationwide extent of his fame that resulted from "Jole Blon," and turned down an offer to go to Nashville and the Grand Ole Opry. Toward the end of his life he left Louisiana and the Golden Triangle of Texas for the most part and worked in central, east, and west Texas and along the Gulf Coast of Texas.

On July 17, 1951, Harry Choates died in an Austin, Texas, jail as a result of complications from his alcohol addiction. Like generations of fiddlers and musicians that have followed him, generations in the future will study his music, trying to unravel the mystery of Harry Choates and his mastery of the music he loved.

In 2004 I did a survey for *My Fiddlin Grounds*, which involved a study of 700+ fiddlers from the western and upper regions of Louisiana who played from 1970 to 2004. Harry Choates's "Jole Blon" was the most popular song among these fiddlers. Harry Choates was the most popular fiddler of these musicians as well—and he had been dead for fifty-two years.

Interviews by Ron Yule: Carrol Broussard (9-21-2004), Tim Knight (4-18-2005), and Crawford Vincent (7-13-2003, 10-10-2003, 4-4-2004, 5-12-2004, and 9-22-2004).

References

Bastin, Bruce. Liner notes. *A Tribute to Harry Choates and his Cajun Fiddle*. Flyright 572, 1981.

Brasseaux, Ryan. *Bayou Boogie: The Americanization of Cajun Music*. Thesis. Louisiana State University, Baton Rouge, 2004.

Brown, Andrew. Liner notes. *Devil in the Bayou*. Bear Family CD, BCD 16355 BH, 2002.

Knight, Tim. Liner notes. *Harry Choates: The Fiddle King of Cajun Swing*. Arhoolie Records 5027, 1982.

———. Letter dated May 13, 2005, with comments on Harry Choates.

Yule, Ron. *My Fiddlin Grounds*. Center for Louisiana Studies, Lafayette, 2007.

CRAWFORD VINCENT ON HARRY CHOATES

Crawford Vincent, a sideman in the Hackberry Ramblers and a sideman and manager in Leo Soileau's Band, knew and played with Harry extensively.

I met Harry Choates in '41; he was playing guitar, mostly with Leo Soileau. They'd rotate with twin fiddles. I actually started jobbing with them in '43 on weekend jobs. He wanted to play French but he didn't know the words a lot of time. He got a lot of those words from Leo Soileau. That Eh-Ha-Ha, he'd run out of words and Leo would say Eh-Ha-Ha . . . Leo just loved him to death, he was his boy, you know. Called him his little boy. He'd quit, go to Houston, Fort Worth. He'd come back. Leo was at the Showboat and he'd tell him [Choates], 'if you ever need a job come back, you got a job.' And he did—that's the kind of man he [Soileau] was. He loved him to death. He was about seventeen. Happy Fats had hired him already.

I'll tell you that feller there; he could put a sound post in a violin the best I ever heard. I asked him one time, how do you fix that sound post? He said 'it's gotta be just a very little behind that bridge.' He could set that sound post with no trouble at all. He was just a talented man.

He could pick the guitar out of this world. Pee Wee Lyons, he played steel guitar with Harry Choates, Lefty Frizzell, and Ray Price. He used to live at my house and told me one time. He said, "We were in west Texas playing and on the way back. The Stan Kenton Orchestra was playing at a big nightclub, they didn't know who he was or nothing. We walked up to the bandstand. Harry Choates asked, 'Can I sit in?' They recognized him 'cause they knew him as a fiddle player. They looked at him and told him, 'We don't play that kind of music.' He said, 'I can play a little guitar if you'd let me.' They said, 'OK, come on in. What do you want to play?' So Harry Choates said, 'I'll play the "Woodchopper's Ball" or "In the Mood" or something like that.' And boy, ole

Harry Choates came in on that guitar up and down that keyboard, you know. Oh, them guys kept looking at him. 'Where in the world is that guy from anyway?' One of these guys says, 'He plays fiddle, he's a fiddle player. He made "Jole Blon" famous. What else you want to play, Mr. Choates?' Harry said, 'I'll play "In the Mood" or "September in the Rain" or something like that.'" [Note: This an unconfirmed story that Crawford cites as happening in Corpus Christi, Texas, in another account.]

Then he organized about a two- or three-piece band. But then after that he moved to Texas. He'd move around a lot . . . he moved to Corpus Christi with Joe Manuel, that was Abe's brother, and they played there. He always wanted me to travel, but I just wasn't ready to travel. I told him, "Harry you just go ahead and find yourself somebody else." To me, he put Cajun music on the map. Before that nobody wanted to hear it. When we played in Creole with the Hackberry Ramblers, and Luderin, it was strictly country like Tex Ritter and Bob Wills . . . Gene Autry, Jimmie Rodgers.

Harry would rather play the electric guitar than the fiddle. He was a genius on the electric guitar. . . . He loved the playing of Charlie Christian.

He borrowed my fiddle many times . . . everybody'd keep saying, "He didn't return it." I'd say, "Ah no, he returned my fiddle."

When I grew up years ago, fiddle players, they were scarce. If you could get one you'd hang on to him. Harry wanted to play that electric guitar. But we hired him for guitar. We eventually put him on the fiddle. He grabbed the fiddle and let me tell you something. That guy there he was just a talented man. He played the guitar a lot. Probably half and half.

He played in B flat a lot. He loved to play in E flat. We played the Rhythm Boys theme song in B flat . . . He recorded a lot of those Cajun numbers in A.

Harry wrote the theme song for the Rhythm Boys [Leo Soileau] to the melody of "Put on Your Old Gray Bonnet." [As sung by Crawford:]

Put on your ole grey bonnet
Come on by cracky
If you want to hear us play

Bring your blues and troubles
And they will bust like bubbles.
The Rhythm Boys will make you gay.

I made two recordings with him, "Jole Blon's Gone" and "Lake Charles Waltz" . . . I played the drums.

I wonder what he would have done with the Cajun accordion? You know he used piano accordion!

He played regular [with Bruner], I believe he played with Cliff Bruner and Moon Mullican in about 1940, before he got popular. Nobody knew who he was. He was just jobbing around . . . He went and worked with Cliff Bruner and Moon Mullican around Beaumont before he joined us. . . . He doubled up [on guitar and fiddle].

You could hum a song and he'd pick it up and play it out of this world. He borrowed my fiddle, especially when we'd play right here in Basile. He'd return it all the time. He wouldn't hock it like some people used to say. He was honest as they come as far as I'm concerned. . . . He'd borrow it when we played at the Green Lantern and he'd return it the same night.

As far as the guitar. He had his own guitar. That fiddle, he'd borrow it from me. [He played] an F-hole. It was a cheap, cheap guitar. The equipment wasn't very good . . . After he started making money he started buying better equipment. It's as simple as that.

He always had a good fiddle. Except, when we made the "Lake Charles Waltz" and "Jole Blon is Gone," he used my fiddle. He didn't have his for some reason or other.

I went and played a few jobs with him in Creole, Cameron, and Lawtell—while we made those records. After that he wanted me to go on the road with him in west Texas and I refused. I could have gone with Harry Choates all over. I had no idea he'd become as famous as he did.

RY: When y'all went in to record, did you know what songs you were going to play?

CV: No sir. He picked those two songs out of the blue sky. "Jole Blon is Gone" and "Lake Charles Waltz."

He almost burned the darn house down one time. He went to bed with a cigarette . . . Smoke was all over the place. The landlady dragged him outa there and he survived. That was about '44 . . . That was in Orange.

I had no idea he'd become as big as he did. He's actually bigger now since he died than he was.

COMMENTS FROM CARROL BROUSSARD

Comments from Carrol Broussard, who played and recorded on steel guitar with Harry in 1949 and 1950. He played steel guitar with many other bands including Robert Bertrand, Cliff Bruner, Moon Mullican, the Sulphur Playboys (with his father, Charles), Rufus Thibodeaux, Jo-El Sonnier, Abe and Joe Manuel, and Cledis Mott and the Tune Toppers. He played on the J. D. Miller recording "Tribute to Harry Choates" with Rufus Thibodeaux, Abe Manuel, and Dorothy Manuel.

I worked for Harry two or three different times, but I started in 1949. When I started with him we had a sit-down job at the Triangle Club here in Lake Charles. After that we moved to Corpus Christi for that summer of '49, came back and worked in Opelousas, in that area.

The first recording was the "Sidewalk Waltz." We went back and recorded with him right before the band broke up . . . must have been in 1950.

Harry took the cure at one time. For maybe about a month and a half he didn't drink. He was a different person . . . He went to "Alex" [Central State Hospital in Pineville]. When he came back he was more businesslike and got along with everybody.

RY: How would you describe his fiddle playing?
CB: Excellent! A lot of his songs were a Bob Wills style of fiddle. He knew a lot of Cajun songs. I don't know if he had a favorite. He liked to play them both. He was a guy who made style. He had his own style. That's really what made him.

Harry never played over people's head. I guess that's what made him. He didn't play too much of that jazz type stuff. He was just playing what people understood. That's what made him.

He played what people liked. There are a lot of great musicians but they play over people's heads. They don't become great . . . they're good musicians. He was a stylist.

"Jole Blon" was in A. He'd played in E flat, B flat, he could play in any key.

If you listen to some of his records, you can still hear the fiddle [while he was singing]. He wouldn't be playing the true melody all the way, but you could still hear the fiddle while he'd be singing. . . . He did it on the bandstand just like he did it on the record.

When we recorded "Sidewalk Waltz" we got $20 a piece. That's probably like $200 today . . . That was fifty-something years ago.

He played with the piano accordion. The "Sidewalk Waltz" was recorded with a piano accordion.

RY: Did he ever play with a Cajun diatonic accordion?
CB: No, not that I know of. I don't believe that he did. It wasn't his style.

Years ago it ["Jole Blon"] may have been played in G. He went to A. What he did—he stepped it up. He put a lot of good licks in there. That's what really made it. If he'd played that old style it wouldn't have made any more than anybody else.

LETTER FROM TIM KNIGHT

Tim Knight, from Port Arthur, Texas, is a professor at Lamar University at Port Arthur and a Choates biographer and writer. He has studied Harry's life, especially his younger life while in Port Arthur. In 1982 Tim wrote the extensive liner notes to Harry Choates: The Fiddle King of Cajun Swing. His forthcoming book on the life of Harry Choates, Poor Hobo, will hopefully be published in the near future. Recently he was chosen to narrate the "Tribute to Harry Choates" by Hadley Castille and the Sharecroppers at the Liberty Theatre in Eunice.

May 13, 2005

Ron,

I can add a few things if that's OK with you. His birth certificate states that he was born December 26, 1922, in Cow Island, Louisiana, a small community near Kaplan. There were no medical personnel available so Idolie Menard gave birth to her "little boy" with the help of a local veterinarian. Some people have laughed at this, but I find it rather sad and touching.

Many have said that Harry was illiterate with no education, however records show that his father, Clarence Choate enrolled him in the Port Arthur Public School System on March 27, 1933. He completed the 7th grade and dropped out at the end of the 7th grade. Harry was 14 at the time and was already making "good money" playing in bars and Bellot's Barber Shop on Procter Street. Even though he had family in Louisiana, his base of operations would be Port Arthur with its wide-open life style and jobs available at the Gulf and Texas Company Refineries.

Everyone listens to some kind of music. The music people listen to explains their personality and if you will, their soul. Harry touched their souls. He died alone in jail surrounded by his personal demons, a helpless victim of alcohol abuse. True he never took care of his family obligations or anything else for that matter. However he did leave a legacy of his music that makes men like Hadley, you, and me travel to a graveyard in Port Arthur to stand and wonder what might have been. The best tribute of all was the fiddle music from the both of you drifting across the cemetery under a bright blue spring sky. These are my thoughts I hope you will understand and let me hear from you.

Sincerely,
Tim

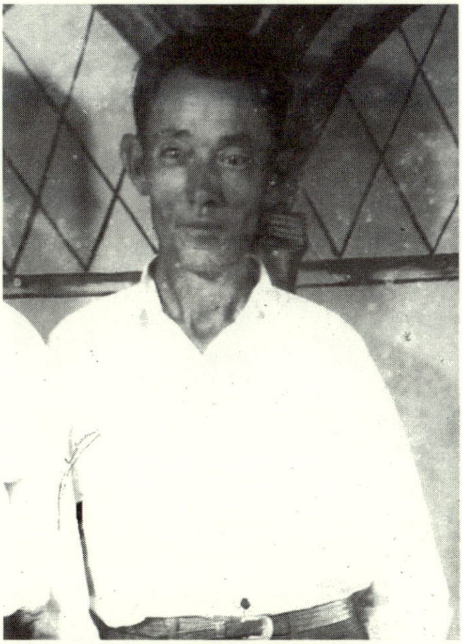

Photo courtesy of Jimmy Coke.

HITER COLVIN

(1900–1975) Dubach

Hiter (Pee Wee) Colvin was one of Louisiana's pioneering fiddle recording artists and professional musicians. He was born near Dubach in 1900 on Boardtree Creek in the Fellowship Community. No one can recall whether his ancestors played music but his father, Thomas, apparently wanted someone in the family to play because he bought a fiddle at a Monroe pawnshop and offered it to the first of his nine children who would learn to play it. Hiter earned the fiddle.

Hiter learned early on that he could make money playing the fiddle, and throughout his lifetime he made a living playing at country dances, barbershops, fiddle contests, serenades, and dancehalls. Although he did hold down a public job near the end of his life, playing music was his major source of income (as well as farming on a small scale). Hiter was a diminutive man and,

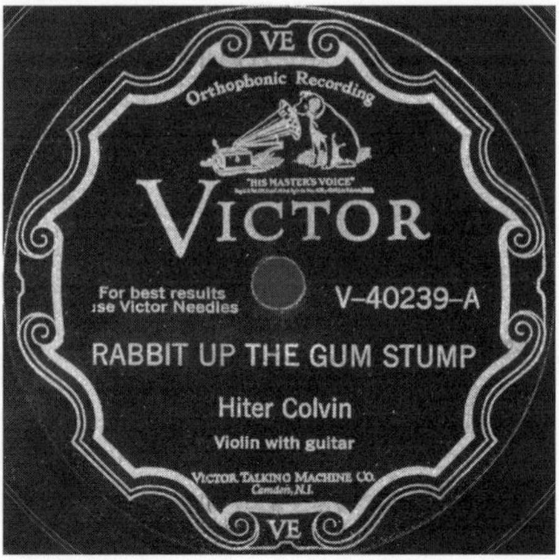

as his great-nephew Jimmy Coke points out, he was not able to do much heavy work.

Hiter had been traveling into southern Arkansas frequently playing dances and on one of his trips to El Dorado in 1921 he met several musicians who would play with him throughout the 1920s and off and on throughout his lifetime. "Pee Wee," as all the musicians knew him, was in El Dorado to entertain with his fiddle and make money wherever he could pass the hat and get a few bucks. Jimmy recalls stories of the group playing with Hiter on fiddle, Hilton Coke (b. 1903) on guitar and fiddle, Pete Coke on mandolin, Jack Westmoreland on fiddle, and "Peg" Simms (nicknamed because of his peg leg) on bass fiddle or guitar.

Not confined to Arkansas, Hiter and Hilton played throughout northern Louisiana and eastern Texas following the "oilfield money" during their 1920s heyday. They played wherever they could gather a group of people, but mainly in bars, dancehalls, and clubs. Jimmy notes that,. with Hiter's talent playing fiddle, it did not take much to gather a crowd. As Hiter's recorded works will attest, he was adept at all the appealing fiddle tune styles of the time, from blues to beautiful double-stop waltzes to foot-stomping energetic breakdowns.

Bronice Colvin Chelette, Hiter's niece, recalls him as very limber even until the day he died. One of his favorite acts was to trick fiddle, playing the fiddle behind his back, behind his head, between his legs, etc. Bornice recalls him playing "Listen to the Mockingbird" during this trick fiddle maneuver, but Jimmy notes he could do this on any tune he played. This was a crowd-pleasing act and probably helped generate a larger pot at impromptu performances.

In 1926 Hiter married Eloise Torrence; they had one son, Hyter, and two daughters, Geraldine and Norma Jean.

Although the circumstances are not known, Hiter began playing with guitar player Herb Sherrill in the late 1920s, probably in the east Texas oilfields. On October 21, 1929, he and his guitarist friend, Herb Sherrill, traveled to Dallas and recorded six sides for Victor records. The tunes, "Indian War Whoop," "Monroe Stomp," " Dixie Waltz," "Old Lady Blues," "Hiter's Favorite Waltz," and "Rabbit Up the Gumstump," were distributed on the Victor Label. Mike Luster, in his tribute to Hiter, "Remembering Hiter Colvin, the Fiddle King of Oilfield and Gumstump," notes "Rabbit Up the Gumstump" was Hiter's "evocative showpiece said to be a portrayal of the dogs pursuing rabbits down along Boardtree Creek." The energetic breakdown tune, which was played in an AEAE tuning, has overtones of other traditional fiddle tunes played throughout the United States, namely "Cripple Creek" "and "John Brown's Dream." Tony Russell also states that "Rabbit Up the Gumstump" was also issued on the Montgomery Ward label as "Rabbit in the Pea Patch." Luster further notes:

> *The records sold well for Victor and they even ran a two-page display ad in one of their catalogs with Jimmie Rodgers pictured on one page and Hiter Colvin on the other, but Colvin saw little money from them and refused to record again. . . . Jimmie Rodgers himself came to town, trying to convince Colvin to join him on the road, but the fiddler refused, opting instead to keep company with his buddy Sherrill or with a peg-legged guitarist and follow the oilfield money.*

Sometime around the late 1920s, Hiter and Hilton began to play more sporadically; by 1933, when Hilton married, caring for their families separated them for a while. Hiter moved back to east Texas to play around Kilgore, again following the oilfield money. Luster cites one story that highlights Hiter's great talent with the fiddle:

> *His honky tonk dances were legendary. On one occasion, he played at a highway nightspot while the celebrated Light Crust Doughboys played to a largely empty house at another across the road. At the end of the evening, the Doughboy bus pulled into the yard at the Colvin house trying to get the man they couldn't lick to join them, but again Colvin chose to stay put to play in the clubs and sometimes even in the Pentecostal church. He remained in Kilgore for seven or eight years, during which time his marriage broke up and his family moved back to Sandy Bend [Arkansas].*

Luster notes that Hiter left east Texas in the mid-1930s, returned to Arkansas, and sometime around 1940 returned to northern Louisiana. Upon his return he continued to play dances, using a nephew, Bill Bagwell, as well as others as accompanists. He also continued to play at fiddle contests and serenades to try to earn a meager living. Hilton Coke eventually moved to the Monroe area, following Hiter to north Louisiana, working in the oilfields, carpentering, farming, and as a mechanic.

After they reunited they played on local radio stations around Monroe, as well as on television station KNOE in the mid-to-late fifties on the *Happiness Exchange,* a weekly Saturday program that featured local talent. Jimmy recalls the group playing at the Old Trading Post on the outskirts of Monroe in the 1950s. These Saturday evening shows were broadcast over local radio and also featured numerous local groups. They played their all-instrumental music everywhere they could: square dances, barbershops, stores, churches, and dance-halls. Jimmy notes that the normal modus operandi was to play a while and gather a crowd and Hiter would pass the hat, and then play a few more and pass the hat again. This would continue until he was satisfied with the take, and then they would move on to another place.

In 1961 Hiter received a gunshot to his face that impaired him for the rest of his life. Various theories as to the circumstances surrounding this tragedy have been proposed by family members, but no one has given a definite explanation as to what happened. His massive injuries led to his hospitalization, and he spent two years in the hospital in Shreveport. Nearing death and in despair with a need to keep his spirits up, as well as the spirits of everyone there, he kept his trusty fiddle by his side and played every chance he could, bringing cheer to the whole ward. Jimmy recalls he could hardly speak and wore a cloth over the wound. To converse, he would write everything down on a pad.

Following his release from the hospital, he moved permanently to Bentley, in Grant Parish, to live with his brother, H. B. (Brown) Colvin, eventually moving to a small home on the property, where he lived alone.

Throughout Hiter's life much of his income came from playing music, but Bronice recalls he worked for the U.S. Forestry Service in Grant Parish during the 1950s, and periodically came to Bentley for visits with the family. After his release from the hospital, he rejoined the U.S. Forestry Service.

Hilton joined him in Central Louisiana and they played together until Hiter's death in 1975. Hiter's playing in later years was mainly confined to playing at the Bentley United Pentecostal Church and at jam sessions among friends, with many of these sessions being held in the yard at Hiter's place.

Pecan Festival Fiddle Contest, Colfax, 1971: Hiter Colvin playing. Fiddlers on deck: Doug Lee, Ray Beebe, Kenneth Tackett, Warren Ferrier, and Fred Beavers. Photo courtesy of Louisiana Pecan Festival/Bill Landrum.

Since Hiter also played guitar and Hilton played fiddle, they would trade instruments during these impromptu jam sessions.

In 1970 and 1971 Hiter entered the Louisiana Pecan Festival Fiddle Contest in Colfax, being taken to the contest by his niece, Bronice.

After a stay in a local nursing home, Hiter passed away in 1975; Hilton followed in 1977. Their musical partnership spanned over fifty years, bringing some of the finest fiddle music to fans and listeners in the three-state area of Arkansas, Texas, and Louisiana.

Jimmy, who played guitar with them at these home jam sessions, recalls that Hiter leaned toward more difficult tunes with many chord changes. He recalled, "He especially liked tunes such as 'Kelly Waltz' and 'Wednesday Night Waltz,' tunes that could be classified as old-time or contest-style tunes."

In addition, numerous inquiries have surfaced concerning knowledge of the guitarist who accompanied Hiter on his Dallas recordings. Attempts to locate and verify Herb Sherrill have been unproductive. During the 1920s, a Herbert Sherrill Sr. lived near Athens in northern Louisiana and his children attended school in Gibsland in the 1950s. One son, Doyle, was a bluegrass musician (mandolin, guitar, and vocals) playing in bands around the Dallas, Texas, area and another, Herbert Jr., was the promoter of the Home Place Acres Bluegrass Festival near Athens in the 1980s and nineties. Since Athens

Hilton Coke and Hiter Colvin, 1940s.
Photo courtesy of Jimmy Coke.

is only a short distance from Dubach, it is thought that Herbert Sr. might be the guitarist on these recordings. No family members recall his musicianship in the early 1900s, and no records are available to verify this.

Hiter's recorded fiddle tunes continue to be released on various old-time compilations. "Indian War Whoop," "Monroe Stomp," and "Rabbit Up the Gumstump" have been the tunes released on BACM (British Archives of Country Music), Roots of American Fiddle Music Volume I, and County Records.

Hiter's impact has been felt throughout the old-time musical community. Modern-day fiddlers who study many of the old recordings have learned several of Hiter's recordings. John Hartford, a student of old-time fiddling in the United States, studied Hiter's music, penning a transcription of "Indian War Whoop" that appears in the Winter 1991 issue of *The Devil's Box*. A recent DVD, *Music for the Sky* by Nikolai Fox, a documentary that features fiddlers from Vermont, showcases Jim Burns playing Hiter's "Monroe Stomp." North Louisiana fiddlers Roy Beckham and Owen Perry both loved Hiter's fiddle playing, considering him the best in the area. Present-day Louisiana fiddler Curry Perkins and nationally known guitarist John Beland have learned several of Hiter's recorded tunes and consider them very challenging. Studies are continuing on the tunes unique to Louisiana fiddlers, and several of Hiter's tunes qualify for this venture by Perkins and the author.

Interviews by Ron Yule: Fred Beavers (7-10-2005), Jimmy Coke (6-14-2007 and 6-27-2007), Bronice Colvin Chellette (6-22-2007), Curry Perkins (7-15-2008), Susan Roach (9-8-2008), Pearl Sherrill (3-25-2008), and Joe Spence (9-9-2008).

References

Colvin, Ethel, and Baker Colvin. *Colvin and Allied Families*. Hurley Printing, 1965, 174.

Fox, Nikolai. *Music In the Sky*. DVD, 60 minutes. Vermont Music and Library Shop, 2008.

Hartford, John. Tune transcription, "Indian War Whoop." *The Devil's Box*, Madison Alabama, vol. 25, no. 4 (Winter 1991).

Luster, Mike. "Remembering Hiter Colvin, the Fiddle King of Oilfield and Gumstump." *Shreveport Sounds in Black and White*. Kip Lornell and Tracey E. W. Laird, editors. University Press of Mississippi, Jackson, Mississippi, 2007.

Russell, Tony. *Country Music Records: A Discography, 1921–1942*. New York: Oxford University Press, , 2004.

Yule, Ron. *My Fiddlin' Grounds*. Center for Louisiana Studies, University of Louisiana, Lafayette, 2007.

Photo courtesy of Steve Conn and Molly Conn Wiley.

VERTIS ROY "PEANUT" CONN

(1919–1964) Pineville

Although Vertis Roy "Peanut" Conn's life would be cut short because of injuries from World War II, he was admired by those who knew and heard him play in central Louisiana. Peanut was born in Copiah County, Mississippi, in 1919, and took to the fiddle at the age of ten. His talent bloomed early, and by the age of twelve he was sneaking off with his brother Hilton to play at various country dances and juke joints in the central Mississippi county south of Jackson. By fourteen Roy had moved to Louisiana and in 1936 was living in Sicily Island. News spread fast of his great talent on the fiddle.

The Henry Casson Clark family, from Alexandria, had been playing string band music since the early 1920s but disbanded their family band, Clark's Stringband, sometime in the early 1930s. Several family members began a band with Millard "Curly" Cupit and Louis Peck, two central Louisiana guitar players, and Curly brought Peanut from Sicily Island to Pineville to play fiddle for them. Peanut stayed with the Matthew "Punk" Clark family and roomed with the Clark boys.

The band, Clark's Hotshots, played a variety of music, from hillbilly country string band to western swing. They traveled all over the area and were even offered a radio program in Dallas for a major flour company, but some of the band members did not want to go. Locally they played weddings, house dances, and local shows. In 1936 KALB opened for broadcast, and the band, renamed Clark's Merrymakers, had one of the first shows, a daily spot (2:30 to 3:00 p.m.). They joined the Jones Brothers, from nearby Colfax, and the Baum Brothers, from Pollock, as well as other local musicians from the area. Their popularity is noted by the fact that, at the peak of their appearances on KALB, they were receiving 100 cards and letters per day. Roy played with the Clarks for the ensuing years until the late 1930s, when World War II took priority. During this period he also freelanced with other bands, such as the Clear Creek Wanderers, and played on KALB and at dances at the Bentley Hotel in downtown Alexandria. Hershel Barron, a member of the Wanderers, recalls that they would play the show at the station in the evening and walk across the street and play the dance, usually for soldiers encamped at local military bases. Herschel states, "We'd leave the radio station and go across the street and play [Wahl Hotel] 'til the curfew . . . that was eleven o'clock." They also played at the Dixie Inn in Cottonport, on Saturday night and the Black Cat in Marksville on Sunday night. He adds, "It wasn't anything to have 300 to 350 couples down there." They had a microphone for the acoustic instruments and vocals and an electric guitar for the lead.

Steve, Roy's son, recalls that Peanut was named "one of the best Swing Violinists in the South and Southwest" by *Melody Maker* magazine in 1941. His demand as an instrumentalist was increasing but, unfortunately, he was drafted into the military the following year, and spent 26 months in the infantry in the South Pacific, eventually fighting in the Philippine Campaign in 1944. In action on Saipan, on the road to Baguio, Peanut was severely wounded, losing his left leg at the knee and severely injuring his right foot. He wore a wooden leg the rest of his life. He received a Bronze Star and a Purple Heart for his service to the nation.

After serving in World War II, Peanut returned to Alexandria and picked up where he left off. He continued playing in clubs, but his style was changing. The influence of the military and the bases around Alexandria brought a need for a different style of music. The music became even more swing oriented,

Mack Hull, Peanut Conn, Pete Carlino, Jimmie Davis, Phil Harding, and unidentified trombone player. Myles Park, Alexandria, May 23, 1959. Photo courtesy of Steve Conn and Molly Conn Wiley.

following the sound of the big bands and Bob Wills and the Texas Playboys. Peanut called this "Hillbilly Jazz."

In 1948 Peanut, along with Dan Welch (steel guitar), Mack Hull (guitar), a bassist, and several horn players, played a club in Cottonport every Friday and Saturday night for two years. Calling themselves the Cavaliers, they played every style from Broadway to country and swing. Wallace Moreau played the sax and clarinet in the beginning, singing the pop tunes while Peanut would sing the country songs. After Wallace left the band, Dan began singing the pop tunes. He notes they did not play Cajun music, even "Jole Blon," which they got lots of requests for. When they first went to the club to audition the crowds were very sparse, and Dan laughingly recalls the conversation with the owner in a November 2006 interview: "Well we can give you boys $20 a night which was good pay back then or you can take the door. [They said] We'll take the $20. And that was a mistake [laugh]." He says they built up the club and always regretted that original decision.

Under several names (including Peanut and the Plantation Boys and the Vagabonds) and with a few changes in instrumentation and personnel, the group played at clubs and dancehalls all around central Louisiana. In late 1949

Phil Harding, a bassist who had played with orchestras throughout the Midwest and Plains states, moved to Alexandria and was approached by Peanut about forming an orchestra. The fifteen-piece Roy Conn Orchestra played around Central Louisiana and at local jazz clubs like the Roof Top and Blue Moon. The orchestra's biggest shows were at the Frontier Club and the Mirror Room at the Bentley Hotel. Roy was the vocalist and fiddler, but he could also play guitar, banjo, and piano. He arranged and scored the music, many times playing big band music as well as jazz. Besides arranging, he wrote several tunes performed by the orchestra, one being "I'm Still in Love with You."

This group played until the later 1950s but Phil remembers that Peanut would play with a combo of any size depending on the needs of the club or promoter. He notes that in the early sixties the band decided to not play on New Year's Eve and a man from Colfax called at the last minute for a replacement band. Peanut and Phil decided to play the gig as a duo. He notes, "We played just the fiddle and the bass from six to nine—and no one went home."

Roy was also known to play with Jimmie Davis and the Sunshine Band (during Davis's 1959 gubernatorial campaign), Herman Scallan, and R. G. Coleman (steel guitarist).

The only studio recordings they made were on "metal plate disc," and they used these mainly for demos to get jobs. They continued to play on KALB and at least one tape of a radio show exists, a live recording of the combo (with R. G. Coleman on steel, Buck Bryant on drums, Hank Bendickson on bass. and Mack Hull on guitar) from the Frontier Hotel in downtown Alexandria in 1952. There is also another recording of the big band from the 1954 pharmacists' convention at the Bentley Hotel.

Even though his orchestra was in demand throughout central Louisiana, Peanut never gave up his day job. He worked as a cobbler after World War II at the Pineville Shoe Shop, at Central Louisiana Electric Company, and Southern Chevrolet before eventually becoming an insurance agent, which was his main occupation until his death.

He continually had to struggle with the injuries he sustained in the war. He developed diabetes and heart trouble, and this, coupled with problems with his prosthesis, caused severe health problems. He passed away in 1964 at the young age of 45.

His son, Steve, is a professional musician playing numerous instruments including the fiddle. He currently resides in Tennessee and is a songwriter, recording artist, and studio musician. Peanut's granddaughter, Jennifer Painter, is an accomplished violinist, with a degree in music from LSU. She is the

Clark's Alexandria Hotshots/Merrymakers; Louis Peck, Peanut Conn, Curly Cupit, and Mathew Clark, announcer, and Lafe Clark. 1936, KALB radio. Photo courtesy of Steve Conn and Molly Conn Wiley.

director of the orchestra at the Nashville School of the Arts. His grandson, Shamus Fuller, and great-grandson, Dylan Fuller, also play the fiddle.

Peanut Conn was an extraordinary musician, teacher, and bandleader and was revered by many of the fiddlers—like Hermon Lasyone and Eddie Friday—who graced the 1940s and 1950s central Louisiana country and dance hall scene. He has a legacy of being a great entertainer, musician, and one of the best swing fiddlers you would ever want to hear.

Interviews by Ron Yule: Bill Clark (6-19-2004), Shelby Clark (6-19-2004), Steve Conn (11-29-2006), Eddie Friday (3-12-2003), Shamus Fuller (12-11-2003 and 2-22-2004), Phil Harding (11-30-2006), Hermon Lasyone (12-15-2002), and Dan Welch (11-30-2006).

Reference

Alexandria Town Talk. "KALB Program News." September 9, 1938.

———"KALB Program Schedule." May 9, 1936; December 1, 1937; November 17, 1937.

Yule, Ron. *When the Fiddle Was King.* Fiddle Country Publishing, DeRidder, Louisiana, 2006.

Photo courtesy of Mitchell Conner.

VARISE CONNER

(1906–1994) Lake Arthur

Varise Conner, like numerous fiddlers in the western corridor, chose to stay home and play the fiddle with family and friends. Playing on the road and making music a livelihood was not his cup of tea. He was a quiet man who worked in the timber industry as a sawmill operator. His fiddling was born from the age-old style of his ancestors but would influence a new generation of fiddlers who appreciated his intricate noting, rhythm, and timing—and with hardly any fanfare whatsoever.

The Conner family migrated from Ireland in the late 1700s, and included in Varise's ancestry was a long line of musicians who had played country dances in south Louisiana since the mid-1800s around Lake Arthur. It is not known whether the original Conner family immigrants played musical instruments, but Varise's grandfather, Octave, played fiddle. His father, Arcene, was a fiddler, and Varise watched and listened to him at old country dances as he played dance tunes common to their ancestry.

Varise learned to play around the age of nine. His first efforts were to sneak his father's fiddle out while his father, a farmer, was in the field working. When he heard the sound of the horse's trace chains as Arcene was coming in from the field, he would put the fiddle up. At a dance one night, an uncle who was playing the fiddle handed it to Varise while he took a break. When Varise began to play, Arcene was astounded and thought he had been born with the talent to just pick up the fiddle and play.

Once his father learned of Varise's interest, he purchased for twelve dollars a copy of a 1713 Stradivarius violin that had belonged to a cousin, Adelard (Adler) Conner. The violin had been left in a local repair shop and Varise and his father paid the repair ticket on it. Although Varise had also learned guitar, and his brothers, Murphy and Valsin, played fiddle, they finally decided that Varise was the best at fiddle and Murphy was best at rhythm guitar, so each played those instruments primarily. Valsin, who had injured a hand in a dynamite cap explosion, played bass fiddle.

With fiddle, guitar, and bass fiddle they played around the house as a string band, eventually venturing out to play at a few country dances, which would net them a little extra pocket money. After playing a few house dances, they decided to play at one of the local dance halls, Lake Arthur's famous Bucket of Blood. One night they went to the dancehall and asked if they could play for the crowd. After getting permission, they played and the crowd liked them, so they were asked to finish the dance. Their reputation spread and they began to play at other country dances and family get-togethers, becoming highly popular around Lake Arthur. Many times they played at dances in places that could only be reached by boat. A first cousin, Arcade Conner, played the fiddle and would come to the dances and play second fiddle to Varise.

George, Varise's son, notes that his father played the same reels, waltzes, mazurkas, polkas, two-steps, and tunes he had heard from his forefathers, in a style he had learned from his family, as well as from other early-twentieth-century sources. He related to Mitchell, another of Varise's sons, that Irish immigrants who worked on the railroad in the early 1900s would hear of a local house dance and attend it, and because many were fiddlers they would join in the music festivities and play for the dancers. During the dances tunes got traded and the local fiddlers learned from different varying outside sources. Varise also learned tunes from other local fiddlers, like Oscar and Valsin Aguillard in addition to learning tunes from commercial recordings and radio.

Varise, Milton, and Murphy Conner, 1958. Photo courtesy of Mitchell Conner.

One of Varise's favorite tunes, "Memphis Blues," was learned from a cylinder recording.

Mitchell notes that Varise played in many different tunings. He played in standard tuning (GDAE), as well as FCGD, a tuning he did not care for. On several tunes, Varise would tune higher so he could reach certain notes. There were various cross tunings he used for certain songs, but the family does not recall what they were.

In 1927 Varise put together his famous composition, "Lake Arthur Stomp," one of several fiddle tunes he penned. The tune was originally called "Lake Arthur Two-Step," but was soon renamed the "Lake Arthur Stomp." George recalls, "It was such a lively dance, everyone would stomp their feet, so they renamed the tune." This tune has been played and recorded by many fiddlers including Ken Smith, Rufus Thibodeaux, J. B. Fuselier, David Greely, and Will Kegley.

In 1928 the recordings of Joe Falcon with accordion became popular and changed the nature of the dance music around Lake Arthur. Mitchell recalls his dad saying that most of the music around Lake Arthur before 1928 was string band, featuring the fiddle and fiddle tunes of Irish and French music. After the introduction of the accordion, everyone wanted to hear it at the

Varise Conner and Edgar Benoit at Mamou fiddle contest, 1980. Photo courtesy of Calvin Ardoin.

dances. Sometime in the early 1930s, J. B. Fuselier moved to Lake Arthur and played accordion with the Conner Boys for several years at dances. Crawford Vincent recalls that, when he was a boy, Varise and J. B. played dances at Savan Roy's in Creole. In later years, he recalled, he jammed with Varise and described him as a "a fine fiddler." Although Varise played at dances with J. B., he never recorded with him. J. B. did record Varise's signature tune, "Lake Arthur Stomp," on February 27, 1937, for Bluebird in New Orleans.

The Conner Boys played with other musicians from the area. One notation in the *Lake Arthur News* in 1934 reports Varise and Murphy playing at a sixtieth wedding anniversary party for Mr. And Mrs. Euzebe Trahan, joined by Sidney Broussard (fiddle), Sidney Broussard Jr. (guitar), Edgar Benoit, and Clarphy Landry.

Mitchell recalls hearing his father talk about the struggles of having a dance band in the troubled times of the 1930s. With the Depression in full bloom and money scarce, the take at dances became less and less. The situation got so bad that sometimes as many as a hundred people would come to the dances and stand outside and listen because they could not afford to come in. On one occasion the dance hall owner began to let the dancers in free, and this did not sit well with Varise. In 1935, Varise quit playing and told the others, "Y'all can play your life away for free if you want to, but not me." In 1940 Varise married, and his fiddle lay dormant until 1956.

In 1956, Varise's daughter, Ethel, who had continually urged her father to take up the fiddle and play, bought him a bow and told him he had no excuse for not playing the fiddle. Varise and Murphy rekindled their music making and began to play around the house and at family gatherings.

Varise soon met the fiddler and violinmaker/repairman, Lionel Leleux, from Lyon's Point near Kaplan. Lionel was a smooth Cajun fiddler who had played with some of the best musicians, including Joe Falcon and Nathan Abshire. Lionel was a friend of Bascom Mouton, another Lyon's Point fiddler, whose dynamic playing Varise loved. According to Mitchell, Bascom would move around a lot, holler, and sing songs in French. Mitchell remembers one of Bascom's favorite announcements before he played a dance: "Friends, I didn't come here to make y'all feel sad." Mitchell recalls his dad commenting about a lively all-evening session with Bascom and his effect on the furniture. "If it wasn't a good chair, at the end of the night he'd have to throw it away."

During the 1960s Varise continued to play and jam with Murphy and his son, Milton. His daughter, Barbara, and sons Mitchell, Andy, and George, learned to play rhythm guitar so they could play with their father. Ralph Jannise, a local fiddler from Gueydan, also jammed when he could.

In 1974 Varise began appearing at local Cajun concerts and festivals, being introduced to a new generation of Cajun musicians. He started attending fiddle contests, winning or placing in most he entered, and was recognized as a stylist by a younger generation of fiddlers. Folklorists and musicians began to study his life and music as those of an originator of a style of music from the turn of the century and earlier. Varise's influence has spread far and wide, with numerous fiddlers such as Ken Smith, Michael Doucet, and David Greely studying his playing style in great depth. Barry Ancelet, the noted folklorist, has authored *Cajun and Creole Music Makers*, which studies the life of Varise Conner and other pioneer Cajun musicians. David Greely writes in a May 2007 correspondence his thoughts on Varise:

> *Barry Ancelet introduced me to the music of Varise Conner. Varise's music was light and lilting, and almost always sounded happy, in contrast to the mournful heartbreak of the prairie songs with their titles like "Dying in Misery." Varise's bow hand was both an inspiration and a challenge, and twenty-plus years later I'm still challenged by his tone and rhythm.*
>
> *Something about Varise's refusal to cater to popular tastes had a powerful appeal to me. It's the repertoire of a musician's musician, with no need for lyrics or singers, no one worried about playing too many waltzes, no accordions to try to outgun—*

just Varise and Lionel Leleux and a few guitars, playing in perfect tune, time, and timbre.

It doesn't get any better. It's fiddle heaven.

Audio recordings from 1970s sessions recorded by Barry Ancelet have been released on Louisiana Crossroads Records. The recording, *Louisiana Folk Masters: Varise Conner* is available from Louisiana Crossroads Records, 211 E. Devalcourt Street, Lafayette, Louisiana 70506.

Interviews by Ron Yule: George Conner (6-25-2004 and 7-24-2004), Mitchell Conner (7-26-2004 and 8-6-2004), and David Greely (November 2003, Dewey Balfa Cajun Music Camp class on Varise Conner's music).

References

Ancelet, Barry and Elemore Morgan Jr. *Cajun and Creole Music Makers.* University Press of Mississippi, Jackson, Mississippi, 1999.

Ancelet, Barry, Michael Doucet, and David Greely. Liner notes. *Louisiana Folk Masters: Varise Conner.* Louisiana Crossroads Records, Lafayette, 2004.

Greely, David. E-mail, May 5, 2007.

Lake Arthur News. "Mr. And Mrs. Euzebe Trahan Celebrate Their Sixtieth Wedding Anniversary." May 4, 1934.

Photo courtesy of Thomas Philyaw Collection.

JOHN W. DANIEL

(1873–1931) Pineville

Editors note: Although his name is John W. Daniel, he is referred to as John W. Daniels in some of the noted accounts. In the accounts that follow the name used by the source (newspaper, census record, audio recording records, Death Certificate, and the Shreveport Directory) will be used (Daniels or Daniel).

In 1922 fiddlers Eck Robertson and Henry Gilliland recorded "Arkansas Traveler" and "Turkey in the Straw" for Victor. This landmark recording session sparked a procession of country fiddlers who would be recorded over the next few years. Within a few years, the names of John Carson, Clark Kessinger, Gid Tanner, Lowe Stokes, Doc Roberts, and many other fiddlers became household names because of their recordings. By the mid-twenties the recording industry moved further west, and many Texas fiddlers, including

Louisiana State Fair Winners, 1925. Shreveport Journal, Nov. 14, 1925. Bob Garrett, 4th; O. C. Storey, 3rd; G. C. Vallery, 2nd; and John W. Daniel, 1st.

Robertson, recorded even more sides; fiddler John W. Daniel would follow in their path and be the first Louisianan to record country music.

John was a perennial contestant and winner at fiddle contests in Alexandria and Shreveport from 1919 until 1930. He even bragged a little on himself in an article in the October 20, 1919, *Shreveport Journal*. "Another old fiddler, John W. Daniels of Pineville, La. entered the contest and accompanying his entry was a letter stating he was a 'red hot' contestant for first prize. . . . Mr. Daniels reports his violin is one of the finest in the land, valued at $1000, and says that after the State Fair he will permit any person to examine it." Accounts speak of his beautiful tone, smoothness, and ability on the fiddle. The *Shreveport Times* of November 7, 1924, stated: "He produced harmony pure and sweet, and there was not a squeak or single discordant note to mar his performances." And: "Mr. Daniels played . . . with such perfection and ease." The November 5, 1926, *Shreveport Journal* noted: "Bob Garrett of Timpson, Texas, one of the most noted old fiddlers, commenting on the award [John W. Daniel's first place prize] said, 'I have played in fiddle contests from New Orleans to Oklahoma and have met the most noted players in the country, but I am free to say that I have never seen or heard a man who could equal John Daniel.'"

John followed the lead of other fiddlers and recorded four sides for Victor in New York City on July 17, 1926. As noted in *The Devil's Box* by Charles Wolfe, this was probably a custom recording session. This session may have been paid for by Daniel or someone who fronted for the session. As far as is known, no copies or recordings of the session exist, because they were never issued. Todd Harvey, a researcher at the Library of Congress, in a recent letter notes that John played, as a violin solo, "Turkey in the Straw Quadrille," "Forked Deer Quadrille," "Charleston Hornpipe," and "Cottage Hornpipe," at this session. Todd's sources include Meade, Spottswood, and Meade in *Country Music Sources: A Biblio-Discography of Commercially Recorded Traditional Music* and Brian Rust in *The Victor Master Book, Volume Two (1925–1936)*. This recording session is a landmark in the annals of Louisiana country music.

John W. Daniel was born in Alabama in 1873 and migrated to central Louisiana before 1900. He joined other relatives who lived in the region. He is first noted as a contestant at the Louisiana State Fair in 1919, and over the last twelve years of his life, he lived briefly in DeQueen, Arkansas, as well as Pineville and Shreveport. He was an engineer, "a blue print expert," while he worked in both Pineville and in Shreveport. In Shreveport he worked for the Blumberg Mercantile Company. When he passed away in 1931, he was working on the Red River Bridge between Pineville and Alexandria.

Besides the tunes he recorded in 1926, he was known to play "Cackling Hen," "Polly Put the Kettle On," "Leather Britches," "Rattler's Farewell," "Can't Saddle My Mule," "Give My Girl a Tater," "Arkansas Traveler," and "Sally Goodin." After the 1922 Central Louisiana Fair he joined with guitarist Fred Randolph of Bayou Cocodrie, and played "Devil's Dream." The *Town Talk* notes, "Mr. Daniels announced that this is a tune which was frequently played by Uncle Vallery Broussard more than thirty years ago."

Over the years, John played with some of Louisiana's finest fiddlers, including Willie Caston, Fleecy Caston Philyaw, Reamey Patterson, J. E Richardson, and Bill Richardson, as well as the best fiddlers from east Texas: Bob Garrett, Jim Pate, Gus Pate, and Dave Page.

In 1926, at the peak of his contest domination, he retired. After the contest was over and he had accepted his award, he announced that he had won fifteen first and second prizes in fiddle contests during the last ten years and he was going to retire. He continued to help with the judging at the state fair, and entered the "Couples Division" in 1930, winning first place with Reamey Patterson.

The Old Fiddlers Club of Shreveport, under the direction of Dr. J. E. Richardson, had begun helping with the Louisiana State Fair in 1925, organizing the entertainment, instrument displays, and dancing as well as the fiddle contest. John Daniel was an active participant in the club, appearing on radio (WGAQ and KTBS), at square dances, and in fiddle contests around Shreveport. Murray Richardson, son of Dr. J. E. Richardson, vaguely recalls John Daniel being associated with his father and the fiddlers around Shreveport. He was a small boy and especially recalls others talking about Daniel and his highly talented fiddling.

Murray Richardson notes that he was an engineer in a recent interview, a point verified by his death certificate and an article in the *Alexandria Town Talk*, December 11, 1931. It reads:

> *Central Louisiana's noted fiddler, John W. Daniel, 58, died today while at his work as a blue print expert on the new Red River traffic bridge. Death was attributed to a heart attack.*
>
> *Every year at the Central Louisiana Fair, Daniel fiddled away to first prize in the "Old Fiddlers' Contest."*

John W. Daniel was a pioneer in Louisiana country music. His landmark recordings and appearances on radio and concerts with the Old Fiddlers Club of North Louisiana mark the beginning point that launched Shreveport into a position as an early front-runner in the country music industry in Louisiana. The Pelican Wildcats and Taylor-Grigg Melodymakers, as well as others, would follow and record and play on local radio stations KWKH, KRMD, and KWEA. North Louisiana fiddler Hiter Colvin recorded for Victor in 1929. Fiddlers Lonnie Hall, Preacher Harkness, and Dobber Johnson (all Louisiana-based fiddlers) playing with Bob and Joe Shelton's Sunshine Boys and additional fiddlers Tex Grimsley, Hank Strickland, Jack Kay, and Larry Bamburg would follow suit and eventually help create what Tillman Franks terms the "50 Mile Magic Circle." John was a part of the original movement that sparked Shreveport to its "glory days in country music" in the forties and fifties.

Interview by Ron Yule: Murray Richardson (2-5-2005).

References

Alexandria Town Talk. "Old Fiddlers in Big Contest." October 14, 1922.

Franks, Tillman. *I Was There When It Happened*. Sweet Dreams Publishing, Many, Louisiana, 2000.

Louisiana State Archives, Death Certificate of John W. Daniel. December 11, 1931.

Luster, Mike. "Remembering Hiter Colvin, the Fiddle King of Oilfield and Gumstump." *Shreveport Sounds in Black and White*. Kip Lornell and Tracey E. W. Laird, editors. University Press of Mississippi, Jackson, Mississippi, 2007.

Shreveport, Louisiana, City Directory, 1925. R. L. Polk and Co., Dallas, Texas.

Shreveport Journal. "Old Fiddlers Ready For Contest at Fair; Rivalry to be Keen." October 20, 1919.

———. "Homemade Violins and One Picked Up From Battlefield Figure in Contest. J. W. Daniel Judged Best Old Fiddler." November 4, 1920.

———. "Jim Pate Wins First Place in Old Fiddlers' Contest at Fair." November 3, 1921.

———. "Dave Page Wins First Place in Old Fiddlers Contest." November 6, 1924.

———. "Thirty-Seven Old Fiddlers Enter Annual Contest at La. State Fair." November 4, 1925.

———. "Winning Fiddlers." November 5, 1925.

———. "J. W. Daniels of Shreveport Wins Fiddlers Contest." November 5, 1925.

———. "Shreveport Man Wins Fiddlers' Contest at Fair." November 4, 1926.

———. "37 Old Fiddlers Stage Fine Show at the 1926 Fair." November 5, 1926.

———. "Winners in Old Fiddlers' Contest at State Fair." November 5, 1926.

———. "Two Shreveport Fiddlers Win at La. Fair Contest." November 8, 1929.

Shreveport Times. "Old Fiddlers Match." October 24, 1919.

———. "Fiddlers Contest." November 5, 1920.

———. "Old Fiddlers Draw Big." November 4, 1921.

———. "Center Texas Man Wins Old Fiddlers' Contest at State Fair For Second Time." November 7, 1924.

———. "Fiddlers Attract Crowd." November 6, 1925.

———. "Shreveport Old Fiddlers Winners in Two Classes in Annual Contest at State Fair Grounds on Thursday." November 8, 1929.

United States Census Records. Alexandria Historical Library, Alexandria, Louisiana.

Wilson, J. L. "She's Fit to Fiddle." *Shreveport Times*, December 7, 1975.

Wolfe, Charles. *The Devil's Box*. Country Music Foundation Press and Vanderbilt Press, Nashville, Tennessee, 1997.

Photo courtesy of the author.

LUDERIN DARBONE

(1913–2008) Sulphur

Luderin Darbone was born in Evangeline, Louisiana, on January 14, 1913, to Eddie (Edval) Darbone and Nora Agnes McFarlain Darbone. They soon moved to Orangefield, Texas, where he was raised. At the age of twelve, he decided to pursue the violin and began lessons via a correspondence course from New York City. He states: "There was no one to teach me. After a while, I began to play by ear instead of note . . . I liked playing by ear best. I could add little things into the songs." Luderin had an uncle who played, but he never heard him.

Luderin says his first fiddle was one his father found in a pawnshop in Port Arthur for twenty dollars. Originally he learned tunes by listening to string bands that played over KFDM in Beaumont around 1926 or 1927. His family moved to Hackberry in 1928 and he began to listen to the various players around the area, such as the Fawvor brothers, Dudley and James. His parents inspired him to begin playing Cajun music and, besides fiddle, he also plays rhythm guitar and harmonica.

In 1933, he decided to form a band and play dances. He met longtime friend Edwin Duhon, a guitarist, fiddler, and accordionist, and they began to play together at parties and socials around their Hackberry homes. Luderin began attending business college in Lake Charles, and radio station KPLC opened about a block from the school, in the Majestic Hotel downtown. Luderin states in an interview from May 2004:

> *I went up there and told them we have a string band in Hackberry and I'd like to get on the program. So the fella gave me a spot on a Monday morning. It must have been about 6:30 or 7:00 in the morning. You can imagine driving from Hackberry and across the prairie. In those days it was slow going. That meant getting up pretty early in the morning.*

Duhon and another local musician, Alvin Ellender, joined playing guitar. The Hackberry Ramblers' first booking was in Basile, followed by radio broadcasts in New Orleans, Port Arthur, Lafayette, Beaumont, and Lake Charles.

Over the years the personnel has changed except for Luderin, who always strived to keep the group and its name intact. By 1935 Duhon was gone, and Luderin moved to Crowley, where he ran a service station. The group appeared on radio from Montgomery Ward in Lafayette, and recorded over eighty selections for RCA on their Bluebird label in the mid-1930s. Their association with Montgomery Ward led to their being known as the Riverside Ramblers on non-Cajun cuts. One tune, "Wondering," was a big hit for the Ramblers. Following the death of his father in 1939, Luderin moved back to Hackberry, eventually forming a group with a new set of musicians. In 1943, Edwin Duhon rejoined the group and never left until he passed away in 2006.

During the forties and fifties the Ramblers played dances throughout southwest Louisiana. Luderin worked at the Swift meatpacking plant until its closure and then at the PPG Plant in Westlake, retiring with seventeen years' service in 1980. One milestone for the group was their appearance at the Berkeley Folk Festival in 1965, one of the first by a Louisiana group at a folk festival. In the early 1980s the group began to explore its Cajun roots: Duhon began playing the accordion, more Cajun music was added to their repertoire, and they began to attend numerous Cajun festivals.

The Hackberry Ramblers, who had previously recorded numerous sides for Bluebird, continued to record, waxing 12 selections for Deluxe in the 1940s;

Hackberry Ramblers: Maxie Sonnier, Butch Ogea, Luderin Darbone, Lennis Sonnier, Edwin Duhon, 1964. Photo courtesy of Luderin Darbone.

four sides for Goldband; a 1963 album for Arhoolie; and three CDs in the 1990s, one for Flying Fish and two for Hot Biscuits. He does some vocals and they include "Un Piastre Ici, Une Piastre La Bas," "Fais Pas Ça," "Oh Josephine, Ma Josephine," "Eh La Bas," "Fau Pas Tu Brai," "Cherie," and "My Little Acadian Girl," all tunes he also wrote.

Fiddlers and historians alike have cited Luderin's impact as an instrumentalist. Andrew Brown notes that Luderin's recording of "Jolie Blon" was the classic cut until Harry Choates's 1946 recording took the Gulf Coast by storm. Luderin and the Hackberry Ramblers were very influential to the movement of country music in southwest Louisiana, with many pickers getting their first touch of country music from seeing or hearing the group perform.

Among his many awards are two Big Easy Awards, Best Country Folk Artists Category, one in 1990 and one in 1997, and the Big Easy Achievement Award in 2000. Other honors include induction into the Louisiana Hall of Fame in 1992; Cajun French Music Association Hall of Fame (Lake Charles chapter), 2001; Governor's Arts Award for Outstanding Lifetime Achievement in the Arts, 1996; medal for being nominated for a Grammy Award, 1998; the Heritage Award from the National Endowment for the Arts; and a certificate for outstanding contributions to country music by the Country Music Hall of Fame in Nashville, 1999. Featured profiles include CNN's "Manner Vogue"; a German magazine in the 1990s; the *Today* show on NBC; and Ann Savoy's *Cajun Music—A Reflection of a People*, in 1984.

Luderin has played Cajun music coast to coast as his contribution to preserving Cajun music and culture. He has played with famous musicians such as Michael Doucet, Jimmie Dale Gilmore, Marcia Ball, and Rodney Crowell. Crawford Vincent noted, "He is a credit to the music."

Luderin states: "I've really enjoyed my life. And because of one thing, the fiddle. If my mother had not talked me into playing the violin and taking that correspondence course I would never have seen Chicago, New York, Nova Scotia, and Holland. I thank my mother for talking me into that." He recalls that his wife enjoyed his playing the fiddle saying, "She especially enjoyed the dances because I gave her a percentage of my take at the dances."

For a more complete history of the Hackberry Ramblers see *When the Fiddle Was King*, a history of early-1900s country bands in western Louisiana. Luderin's impact on fiddlers of the past seventy years has been enormous. Fiddlers and country musicians alike were inspired to play country music from hearing the Hackberry Ramblers in performance and on record. Luderin continues to inspire with his youthful approach to the music he loves.

Luderin passed away on November 21, 2008.

Interviews by Ron Yule: Luderin Darbone (5 10-2004, 6-8-2004, and 8-27-2008) and Crawford Vincent (4-4-2004).

References

Brasseaux, Ryan A., and Kevin S. Fontenot. *Accordions, Fiddles, Two Step and Swing: A Cajun Reader*. Center for Louisiana Studies, Lafayette, 2006.

Brown, Andrew. Liner notes. *Devil in the Bayou*. Bear Family CD, BCD 16355, 2002.

Savoy, Ann. *Cajun Music: A Reflection of a People*. Bluebird Press, Eunice, Louisiana, 1984.

Yule, Ron, et al. *Cajun French Music Association Hall of Fame (Lake Charles Chapter)*. Fiddle Country Publishing, DeRidder, Louisiana, 2004.

Yule, Ron. *When the Fiddle Was King*. Fiddle Country Publishing, DeRidder, Louisiana, 2006.

Photo courtesy of David Simpson, LSU-E.

MICHAEL DOUCET

(1951–) Scott

An astute student of the masters of Cajun fiddling, Michael Doucet has blended the feel of the fiddling of the past with his musical inner voice to produce a sound that is uniquely his own. In his career he has played nearly every style of fiddling and music in the country, bringing himself and his listeners to new heights in musical enjoyment.

Michael was born in Lafayette in 1951, and spent the first twenty years of his musical life hearing and experimenting with various forms of music. By the age of six he was absorbing the sounds of Elvis Presley and requested a guitar to accompany his singing, but he was presented a banjo instead. After a run at the drums, he played trumpet with an aunt, Jessie Greig, who played piano accordion around the Lafayette area with her husband's swing band, the Harry Greig Orchestra. And he finally got a guitar.

Around the age of ten, his uncle, T-Will Knight, a dance band fiddler who also played banjo and bass fiddle, began showing him a few tunes on fiddle. He recalls he eventually learned three tunes: "Allons a Lafayette" in a Harry Choates style, "Jole Blon," and a Cajun version of "St. Louis Blues." Will did not call the song "St. Louis Blues," but when Michael learned all the parts Will had shown him and played it for someone, they identified the song as "St. Louis Blues." Mike recalls Will told him, "If I could learn those three styles I could play anything." Learning the fiddle was a frustrating experience in those early years. T-Will would not allow Michael to take the fiddle out of the house and he did not own a violin, so his only practice came when he went to the Knights' home or was playing with musicians who had a fiddle, and he would play his three tunes. Doucet never acquired the fiddle for himself, but finally had the fiddle repaired, and presently T-Will's fiddle is hanging in the State Museum in Baton Rouge. Besides the influence of the Cajun fiddle from T-Will, Mike was further influenced by his aunts who sang French ballads.

By the time he graduated from high school in 1969, he had been around Cajun music and had spent time with some of the older musicians around the area. He attended LSU and several incidents finally got him on track to play the Cajun fiddle style. First, he took a class on Anglo-Saxon folklore and realized that the music of French Louisiana was not addressed when the teacher told him that "Cajun songs were just translated English songs." Knowing that this was not true and curious, he dug out a 1939 thesis by Irene Whitfield that documented his premise that these songs had survived from French and Acadian songs.

Second, a friend played violin in the orchestra and Mike asked him to let him play on it. His interest was piqued and his journey was set: to immerse himself in the French Louisiana culture he loved, and all while playing fiddle.

He realized early on that he had to seek out the masters of Cajun fiddling and learn the music of old so he could assimilate it into his own style. He also realized that he must directly study the masters of the music he loved to get a direction and feel for his music. His list of masters reads like a Cajun Fiddlers' Hall of Fame.

Mike's first influences were fellow Scott fiddler Doc Guidry, who played in a smooth, more country style, and fiddlemaker/fiddler Lionel Leleux. Mike notes: "Doc Guidry, he was closer and I knew his style. Then Lionel Leleux, I'd go over to his house and we'd talk for a long time. And he played with one of my neighbors, Don Montoucet, an accordion player. So, there were always

Beausoleil avec Michael Doucet: Jimmy Breaux, Billy Ware, Tommy Alesi, Michael Doucet, Mitch Reed, and David Doucet. Photo by Rick Olivier, courtesy of Michael Doucet.

jams there." Mike notes that Lionel played in a standard tuning, and he learned about playing parallel "eighths" or octaves and Lionel's impeccable timing.

As he began knocking on more doors, he landed in Eunice at Dennis McGee's. Dennis had a connection to the fiddling styles and tunes of the 1800s (before the introduction of the accordion), and many of his records from around 1930 indicated this. Besides learning over 150 tunes from McGee's repertoire of contradanses, reels, mazurkas, and other Acadian tunes, Doucet began learning the art of seconding on fiddle. This method of chording and playing rhythm had been the method of choice in many cultures where, early on, two to four fiddles were used at a Saturday night house dance or party. He recalls that when he met Dennis, "It was a whole different style of music, so I had to actually almost re-learn how to play."

Another influence, Varise Conner of Lake Arthur, had been a string band fiddler in the twenties and thirties and played with a true, clean tone. Michael notes that, from Varise, he mainly learned the use of the bow arm to get intricate patterns and the proper touch and feel of a song. He described Varise's playing: "He knew how to make the notes speak to you instead of just sawing back and forth."

Studies with Creole fiddlers Canray Fontenot (Welsh) and Bébé Carrieré (Lawtell) allowed Michael to learn some of the bluesy and rhythmic aspects of these legendary fiddlers. He notes that Bébé played in an AEAE tuning, a new experience for him. Another source for learning the blues was Eunice fiddler Wade Frugé, who still played the older styles.

Grand Louis fiddlers Dewey and Will Balfa gave Mike a chance to learn the use of drones in his music. As a cultural ambassador for French Louisiana, Dewey teamed with Doucet to educate the south Louisiana secondary schools about their culture and heritage, especially musical. This program, sponsored by the National Endowment for the Arts, was a success and a starting point for a soon-to-explode interest in Cajun music. Although they did not teach fiddle to the students, they were available in case any showed an interest.

Other local fiddlers, Hector Duhon and U. J. Meaux, were a big influence. Mike played with Hector's son, Bessyl, and learned Hector's unique double stops and style of seconding while playing behind the accordion. Recalling Hector's fiddling Mike says, "He infrequently took leads or rides, but when he did it was very bluesy and soulful."

Sulphur fiddler Luderin Darbone also influenced him, especially his 1930s recordings with the Hackberry Ramblers and Riverside Ramblers.

Mike recounts his underlying experiences with these pioneering fiddlers.

> *It was more than the music, it was the people I learned a lot from—the individuals themselves. How they lived their lives and how they dived around the music and what would be the central core of their music. You hear somebody play for an hour, two hours, you kinda pick up some of the same things they might play around the songs in a certain style. I was really looking for stylistic differences, which is very easy to find, because you can go twenty miles from Lafayette and people play differently, well they did thirty years ago at least. It wasn't such a quote/unquote Cajun style; it was a very individual style. So that's what I was looking for in everybody. The individual touch.*

Throughout these many studies Mike was playing music, taking his newly acquired fiddle and playing it in dancehalls or almost any venue he could find an audience. As the driving force behind several bands for the last 37 years, he has always kept an open ear to many styles of music, finding a place for himself and his bands in the midst of these yet keeping his feet in south Louisiana. Early bands included his first Cajun band, the Bayou Drifters, and the 1975 formation Coteau, a band that fused Cajun music with rock.

Lawtell Playboys: Mike Doucet, Delton Broussard, Linton Broussard. Festival Acadiens, 1980. Photo courtesy of Calvin Ardoin.

In 1976 he joined forces with his brother David, Billy Ware, Errol Verret, and Tommy Comeaux to form Beausoleil ("good sun"). They made tours into France, where their interest in the roots of their French music was rekindled. An album they recorded led to a grant to bring Cajun music into the schools of south Louisiana. For more than twenty-five years the band has had a no-boundaries approach to music, incorporating many styles of rhythm and musical forms into their recorded projects, network TV shows, and stage shows, yet with a Louisiana touch. They appeared in a movie, *Belizaire the Cajun* and were on the soundtrack of two others. Countless appearances at venues throughout the world have dotted their itinerary. After eleven Grammy nominations (and one win, for *L'amour ou la Folie* in 1998), and their record and video performances on Mary-Chapin Carpenter's Grammy-winning single "Down at the Twist And Shout," their recorded projects continue to incorporate creativity and a love for music.

Michael's family shines with creative and musical talent. His wife, Sharon, is a highly acclaimed writer, having penned numerous books on various aspects of the French culture. Her novel *Fiddle Fever* should be required reading for any aspiring fiddler. Son Matthew Jacques, born on Beethoven's birthday, plays fiddle, accordion, and guitar; besides occasionally playing with Beausoleil, he has played with numerous young Cajun groups including Joel and Wilson

Savoy, the Lost Bayou Ramblers, and while apprenticing violin making in Portland, Maine, started his own Cajun group, Douce. He has made eight violins. Son Ezra Amédé Doucet plays jazz piano and acoustic bass.

Michael has never rested on his laurels nor has he been a one-horse musician. Tours and recordings with other musicians have always weaved in and out of his career. He joined forces with his old friends Ann and Marc Savoy to record several CDs focusing on the roots music of Louisiana. He has also toured and recorded with two all-star fiddle troupes, The Fiddlers 4 and The Masters of the Folk Violin, incorporating many of the fiddle styles of North America in their programs. He has recorded at least twenty-eight projects plus a CD/DVD, *Learn to Play Cajun Fiddle.*

When you hear Michael Doucet play, you hear a deep love and understanding of the great masters of the music he loves. It is in his soul; it has fused with his own great musicianship—and man, it sounds good.

Interview by Ron Yule: Michael Doucet (3-6-2007).

References

Ancelet, Barry, and Elemore Morgan Jr. *Cajun and Creole Music Makers.* University Press of Mississippi, Jackson, Mississippi, 1999.

Ancelet, Barry. "Dewey Balfa: A Cultural Ambassador." *Accordions, Fiddles, Two-Step, and Swing,* Ryan A. Brasseaux and Kevin S. Fontenot, editors. Center for Louisiana Studies, Lafayette, 2006.

Savoy, Ann. Liner notes. *The Savoy-Doucet Cajun Band: Home Music with Spirits.* Arhoolie CD 389, 1992.

Simmons, Michael. "Michael Doucet: A Fiddler's Education." *Fiddler Magazine* vol. 8, no. 1 (Spring 2001).

———. "Michael Doucet on Beausoleil." *Fiddler Magazine* vol. 8, no. 1 (Spring 2001).

Willey, Robert. Transcript of interview with Michael Doucet. Music Industry Lecture Series, September 25, 2002.

Wilson, Joe. Liner notes. *Masters of the Folk Violin.* Arhoolie CD 434, 1995.

Photo courtesy of the Louisiana Pecan Festival/Bill Landrum.

WARREN FERRIER

(1929–) Montgomery

Warren Ferrier's playing was best described by Troy DeRamus when he said, "Warren is such a smooth fiddler he could step into any studio and record with any country singer." This is the consensus among those who have played or heard him. From a smooth, flowing breakdown and waltz style to a complementing country/bluegrass backup style, Warren can do it all.

Warren was born in 1929 and lived around Montgomery most of his life. Warren states, "I had fiddlers on both sides of the family." The first fiddler he ever heard and his first influence was Jimmy Roberts, his grandpa, who played at country dances around Grant Parish and in local fiddle contests, winning third place at the 1921 Community Fair in Colfax. Warren also recalls hearing the Jones Boys from Colfax, who also played at country dances in the late 1930s. He especially recalls their jug player and the homemade bass the Jones

Boys carried in their band. His father, Floyd, and mother, Maude, played fiddle and guitar at country dances, but they had quit by the time he began learning. He said his father, even after he quit, could still chord a guitar and play rhythm very well. After attending dances he became attracted to the sound of the fiddle and bought one for eight dollars. Around the age of eight he began learning his first tunes, "Rubber Dolly" and "Blues in A."

His whole family was musically inclined; his brothers Al (guitar), James (guitar, mandolin, and fiddle), and Brian (guitar and mandolin) began to play at an early age. Warren recalls Al and Brian learning to play the guitar and laughingly says he would hit them with his fiddle bow when they missed a chord on the guitar. By the early 1940s, they began playing as a family band around the Montgomery area. James was killed in the service during World War II. Warren says he was a great mandolin and guitar player.

They played at a few dances, but Warren remembers that their favorite form of musical entertainment was serenading throughout the community on Saturday night. This form of entertainment was popular among country and rural musicians in central and north Louisiana. The Grigg, Baum, and Hood families all were active as serenaders within their communities. He said in a 2005 interview: "We'd go from house to house and play a couple songs at each. They'd want us to play more but we'd tell them we had more houses to play for. Sometimes it would be after twelve before we got home ... They'd want us to stop and eat, but we'd just keep going." He recalls that most of the songs they played were popular songs from artists like Johnny and Jack.

Their music playing was not too serious until the early 1950s, when they began to play dances and clubs around central Louisiana as the Ferrier Brothers. To round out the Ferrier Brothers sound, Brian switched from mandolin to lead guitar. For about a year and a half, they played with Clyde Baum as the Bayou Boys at school shows, eventually landing a spot on KALB television.

They continued to play as the Ferrier Brothers and continued to work by day in the woods. With the advent of rock and roll on the musical scene in the early 1950s, the Ferrier Brothers began to lean in that direction. Al, who was the vocalist, began to sing rock and roll songs and the group soon became more popular as a rockabilly band than a country band, so they changed the name to Al Ferrier and His Boppin' Billies. The need for a fiddle was diminished with the change in music styles and Warren played bass fiddle on most of these shows, as well as fiddle.

Al became so popular that he began recording with Eddie Shuler at Goldband Studios in Lake Charles. This launched their recording career and

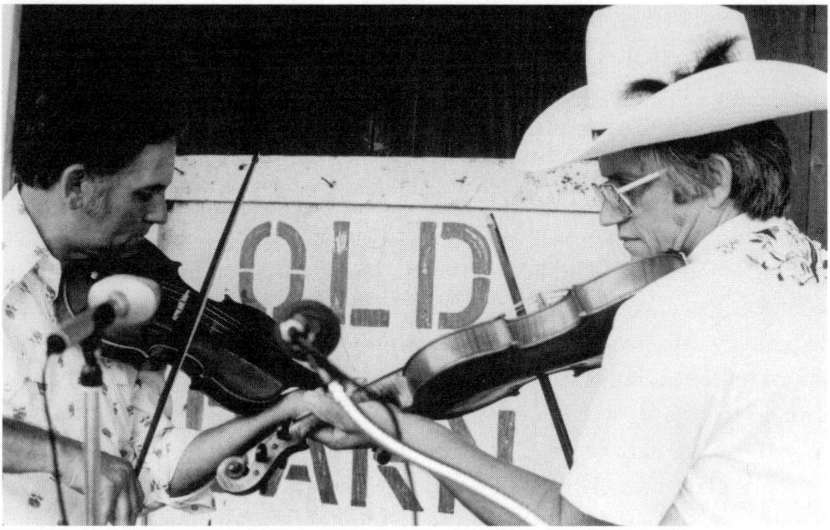

Jamesette Kile and Warren Ferrier at the 1981 Louisiana State Championship, Boyce. Photo courtesy of Susan Roach.

also led them to the Louisiana Hayride. Eventually Al recorded for J. D. Miller, and Warren played on some of these recordings as well. Warren recalls, "He had one song I played twin fiddles on. I can't remember the name."

They were becoming more popular, so Eddie took them to Shreveport for the first of three appearances on KWKH's nationwide country radio show, the Louisiana Hayride. Warren recalls, "When we were on the Hayride we'd play several shows each night. I'd play the fiddle on the country songs and bass fiddle on the rock and roll songs. We'd usually play the country songs first." He added, "There were people everywhere. Girls lined the front of the stage. The balcony was full." Warren recounts they were so popular that they even backed Elvis on one of his shows.

Warren also played some during the 1950s with Jelly Elliott and the Singing Cowboys, at shows and on KALB. The Ferriers were playing at clubs all over Louisiana and, by the late 1950s the toils of the music business and problems with exhausting travel caused Warren to leave the band.

After the split, around 1960, he left the country music scene except for an occasional recording session with his brothers. This pattern has seemed to follow Warren's music career throughout the years. Warren notes, "I didn't play all the time. I'd play a while and then quit for a while." He began working with the Louisiana State Highway Department in 1962; after a while, he went back into the woods to haul poles. In the early 1970s he re-entered state employment, eventually retiring from the highway department.

In 1969 Rubel Wright and Bill Landrum left Don Wiley's Catahoula Playboys and his Catahoula Country Show in Jonesville, and started the Louisiana Jamboree at the old Wayne Theater in downtown Colfax. Warren came out of retirement and played occasionally, eventually becoming the full-time fiddler in the staff band until the show ceased in 1974. Bill and Warren recall not only local bands and local singers entertaining at the theater, but that many Grand Ole Opry stars like Jim and Jesse and the Virginia Boys, Junior Samples, and Ray Pillow appeared there often.

In the early 1970s he re-entered the music scene, playing with some of central Louisiana's most popular country bands. He appeared off and on with Rubel Wright and the Wright Beats, Don Wiley and the Catahoula Playboys, and Troy DeRamus and his Big D Band. During this period he worked with some of Louisiana's finest fiddlers, including Eddie Raxsdale, Ray Beebe, Jamesette Kile, Herbert Meche, and Eddie Friday. These bands appeared throughout the area at shows and dancehalls, and made appearances on KALB television and local radio stations in Alexandria and Natchitoches.

Warren's skills as a contest fiddler began to emerge around 1970. He entered and won many contests throughout the central Louisiana area, including the Louisiana Pecan Festival (where he was a perennial winner), Fish Creek Campgrounds, Montgomery Fourth of July Celebration, Natchitoches Christmas Festival, Columbia Arts and Crafts Festival, the Winn Parish Forestry Festival, the Backwoods Inn at Readheimer, and in Branson, Missouri. His reputation was so well known at the Colfax contest that they retired him from competition. He also was a divisional winner at the Louisiana State Championship once and a finalist on several other occasions. Ray Lasyone, who was associated with the Louisiana State Fiddle Contest at Boyce and Marthaville, once commented, "When you saw Warren Ferrier come in packin' his fiddle, somebody'd better get ready to play."

As a member of Troy DeRamus's Old Barn Dance Band, he appeared at the New Orleans World's Fair in 1984 and at the New Orleans Jazz Festival on several occasions. Besides his television work in the fifties and seventies on KALB, he appeared on Channel 11, Alexandria, in the early 1980s. Until recently he was the staff fiddler at the monthly country show at Colfax.

Although he is an accomplished waltz and breakdown fiddler, Warren's forte is the backup fiddling he provides for a singer. He is adept at the styles of mid-century fiddlers such as Tommy Jackson, Buddy Spicher, and Benny

Ronnie and Warren Ferrier. East Texas Jamboree, Broaddus, Texas, 2000. Photo courtesy of Bonnie Ferrier.

Martin, and has become a good band fiddler in this style. Of Warren's large cache of fiddle tunes, his favorite is "Black Mountain Rag."

Besides his brothers Al and Brian, his son, Ronnie, plays guitar, bass, steel, and even fiddles a little. Ronnie notes, "If we need a second fiddle at our show, I'll jump up and play the second part." For the last several years Ronnie has pursued music professionally and worked in entertainment centers like Branson. Currently, he is the manager of the East Texas Jamboree at Broaddus, Texas, where he plays steel guitar on their weekend shows. When he feels up to it, Warren plays on the Jamboree with his son, making music just like they did when Ronnie would sit around the house and second on guitar for Warren on one fiddle tune after another.

Interviews by Ron Yule: Troy DeRamus (no date), Ronnie Ferrier (4-21-2005), Warren Ferrier (5-3-2005 and 8-5-2005), Bill Landrum (8-5-2005), and Ray Lasyone (2-13-2003).

Photo courtesy of Louisiana Folklife Center, NSU.

CANRAY FONTENOT

(1923–1995) Welsh

Canray Fontenot has been hailed by many as the greatest black Louisiana French fiddler of his time, with a unique style that dated back to the early part of the century. Taking the cue from his ancestors, he played this early music in a way that made him special among his peers. Michael Doucet notes that "He was a living bridge between turn-of-the-century musical styles and today's younger musicians."

Canray was born on October 16, 1922, into a farming family in L'Anse aux Vaches. Both his mother, Ozémire, and father, Adam, played accordion, and an uncle, Joel Victorien, played fiddle, so it was a good bet he was musically talented. Early on he was influenced by the music not only of his father but of Creole accordionists Amédé Ardoin and Sidney Babineaux. Another influence was the recordings of Ardoin, Amédé Breaux, and others he listened to on his

Unidentified, Ed Poullard, Canray Fontenot, unidentified, Bois Sec Ardoin, unidentified. Canray Fontenot Appreciation Day, 1995, Welsh. Photo courtesy of Ervin Lejeune.

grandfather's record player. During these formative years he attended dances with Amédé Ardoin and his father, listening to their music.

Even though he began to like music, he never cared to learn the instrument of his parents. Instead he chose the fiddle. With no access to an instrument, Canray and a friend, Joe Bellard, both decided they wanted to play fiddle. Joe's cousin, Douglas Bellard, played fiddle and owned one, so when he was not around they would sneak his fiddle down and play it. Using their creative talent, they made a couple of cigar-box fiddles so they would have their own instruments: screen wire was used for strings, the bow was a peach tree limb with sewing thread, and they harvested the rosin from a pine tree. Canray continued to listen to Douglas and practice on his homemade violin. Finally, when Canray was around the age of eleven, an uncle gave him a fiddle in exchange for some work he needed done on the farm. He began playing with his father and eventually formed a string band with George Leonard for a while. In his early teens he began playing with his lifelong friend, Bois Sec Ardoin, an association that would last throughout their lifetime. In 1937 Amédé Ardoin invited Fontenot to travel to New York and play on his recording of "Les Portes de la Prison." Much to Fontenot's dismay, however, his mother refused to let him go, telling him he was too young to go to New York.

Adam Fontenot passed away in 1938, creating hardships for the family. Consequently, Canray's was a life of hard work and struggle to make ends meet. He farmed, worked in the woods, and finally in his later years worked at Marcantel's Feed Store in Welsh.

Painting of Canray Fontenot on the wall of a building in downtown Welsh. Photo by author.

He continually supplemented his income by playing a few house dances and dances at clubs in Durald, Opelousas, and around south Louisiana. His musical experiences became broader and during the late 1940s he fronted a string band, Canray and the Basile Boys, while continuing to play with Bois Sec at local dances. During this period he developed his love for ragtime and the Bob Wills–style music prevalent in some local clubs.

In the mid-1960s, Ralph Rinzler came to Louisiana looking for entertainers who were authentic artists of the Cajun culture for the Newport (Rhode Island) Folk Festival. In 1966 Canray and Bois Sec were chosen to represent Louisiana at the festival. In 1974 they made an appearance at the Tribute to Cajun Music Festival in Lafayette, and this jumpstarted tours that included appearances at festivals throughout Louisiana, the United States, Canada, and Europe.

Numerous recordings document Canray's playing with many of his musical friends including Bois Sec Ardoin, Beausoleil, the Carriere Brothers, and the Ardoin family. Several are still available on Arhoolie Records. Many awards have come his way, with the most prestigious being the National Heritage Award from the National Endowment for the Arts, in 1986. He also appeared in the documentary film, *J'ai Ete Bal.*

Michael Doucet, who began studying Canray's fiddle style in 1973 and continued throughout his career, honored Canray and his fiddling in a eulogy (unpublished) written for *Fiddler Magazine.*

Canray's unique style was bluesy, yet melodic. His wild slides and gravelly vocals were always accompanied by his mile-wide grin. Canray originals such as "Joe Pitre a Deux Femmes," "Les Barres de la Prison," and "Bonsoir Moreau" have become standards in the Cajun and Zydeco repertoires.

He and his wife, Artile, raised six children, four of whom went to college and one of whom is a lawyer. Canray played and traveled to the end, teaching and performing with long-time partner Bois Sec Ardoin at Port Townsend, Washington, shortly before he died. That night, Canray played old Creole fiddle tunes, waltzes, mazurkas, string band numbers, New Orleans jazz numbers, blues, original songs on fiddle, guitar, harmonica and jaws harp. Then he began singing unaccompanied ballads in French that sounded so ancient but so natural. He could make his fiddle cry, then he could make it laugh with trilling double stops! Perhaps the most amazing aspect of Canray's talent was how he could blend ancient French songs with his own Creole rhythms to create his own recognizable style in new songs. For example, his "Bonsoir Moreau" was unusual to Louisiana French music in that it was played in a minor key. Canray played it effortlessly in third position with so much emotion, and the bluesy context of the song really set it apart. Humorous neighborhood stories like "Bee de la Manche" were put to music and told the story of how Bee resorts to stealing sheep and is eventually jailed, all because the widow, Adelina, is costing him a great deal of money.

Canray Fontenot, sitting in his favorite rocking chair with fiddle in hand, singing and tapping out the rhythms on his hardwood floor with his bare feet, smiling and passing on forgotten songs whose poetry he lived through. His life was not easy, but he expelled his troubles through his music, a gift which he shared with his neighbors and the world. We mourn not just the man and his talent, but a soulful eyewitness to our musical history. His voice has left us, but his soulful songs remain to remind us of what his grandfather used to tell him: "If you remember my song, you'll remember me."

Interview by Ron Yule: Michael Doucet (3-6-2007).

References

Ancelet, Barry, and Elemore Morgan Jr. *Cajun and Creole Music Makers*. University Press of Mississippi, Jackson, 1999.

Bradshaw, Jim. "Canray Learned from His Father." *Daily Advertiser*, December 29, 1998.

Doucet, Michael. Unpublished Canray Fontenot eulogy written for *Fiddler Magazine*, 1995.

Doucet, Michael. Liner notes. *Louisiana Hot Sauce, Creole Style*. Arhoolie CD 381.

Doucet, Sharon Arms. "If You Remember My Song You'll Remember Me." *Fiddler Magazine* (Fall 1995).

Martin, Shawn. "Canray Fontenot." *Lake Charles American Press*, July 30, 1995.

Savoy, Ann. *Cajun Music: A Reflection of a People*. Bluebird Press, Eunice, Louisiana, 1984.

Photo courtesy of Georgia Yule.

MERLIN FONTENOT

(1923–) Eunice

As with many of the musicians in the Eunice area, Merlin Fontenot was born (September 26, 1923) into a family of highland farmers, with their main crops being cotton, sugar cane, and potatoes. His father, Enos, played accordion, so it was natural that Merlin developed a love for music. After first trying the accordion when his "feet would not touch the ground sitting in a chair," he took a liking to the fiddle at the age of seven or eight. He structured a cigar-box fiddle with a cow-horn tailpiece and a primitive limb bow complete with sewing thread. He admits, "It sounded bad."

He eventually bought a fiddle from Sears Roebuck for nine or ten dollars" and his musical journey began. This journey would lead not only to a great knowledge of Cajun music, but would thread him through the many intricacies of western swing and country fiddle styles. He is especially fond of old

Mary Grimsley and Merlin Fontenot. Natchitoches/NSU Folklife Festival, 1988. Photo courtesy of Mary Grimsley.

pop tunes and feels at home with any of these styles, having a special love for playing harmony and "second fiddle."

By his teens he was playing at house dances that he describes as "rough," with plenty of fights and mischief. They played nearly every weekend, playing in various combinations from two fiddles to a fiddle, guitar, and four-string banjo. Musicians he recalls include Nolan Fontenot and Sidney and Zem Courville. He also notes that accordion was sometime used at the early dances. In his late teens he was playing at dancehalls around Eunice, many times walking the three miles to town from their farm. By 1940 he began playing with his father-in-law, Ambrose Thibodeaux, and an uncle, Lawrence Thibodeaux.

With the advent of World War II, Merlin was drafted into the U.S. Navy, eventually serving in the Pacific campaign. He vividly recalls the day "the bomb" was dropped on Hiroshima, which he feels may have not only saved him and his battalion from a lot of fighting, but may have saved their lives. During this campaign, Merlin and some of the other soldier/musicians entertained the troops playing on the *Dry Gulch Program* over Armed Forces Radio.

Following the war he and his wife, Lillian, settled in Jacksonville, Florida, where he worked at various jobs for the next twenty-five years and played

Courtesy of Ervin Lejeune.

country music with bands in the area. He played briefly with Glen Reeves, but most of this playing was done with the Jacksonville-based Jimmy Strickland Band. They appeared on Channel 4 (Jacksonville) and, after four years, bought a Greyhound bus and hit the road, playing throughout the southeastern United States. In the late 1950s they made two appearances on the Grand Ole Opry, a big thrill for Merlin and an event he will always cherish.

Although he does not care for playing in fiddle competitions, he vividly recalls his only entry, a large contest in Jacksonville with twenty-five entrants and some stiff competition. The second-place fiddler was a lady fiddler who played the instrument on her knee like a cello: Louisiana fiddler Fleecy Philyaw, who also was living in Jacksonville at the time. Merlin took the top prize with rousing renditions of "Orange Blossom Special" and "Jole Blon."

In 1971, as if he knew that Cajun music was going to become more visible to the listening public, they moved back to Louisiana to be near their families. He began working as a carpenter and throughout the early seventies played with various bands at Etley's Lounge in Eunice, with Davis Lee Guidroz, Dulis Landry, and George Boles. The drummer in the band was Wade Benson

Landry, a current professional fiddler and one of Merlin's first students. Merlin also recalls a young Ken Smith coming and sitting in with the band.

Merlin played and recorded with what could be termed as a Who's Who of great Cajun musicians. Various projects included stints with Jo-El Sonnier, the Balfa Family, and Nathan Abshire, as well as many others. He played at numerous folk, jazz, and Cajun festivals, restaurants, and Cajun music centers. His father-in-law, accordionist Ambrose Thibodeaux, recorded three LPs that feature the fiddling of Merlin. One, *Authentic French Acadian Music*, was recorded on one of Merlin's many trips back to the area in the 1960s. Two more, *Ambrose Thibodeaux* and *Authentic Cajun French Music and Folksongs*, followed in the 1970s. This led to one solo instrumental project on La Louisianne Records featuring Merlin's own fiddling titled *Fiddlin' Cajun*. His only vocal output was on the Nathan Abshire LP where he sang third part on one of the waltzes.

After humble beginnings on a homemade cigar-box fiddle, he acquired an 1813 Schweitzer violin from a brother-in-law who fought in Normandy and Germany during World War II. Merlin recalls the story: "He gave an old German two bars of candy for that fiddle . . . and I treasure that thing. I used to use it a lot but now I play it only at home. A time or two I played it at a funeral." He currently plays a copy of the Schweitzer made by local fiddlemaker Woody Breaux.

In 1996 he began a venture that accents his importance to Cajun fiddling when he was selected to perform at Vermillionville, a Cajun cultural center in Lafayette featuring various aspects of Cajun life, including music. Merlin performs as a solo act twice weekly at the center's school building. Saturday nights are spent playing with the house band at Bubba Frey's Restaurant south of Eunice, where he plays with one of his most recent fiddle students, Bubba Frey. In the last few years, he has performed with Cajun artists Kermit Venable, Reggie Matte, and Lee Benoit.

Cajun fiddlers play in various tunings depending on the key of the accordion. Besides the standard GDAE tuning, many tune down one step and use a C tuning or in many cases an F tuning. Uncommonly, Merlin has refrained from this and plays in standard tuning no matter what the tuning of the accordion. He admits, "It doesn't sound as full sometimes, but it comes out." He says playing in B flat has a lot to do with the accompanying musicians: "When you got the mules to pull the wagon, it's not too hard." Another aspect of Merlin's playing, which stems from his earlier years as a country musician, is that he loves to play harmony to a lead fiddle, something not common with many

Cajun fiddlers who primarily "bass" or "chord" behind the accordion. In his days playing with the Balfas, he introduced this approach to their sound. He especially enjoys playing harmony to the accordions of Reggie Matte or Nolan Cormier.

No matter what style he plays, he likes to play Cajun or country music in a traditional vein. At the age of eighty-four, his dance band gigs have diminished but each weekend finds him playing music at restaurants like Randols or Bubba Frey's, entertaining at Vermillionville, or sitting in with some band at a local festival. He is glad to be able to continue playing at his age, entertaining, and demonstrating the musical culture of his heritage.

Interviews by Ron Yule: Merlin and Lillian Fontenot (1-14-2007 and 4-17-2007).

Reference

Ancelet, Barry. Liner notes. *Fiddlin Cajun*. La Louisianne Record LL-142, Lafayette, Louisiana.

Photo courtesy of Eddie Friday Collection.

EDDIE FRIDAY

(1921–2008) Pleasant Hill

In central Louisiana, mention of the mandolin in fiddle circles brings the name of Eddie Friday to the fore. He was noted for his fine rhythm and lead picking in the country scene around Alexandria from 1946 to the mid-1980s. He played fiddle, usually as a second, and for this reason his fellow band musicians were aware of his talent and presence on fiddle. He played in a very relaxed manner at a nice country pace, prompting fiddler June Reeves to once comment, "How does he play so smooth?" In his latter years, he was revered in fiddle circles and attracted quite a crowd when he joined jam sessions at the bluegrass festivals and shows he attended when his health permitted.

Eddie was born in 1921 to a very musical family in Pleasant Hill, Louisiana. Fiddle music constantly rang from the home with his father, C. E., and uncles, Jim and Robert, playing all the old tunes. His brother, Mike, and sister, Vivian, also played fiddle. The whole family knew various other stringed instruments as well as the fiddle. He said there was music in his home all the time and they would play with friends or at local house dances or parties.

Eddie recalled that Ross Mayes, the fiddler with the Pelican Wildcats, would come to the Ajax community in north Natchitoches Parish just to learn tunes from his father, Charlie. Ross was kin to the Powell family who lived nearby in the Wallace community. Ross and Docs Bass, Eddie's cousin, would travel by wagon and stay several days, usually playing on the Powell's front porch. Eddie said, "They'd play all day on Saturday and Sunday." Eddie also remembers that Docs Bass played the guitar and Ross played the mandolin, as well as the fiddle.

Eddie recalls the story of his first encounter with fiddle playing at the age of eight. The family had gone to a funeral and when he arrived home he took out the fiddle and learned a tune he had heard at the funeral. He promptly played it for his mother.

A mention of country dances and house parties brought back many memories for Eddie. Eddie explains, "My dad played many of his dance tunes in C, F, and B flat, and I played the rhythm guitar. It was difficult to play chords the way those old guitars were set up, with high strings and half of the strings missing." Eddie learned them all, but over the years tended to play the mandolin more and more. He met his future wife, Lurlene Knotts, a rhythm guitar player, in 1940, and they played at house dances around Pleasant Hill for three years before they were married in 1943. He also recalled added accompaniment: "For more rhythm, someone would put rosin on the end of a broomstick and rub it on the floor in time to the music. It sounded just like a bass fiddle."

He joined the service in 1943 and served with the Army Air Force as a staff sergeant. He was in combat on Iwo Jima and was decorated with four Bronze Stars and one Bronze Arrowhead.

After his discharge from the service, he and Lurlene along with several other pickers joined Ed Barnes, who had a portable movie picture show, playing throughout the region. They appeared in Marthaville, Keatchie, and all over west central Louisiana as a part of his tent show. They also played at the Taylor Theatre in Pleasant Hill. He notes, "We'd play and get the crowd to come to the movie . . . or run them off, one [laugh]."

He and Lurlene settled in the Alexandria area, where he worked as a machinist and mechanic throughout his career with Blotner Brothers and Coca-Cola. As a sought-after musician he played with numerous groups; he played music as a hobby and never gave up his day job.

Standing: Eddie Friday, Clyde Baum, Hermon Lasyone, and Kenny Guillot. Kneeling: J. W. Thompson, unidentified, and Sidney Ray Cole. J. W. Thompson Show, KALB, 1953. Photo courtesy of Hermon Lasyone Collection.

Soon after settling back into central Louisiana, he formed a band, the Eastern Stars, with Louis Peck (guitar), Buster Carter (fiddle), and Lammie Gaspard (bass). They were all local pickers, with Carter being from Lena. They played country and western–style music, appearing on KVOB early in the morning and at school shows and store promotions. He recalls that Norm Nettles played with them on one radio show. In 1948, they began to play on KALB. Louis Peck then left the group to play with J. W. Thompson's country band.

Eddie also played with the J. W. Thompson Band on many radio shows and accompanied them on several of their tours. One of these tours eventually lead them to Nashville and an appearance on the Ernest Tubb Record Shop radio show after the Grand Ole Opry.

Following World War II, they also played live music at many square dances around the Alexandria area, many times using Eddie Raxsdale or Ray Beebe on fiddle. Mel Hinkley, a transplanted Canadian, was the caller, and they played at square dance hotspots like Myles Park, Camp Polk, the Plantation Ranch, and Camp Beauregard.

In 1949 he joined Mel at the Old Barn and began a thirteen-year run, playing every Saturday night at the barn, many times being broadcast on KSYL. This stint entailed playing square dance music over a microphone, much like they had done after the war. In 1951 Charlie Walding, a fiddler and square dance caller, bought the Old Barn Dance from Mel. The format stayed the same and most of the musicians stayed throughout its eleven-year run.

Like most musicians and sidemen, they played when someone needed them, many times playing with several groups; Eddie continued to appear with J. W. Thompson at Friday night school shows, which were big at the time. In the early 1950s he joined Thompson on fiddle and mandolin when they first opened the KALB television studios. Members included Hermon Lasyone (bass), Eddie (mandolin and fiddle), Clyde Baum (mandolin), Sidney Cole (guitar), and Kenny Guillot (guitar).

Square dancing lost a lot of its popularity and the crowds began to dwindle, so in 1962 Charlie sold the Barn Dance to the Moose Lodge, and the musicians went their own ways. About that time Leon Melder opened the 112 Club south of Hineston and held family style dances. It became the hotspot in the southern part of Rapides Parish, and Eddie migrated to the 112 Club, where he played off and on until it closed in 1970. His main playing was as mandolinist and occasional second fiddle with Leon's house band.

When he was available, Eddie played fiddle with Jay Chevalier, who was Earl Long's driver and band manager on shows on the 1959 gubernatorial campaign trail. He recalls he also joined the group in the studio to play twin fiddles with Jack Kay on the popular "The Ballad of Earl K. Long." Earl liked the band. Eddie recalled, "After he [Earl] heard us, he called Blaze Starr on the phone and told her, 'I've got a band up here that will make J. J. throw his banjo in the lake.' He thought Jay Chevalier played a banjo [laugh]." Besides the Earl Long campaigns, he appeared with other bands around Leesville and Alexandria. Eddie also recalled traveling to a club west of Leesville in the late 1950s to join The Jeter Boys. He played twin fiddles with Jack Kay on these club dates.

In the 1960s, Eddie and other local musicians continued to play on KALB television. Many had their own show for a while. They would hustle their own advertisement, handle the production, and go on the air for their weekly show.

Eddie did not play professionally during the 1970s until Troy DeRamus called him around 1980 to play at the Old Barn in Boyce. Ray Beebe, Troy's fiddler, had come down with terminal cancer and he used Eddie, Herbert Meche, Eddie Raxsdale, Warren Ferrier, and Johnnie Lee DeRamus off and on to play fiddle for the next four years. Each year the band played the Jazz Festival in New Orleans, and in 1984 they played at the New Orleans World's Fair—as Eddie put it, "Twenty-one shows in seven days."

Following the closure of the Old Barn in 1984, Eddie continued to play in Troy's band when they played shows at the Louisiana State Fiddle Championship and local festivals. After the disbandment of the band, Troy and Eddie played shows to demonstrate and promote Troy's books and folklife ventures.

In his later years he played in jam sessions and at bluegrass festivals as his health permitted. Anytime he pulled out the "old fiddle," he was surrounded by listeners hungry for the old-time sounds of the country music of yesteryear. He was usually deluged with requests for Howdy Forrester's "Weeping Heart," "My Mansion's in the Sky," and many of the old hoedowns like "Leatherbritches."

Eddie passed away on February 11, 2008.

Interviews by Ron Yule: Eddie Friday (11-1-2005 and 11-4-2005), plus numerous informal conversations.

References

Kline, Barbara W. "And When the Music Stops . . . an Era Ends." *Alexandria Town Talk*, February 12, 1984.

Liebman, Amy. "Anthropologist: Culture Difficult to Teach in the Classroom." *Alexandria Town Talk*, May 2, 1982.

Photo courtesy of Chris Strachwitz. Photo © Chris Strachwitz. All rights reserved. Courtesy Arhoolie Records, El Cerrito, Ca.

WADE FRUGÉ

(1916–1992) Eunice

Like many of the influential fiddlers in Louisiana, Wade Frugé did not perform prolifically in dancehalls, preferring the more intimate setting of jam sessions, house parties, and small groups. His legacy was the vast regional influence he had on the many traditionalists and purists of Cajun music. His style was steeped in old-time tunes, and he never really changed throughout his lifetime.

Wade was born in 1916 in Tasso, a community near Eunice. His family had a rich heritage in early Cajun music; his main source for learning the fiddle was his grandfather, Napoleon "Babe" Frugé, with whom he lived off and on from the age of thirteen. From him, he learned tunes that were in existence in the early part of the 1800s. One uncle, Artemon Frugé, played fiddle and his cousins, Artemon's sons, Atlas and Houston, played steel guitar and rhythm guitar with some of the biggest stars in Cajun music.

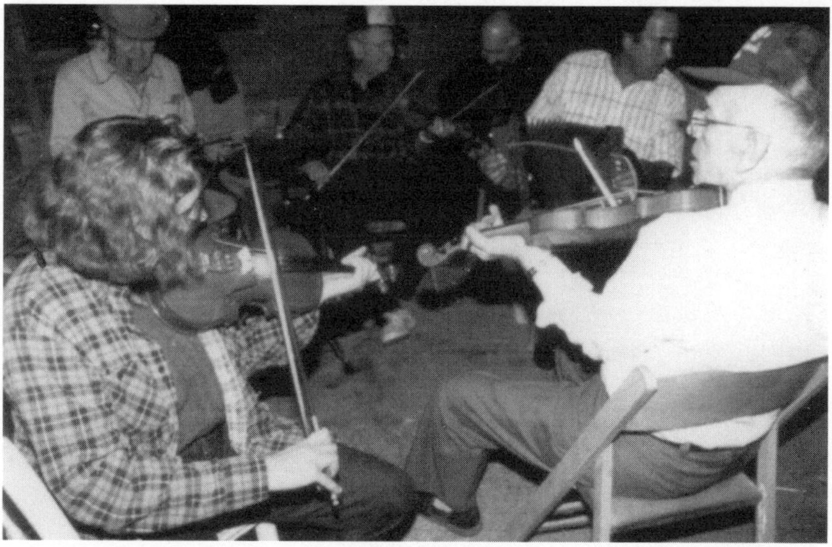

Informal music in Marc Savoy's barn on a boucherie day in the mid-1980s with Tina Pilione, Shelton Manuel, Dewey Balfa, Mike Doucet, Marc Savoy, and Wade Frugé. Photo courtesy of Tina Pilione.

Wade's style was based on the styles of Cajun fiddlers of old, but like many fiddlers he borrowed a little from every fiddler he met. His unique bluesy style is attributed in part to his association with tunes he learned from blues fiddlers like Douglas Bellard and an unnamed left-handed fiddler he heard in front of Nick's Bar in Eunice.

Rather than the string band sound of many early musicians, Wade preferred to play with an accordionist. Throughout his lifetime, Wade played house dances and parties with Artemon and an accordion player, his uncle Hiram Courville. He was also known to play with another uncle, accordionist Toval Frugé. On some occasions he was known to play lead fiddle with Maxim Rozas on second fiddle. Wade continued to play with local musicians while working as a horse trainer and farmer.

Marc Savoy recalls him playing at his father's home in 1959 and played with him many times until Wade passed away on June 23, 1992. In the later years of his life, Wade played at Savoy's Music Center in Eunice with Ann and Marc Savoy and Tina Pilione. In 1988 this association resulted in an important recording of this old-style fiddler, helping preserve this musical style for future generations. Entitled *Wade Frugé: Old Style Cajun Music*, on Arhoolie Records, it featured legendary Cajun fiddler Michael Doucet and old-style Cajun singer Vorance Barzas of Mamou Playboys fame, as well as Tina Pilione and Marc and Ann Savoy. In the late nineties additional tracks were added when the Arhoolie production came out as a CD (Arhoolie CD 476).

In Wade's later years, numerous historians and fiddlers such as Will Spires and Delilah Lewis came to study informally with him to learn about early Cajun fiddling. In the early 1980s, noted Cajun music historian Ann Savoy received a grant to study his fiddle style. Tina Pilione studied his style in detail and hopes soon to release a DVD on the Wade Frugé style of Cajun fiddling as part of her Cajun fiddle instruction series.

Marc Savoy and Tina Pilione relate their thoughts on the fiddling of Wade Frugé in an e-mail dated March 21, 2007:

> *He had a unique style with very beautiful and delicate ornaments. He played with a lot of feeling and had a very rhythmic style. He played in unison with the accordion. That was because he played with his uncles since childhood and they really knew each other's music.*
>
> *He liked the melody, played it well, with just enough—never too much. He liked to play the melody in unison with the accordion, not just seconding.*

The influence of Wade Frugé looms far and wide, affecting fiddlers throughout the country as well as locals from Richard Burgess to Tina Pilione and Ann Savoy. Via recordings and future music culture projects, his influence will continue.

Interviews by Ron Yule: Vorance Barzas (2-28-2007), Richard Burgess (undated informal conversation), Houston Frugé (2-27-2007), Tina Pilione (7-3-2007), and Ken Smith (2-24-2007).

References

Pilione, Tina. E-mail (3-1-2007), re: Wade Frugé.

Savoy, Ann. *Cajun Music: A Reflection of a People, Volume I.* Bluebird Press, Eunice, Louisiana, 1984.

Savoy, Ann. Liner notes. *Wade Frugé: Old Style Cajun Fiddler.* Arhoolie CD 476, 1998.

Photo courtesy of CFMA Hall of Fame Collection, Lake Charles.

J. B. FUSELIER

(1900–1976) Oberlin

Jean Batiste "J. B." Fuselier was born in Oberlin, Louisiana, in 1901, and began playing the fiddle at the age of four. He stated, in a 1973 interview with Sam Tarleton, that his arms were so short he could not pick the fiddle up to play it. Since the fiddle stayed on the bed all the time, he would crawl up on the bed and "see-saw" on it while his sisters would dance on the floor. A first cousin, Gilbert Duplechain, suggested that they sit him in a chair so he could hold the fiddle. His fingers were so short at the time, he learned to play with only three fingers and never learned to use his fourth finger during his career. He states, "All that money I made, I made it with three fingers." By the age of nine, he began playing accordion, which he learned with four fingers.

By the age of ten, he had played his first house dance at Tophey Guillory's, near Mamou. He states, "I played my first dance . . . for fifty cents. The violin by myself.... A country dance in a house. I was so hot. The sweat was pouring in my shoes. I was not quite ten years old. That's the first time I got money to play." J. B. would return from the dances tired, so his father bought another violin and his brother began playing at the dances with him. They had to coax him, because J. B. stated he would rather dance than play the fiddle. They each got fifty cents. He also notes that if they played all night they got fifty cents more.

When he got older and began booking dances himself, he got five dollars for two musicians. He played accordion with a single fiddle accompaniment; he got three dollars because he was supplying the transportation, and the fiddler got two dollars.

By 1925, he states "I'd get 10, 12, 15 dollars . . . that was for the whole band . . . In them days that was a lot of money." Sometimes he got five dollars, again because he was supplying the Model T for their transportation. This band consisted of his brother Clarice, a left-handed fiddler, J. B. on accordion, and his wife on guitar. Arthur Leger recalls that another brother, Furgis, also played fiddle at country dances around Pine Island.

Adam Johnson, a Lake Charles fiddler, recalls seeing J. B. play in 1925 at house dances in Durald and a dancehall in Eunice. These events sparked Adam's interest in learning to fiddle, and he eventually played with J. B. at a few dances and jam sessions.

In the early 1930s, J. B. moved near Lake Arthur and joined the Conner Boys (Varise, Valsin, and Murphy), playing accordion. Joe Falcon's recording of "Lafayette," in 1928, had introduced the accordion to a new audience and the Conner Boys, a string band with fiddle, guitar, and bass, needed an accordion to meet the crowd's demands at dances. Many of these dances on the southern end could only be reached by boat. Crawford Vincent recalls J. B. coming to their home in south Cameron Parish in the early 1930s and eating with his family, prior to playing a dance at Savan Roy's with Varise Conner. By 1935 the Conner Boys retired from playing dances.

During the mid-1930s, J. B. joined a young guitar and tenor banjo player named Beethoven Miller and Preston Manuel, a rhythm guitarist with whom he had been playing since 1932. They called themselves Miller's Merrymakers. Beethoven's father drove the group to New Orleans, where they cut a total of sixteen songs for Bluebird. An unknown string player, M. J. Achten, sometimes joined the group for these recording sessions.

J. B. was the first person to record the popular "Chere Tout-Tout," which was written for his daughter, Myrtle. "Lake Arthur Waltz" and "La Valse Du

Atlas Frugé, J. B. Fuselier, Nathan Abshire, Jimmy Baker, and Preston Manuel. Unknown location, ca. 1950. Photo courtesy of Bernella Frugé Collection/Lyle Ferbrache.

la Compaign" are other songs he composed. "La Valse Du la Compaign" was composed on a tractor. He states, "Me and my first wife were separated. She blamed my mother . . . I let her know it wasn't like that at all—on that record."

When Beethoven left the group, J. B. took over as bandleader and changed its name to J. B. and the Merrymakers. Once the recordings were released, the group became very popular and drew large crowds at the Allen Parish Fair, Step Inn Club (Lawtell), and the Fais Do Do (Ville Platte), as well as other venues throughout south Louisiana.

Several of these recordings were translations into French of popular blues and country songs, "Corrina" and "Birmingham Jail." One of their most popular on the Bluebird label was "Ma Chere Bassette." He cut thirty-four sides in New Orleans between 1936 and 1938. Besides the popular "Ma Chere Bassette," some of his other records included "Lake Arthur Stomp," "I Can't Forget You," "Open House Door," "Elton Two-Step," "Round-up Hop," "Anna Mae Waltz," "Cajun Breakdown," "Ma Julie Noir So," "Redell Breakdown," "Ponce a Noir," "Valse de Rebot," and "Gueydan Two-Step." He states in the Sam Tarleton tapes: "When we'd go to New Orleans to make some records . . . part of the road was gravel, part of the road was dirt. The last time I went to make records in New Orleans I had a Model A. We went in a Model A—four of us."

Preston Manuel in Raymond Francois's *Ye Yaille Chere*:

> *When I first started playing, I was about eighteen or nineteen years old, my first dance was in Iota, Louisiana. I started playing with J. B. Fuselier and the Merrymakers, just a little group. The first record I made for RCA Bluebird was in 1936 in New Orleans. We made, I think, about nineteen records there. I played about twenty-five years with J. B. and the Merrymakers.*
>
> *The first record that I remember making with J. B. Fuselier was "The Lake Arthur Waltz," because we played at a little place in Lake Arthur. Then we played in Pine Island there, so on the other side we made "Pine Island Two-Step." Then we made "Chere Bassette, Ou Toi T'es" for his wife who was given this nickname because she was very short. Then we made "Chere Tout-Tout." We were the ones who made that for the first time; that was for his little daughter who had been given the nickname "Tout-Tout."*
>
> *We made four recordings per session. The man in charge for the recording sessions was Mr. Eli Oberstein. He came from New York and he'd call us; then we'd go to the St. Charles Hotel in New Orleans. We'd make records there; then, at the end of six months, he'd come back and we'd make four more records. I think we made 18 or 19 records for RCA. We slept in the Monteleon Hotel, then the next day we'd go to the St. Charles Hotel, the third floor I remember, and we'd cut these records there. It wasn't tapes, it was thick wax records.*
>
> *When we'd make a record, the fellow would ask us, "Do you want to hear your voice back and see how it sounds?" I'd say, "I'd be tickled to death to hear that!" So he'd replay it and say, "That's perfect, but you'll have to cut another one because that one is ruined!"*

In dancehalls throughout southern Louisiana, many promoters and hall owners would host contests prior to the Saturday night dance; musicians were invited to compete to see who played the dance. Sometimes represented as accordion contests, other times as band contests, these competitions not only picked a winner, but made money for the owners who invited the crowds to come to the club and drink and finally judge by their applause. J. B. and the Merrymakers participated in these contests several times.

Tonice LaFleur, a member of the CFMA Hall of Fame in Lake Charles, played off and on with J. B. while Tonice was living in Durald from 1933 to 1943. He recalls hitchhiking and walking to many of the house dances in the early 1930s; as he puts it, "We were afoot." In addition to J. B. and Preston Manuel, Tonice recalls Preston Fontenot, from Eunice, occasionally played guitar and sang with the group. He notes that they played at the Avalon Club in Basile, George Pierrsonne's in Mamou, the Woodlawn Dance Hall, Abe Boudreaux's Dance Hall in Eunice, and also Port Barre and Cottonport. He notes, "We had four dances a week that we played." They'd travel to the dances in J. B.'s four-door Ford. Tonice recalls when J. B. wrote 'Ma Chere Bassette" for his wife. He said, "He named it after her. I drove the car to Cottonport and he practiced it in the back seat of the car."

He continues, "Every dance we'd play one or two Cajun songs [on accordion]. We played anywhere we could get a little money." Some of the country and hillbilly songs he recalls them playing included "Wondering" and "Corrina, Corrina," and Bob Wills favorite "Maiden's Prayer." "Sometimes we'd get five, sometimes ten dollars . . . apiece." He further recalls, "I was supporting my family when I left J. B. in 1943." Tonice left Durald and went to work in Lake Charles.

J. B. is credited by many as being the first to use a steel guitar in a French band by hiring Atlas Frugé (ca. 1940). The Merrymakers were a string band, but played many Cajun songs because of J. B.'s accordion playing. Atlas Frugé credits J. B. with the revival of Cajun music because of his continued playing of Cajun music in the dancehalls. They played both hillbilly and French music.

J. B. recalled in the Sam Tarleton tapes of 1973 that he was running a restaurant on the "main drag" in the middle of Eunice around 1945 when he first met Iry Lejeune, when Iry would come in and eat and drink coffee. At that time, J. B. was playing nearly every night and soon began taking Iry to the dances, where Iry would play accordion. He says, "Iry, you feel like ridin' tonight?" Iry would respond, "Yeah." He would go to the dances and J. B. would call him up and he'd play a few numbers. J. B. notes, "That's when he took a likin' to me." J. B. recalls him saying, "Any time he wanted to go play music he'd just go meet ole J. B. Fuselier."

After J. B. moved to Lake Charles, Iry and his band, the Calcasieu Playboys, were playing at the Blue Moon and the fiddler (Wilson Granger) had quit. Around nine that night he called J. B. and asked him to come play with them. The guitar player, Alfred Cormier, said, "I think we're gonna keep that man on the violin, he's as good as you ever did have." Iry told him, "I told you that. How good he was." Cormier replied, "I know, I used to hang around with him." They played together after that at various clubs in the area. Every Friday night he would pick Iry up and go to Eunice and play at the Green Wing Club with some of J. B.'s "old players." The club usually closed at midnight. When they played on Saturday night, he would pick up Iry and go to their scheduled dance. The band at that time consisted of Alfred Cormier, an unidentified steel guitar player, and an unidentified drummer. J. B. played with him until the tragic car wreck.

Iry was with J. B. on October 8, 1955, when a car rammed Fuselier's parked car while they attempted to change a flat tire. They were returning from an engagement at the Green Wing Club in Eunice. The accident occurred five miles west of Eunice on Highway 190 and cost Iry his life. Although J. B. suffered serious injuries (numerous broken bones and a head injury), once he recuperated from this accident, his group continued to play music.

One of the best-known lineups of the Merrymakers consisted of J. B. on fiddle, Desbra Fontenot on steel, Norris Courville on drums, and Preston Manuel on guitar. Crawford Vincent sometimes sat in on the drums after J. B. moved to Lake Charles. Crawford noted that J. B. was a smooth fiddler, especially on "Chere Tout Tout." He recalled that J. B. played many accordion numbers during the dances they played in towns including Pine Island, Lake Arthur, Lake Charles, and Port Arthur, Texas. Over the years, J. B. played with many other musicians including Nathan Abshire, Will Kegley, Shelton Manuel, Ellias Soileau, and Jimmy Baker.

Ernest Thibodeaux, a CFMA Hall of Fame vocalist, recalls from his childhood in the early 1930s that J. B. rode his bicycle to their house in Welsh to play with his father, Clobue, and would carry the accordion in a pillow sack in the basket of his bicycle. He would stay most of the day and play on the porch, with Clobue on fiddle and J. B. on accordion. He did not know where J. B. lived at the time. In the mid-1940s, Ernest joined Will Kegley to play with the Pine Grove Boys and notes that J. B. played with them at clubs in Basile and Lawtell.

Adam Johnson told a story about the last time he played with J. B. Fuselier. Adam thought that J. B. had also been killed in the accident that took the life of Iry Lejeune. Adam and his wife were riding around Lake Charles, off of Highway 14, one day in the late 1960s. Adam passed a house and saw a man sitting on the porch that looked just like J. B. Fuselier. After driving down the street, curiosity got the best of him. He went back, and to his surprise, found it was J. B., who insisted that Adam go home and get his fiddle, and they sat on the porch and played a few tunes.

J. B. was an influential fiddler, vocalist, and instrumentalist. He played music for a living most of his life, leaving many recordings and musical memories to his listeners.

Interviews by Ron Yule: Adam Johnson (10-24-2003), Tonice LaFleur (3-8-2004), Arthur Leger (7-22-2005). Delmar Sonnier (6-2-2003), Ernest Thibodeaux (3-23-2003 and 12-4-2005), and Crawford Vincent (8-25-2004).

References

Francois, Raymond E. *Ye Yaille Chere*. Swallow Publications, Ville Platte, Louisiana, 2000.

Sam Tarleton Tapes. McNeese State University Archives, McNeese State Library, Lake Charles , Louisiana.

Savoy, Ann. *Cajun Music: A Reflection of a People*. Bluebird Press, Eunice, Louisiana, 1984.

Yule, Ron. *Iry Lejeune, Wailin' the Blues: Cajun Style*. Fiddle Country Publishing, DeRidder, Louisiana, 2007.

———. *When the Fiddle Was King*. Fiddle Country Publishing, DeRidder, Louisiana, 2006.

Yule, Ron, et al. *Cajun French Music Association Hall of Fame, Lake Charles Chapter*. Fiddle Country Publishing, DeRidder, Louisiana, 2004.

Photo courtesy of Wilson Granger Collection.

WILSON GRANGER

(1921–2005) Big Lake

Wilson Granger was a fiddling figure who experienced all the many twists and turns in Cajun music for eighty-plus years—a sideman who kept the music going and played on some of the most influential recordings in Cajun music. Born in Durald in 1921, Wilson took up the fiddle at age four after the family moved to Black Bayou. His major influence was his brother, Sidney, sixteen years his senior. His father, Salus, although considered a minor influence on his playing, would eventually be a major influence on his recording career. Salus was mainly an "at-home fiddler" who did not play at dances and socials like his two sons.

In 1925 Salus, a highland farmer raising cotton and corn, moved his family to the Black Bayou community south of Lake Charles, where he continued to farm. After sharecropping on Black Bayou for a while, the family moved to another farm closer to Lake Charles near modern-day Lake Street and Tank

Musical Aces/Pine Grove Boys: Earl Demary, Wilson Granger, Coon Guidry, unidentified, Nathan Abshire, and Ernest Thibodeaux. Crystal Grill, 1948. Photo courtesy of Wilson Granger Collection.

Farm Road. With Cajun fiddle music around the house, on the front porch, and at country and house dances on Black Bayou, Wilson became interested in the fiddle, and Sidney became his teacher.

By the late 1920s, Wilson and Sidney began playing house dances together. Wilson was usually given a chair to sit or stand in so he could be heard and seen. This is where he got his nickname, Pagro. He said, "I was so small I'd sit in a chair." Unlike many fiddlers of the period, the Grangers played in unison. Others played as a duet with one seconding on the fiddle while the other played the lead. Wilson notes, "We played exactly the same. It sounded like just one fiddle. We were so used to playing together." They used no accompaniment in their duet band.

In the late 1920s, Sidney joined some neighbors, the Credeurs, and played at Patin's Club in Goosport. Because of his age, Wilson was unable to attend. The group included Sidney (fiddle), Anatole Credeur (accordion), Levi Credeur (jug), Theo Young (guitar), and Ada Credeur (triangle).

After honing his skills and learning more from Sidney, the brother duet began to play in clubs, namely Luke Richard's (Cameron), Savan Roy's (Grand Chenier), and Private Miller's (Grand Chenier). These dances were played usually with two fiddles and an accompanying accordion. Anatole Credeur, or his son Pierre, usually provided the accordion accompaniment. "We played tunes like 'Jole Blon,' 'Chere Tout Tout,' them old songs. They're still playing them," said Wilson. "We played no bluegrass songs, no English songs. We didn't have a radio back then." He added that they did sing—or, as he put it, "sing and holler." He recalled people would come to the dances by walking, horseback, or wagon and added, "That was during the Depression, very few people had cars back then."

Wilson recalled, "One night we played a wedding dance in Grand Chenier and what they did . . . they had some rafters—they didn't have a ceiling, just rafters. They put some boards on the ceiling rafters for a platform, put a ladder for us to climb on. That's where we played the dance." Wilson's family did not have a car but his brother's friends had cars, and they usually carried them to the dances. Many times the family hosting the dance would come and get them and take them to the dance.

Wilson recalled one particularly rare occasion: "In fact we played a colored dance one time. In fact that was the only colored dance I ever played. In a house. It was one of our neighbors. He was holding a dance at his house. So we went."

Pay for the musicians usually consisted of whatever they could take up when they passed the hat, sometimes "a couple dollars." "You know people worked all day for a dollar back then. You did a day's work, you got a dollar. It wasn't much. Now when you play in the halls, the dance halls, they paid us . . . I remember I went with my brother. We played two dances in Grand Chenier and then Cameron, you know, Saturday and Sunday night. And they gave me four dollars. Two dollars a night. And, I bought me a BB gun."

This pattern of house dances and a few dance halls continued throughout the 1930s. Wilson recalls that the dances continued to include accordion, usually Pierre Credeur, unlike other bands that had abandoned the instrument. This was a good training ground for Wilson, who would be able to quickly adapt to the changes in Cajun music that would appear after the war.

In 1939 Wilson left the farm and joined the merchant marine, working out of Port Arthur. He continued this until after World War II, traveling to the East Coast many times and as far north as New York City. Between trips and when he was home, he played music with various musicians.

By World War II Sidney had quit playing and had given Wilson his fiddle, so Wilson struck out on his own to play music in the Lake Charles area. He fell right into the resurgence of the accordion as Cajun music began to distance itself from string band music, which had dominated during the 1930s and early 1940s. Wilson soon became directly involved with some of the major

Oldtimers Band, 1984: Tonice Lafleur, Wilson Granger, Ned Melancon, Pierre Crader, and Ophey Credeur. Photo courtesy of Wilson Granger Collection.

happenings on this front. His career would include playing and recording with such notables as Nathan Abshire, Ernest Thibodeaux, Atlas Frugé, Will Kegley, Earl Demary, Robert Bertrand, "Duckhead" Cormier, and Iry Lejeune, to name a few.

Following World War II, Wilson recalls he played on an Israel LeFleur–produced show with Ellias Thibodeaux on accordion. The father of Cajun fiddling standout Rufus Thibodeaux, Ellias had played accordion at house dances, with the Musical 4+1 Band, and at the famous Bucket of Blood in Lake Arthur. The production was a novel idea to Wilson. He says they would play their show at an empty building in Sulphur, and the music would be sent by telephone to Jennings, where it would be broadcast over KJEF.

Also during this time, Wilson met Earl Demary, a local guitarist and singer, and they teamed up for several years. Earl drove a Lake Charles city bus and was known as the "Singing Bus Driver." They played dances on the weekend, traveling throughout the area and into Texas under the name the Musical Aces. Nathan Abshire was having a hard time keeping a band together, so at the request of Quincy Davis from Eunice, they began playing with Nathan Abshire seven nights a week. A typical week would include playing five nights at the Crystal Grill in Lake Charles; then on Saturday they would go to the Avalon Club in Basile. He states, "We made ten dollars a night. That was good money back then. . . . At one time we use to broadcast here at KPLC every day at noon for one hour. That's how I got to playing with Nathan. . . . Will Kegley would play for thirty minutes with Nathan, the next thirty minutes I'd play with him. He had us both playing."

Abshire's first recording of "Pine Grove Blues" was made with Wilson on fiddle. Lyle Ferbrache writes in an unpublished *History of the Pine Grove Boys*:

> *In 1949, Virgil Bozman recorded Nathan Abshire (accordion and vocals), Wilson Granger (fiddle), Jimmy Baker or "Coon" Guidry (bass fiddle), Ernest Thibodeaux (guitar and background commentary), and Earl Demary (guitar). Together they recorded a raucous and infectious version of "Pine Grove Blues" (backed by the Kaplan Waltz). It was recorded at radio station KPLC in Lake Charles and pressed on Bozman's OT (Oklahoma Tornadoes) label. The record was a sensation.*

The "Kaplan Waltz" was on the flip side. Wilson also recorded "Bayou Chicot Waltz" under his own name with the same band. Wilson further noted that Abshire recorded "Pine Grove Blues" many times and subsequent recordings featured fiddlers like Dewey Balfa and Merlin Fontenot.

Wilson's first stint with Iry Lejeune was around 1948, when Earl Demary occasionally would hire Iry to join the Musical Aces for dances around Lake Charles and southeast Texas. Besides playing with Iry in the Musical Aces, he played with Iry for two stints in the 1950s. Wilson noted that they played throughout southwest Louisiana and southeast Texas at places including Breaux Bridge; the Blue Moon and Hi-Mount Clubs in Lake Charles; the Clover Club in Lacassine; Bailey's Fish Camp in Bridge City, Texas; the Red Barn Club on Highway 90 in China, Texas; and B.O.'s Sparkle in Port Arthur, Texas, to name a few.

Wilson recalled that he recorded several songs with Lejeune. Eddie Shuler recorded these far from the Goldband Studios. "We made those records at Iry's house. He had the recorder on the kitchen table. . . . On one of the records. Iry had a dog. He was under the house. Somebody walked up. That dog barked. It's in the record." The tune, "Durald Waltz," did not feature the accordion. Wilson had this tune in his head from hearing his father play it on the front porch and around the house. With Iry being the talented musician he was, he put words to it, and they recorded it. Wilson stated that many people thought that J. B. Fuselier played on these records because Wilson left the group soon after the recording, and Iry began playing with J. B. until the fatal accident that took Iry's life.

Wilson's recorded output with Iry included "Grande Bosco," "Durald Waltz," "J'ai Ete Au Bal," "Made a Big Mistake," "Come and Get Me," "Don't Get Married," "Convict Waltz," "It Happened to Me," and "Parting Waltz." Except for "Durald Waltz," these were recorded with Iry on accordion and Alfred "Duckhead" Cormier on the guitar.

Wilson continued to play with various groups while keeping his television repair business going, and in the 1970s began to enter fiddle contests at the urging of fellow Cajun fiddler Herman Fontenot.

In the 1980s he joined with Cajun music pioneers Tonice LaFleur, Dudley Rozas, Pierre Credeur, and Ned Melancon and others to play at nursing homes as the Old Timers Band.

Wilson passed away on September 3, 2005, and was posthumously inducted into the Cajun French Music Association Hall of Fame, Lake Charles Chapter.

Interviews by Ron Yule: Louis Fournerat (3-26-2006), Wilson Granger (5-25-2005 and 6-2-2005), Tonice LaFleur (9-20-2004), and Milton Vanicor (2-7-2006).

References

Ferbrache, Lyle. "History of the Pine Grove Boys." Unpublished manuscript in possession of author, 2007.

———. "Musical 4 + 1." *Blues and Rhythm* 206 (February 2006).

Yule, Ron. *Iry Lejeune, Wailin' the Blues: Cajun Style.* Fiddle Country Publishing, DeRidder, Louisiana, 2007.

———. *When the Fiddle Was King.* Fiddle Country Publishing, DeRidder, Louisiana, 2006.

Photo courtesy of David Greely.

DAVID GREELY

(1953–) Denham Springs

Unlike most Louisiana-born Cajun fiddlers, David Greely (b. 1953) did not learn Cajun music in his youth, but his bayou roots manifest themselves in the middle of his career. A direct descendant from France via Nova Scotia, his grandfather Eddie Theriot, from Darrow, played the fiddle at house parties and family gatherings in the community. Always blessed with a unique musical voice, David recalls singing "Sixteen Tons" at three years of age for house-guests at his home and learning some piano by ear from hearing his sister play while she practiced the piano. In his early teens, he sang with a gospel quartet at Baptist revivals around Livingston Parish, and in his later teens he learned to accompany himself on the guitar, leaning toward rock and roll like most youth of the sixties.

As he neared the end of his studies at Denham Springs High School, one evening he loaded into the back of a pickup with his friends to attend a Black

Cornbread, 1976: David Greely, "Dminor" Bennett, and Leo Thomas. Photo courtesy of "Dminor" Bennett.

Sabbath concert in New Orleans. The three-band bill featured Seatrain, a band fronted by ex-Bluegrass Boys, Peter Rowan and Richard Greene. Greely was immediately taken aback by this folk-rock band and the fiddling of Greene, a classically trained fiddler who played well in almost any music genre. David was so impressed he notes, "I never really paid much attention to Black Sabbath after that."

He promptly bought a plywood Japanese fiddle and two bows from a Baton Rouge pawnshop and set out on a trial-and-error experiment, initially impeded by a self-created GDBD tuning that he calls a "G tuning." He purchased a Seatrain LP and began learning "Sally Goodin," making up tunes on his own, and eventually buying a Flatt and Scruggs LP featuring Earl Scruggs and Paul Warren on "Pike County Breakdown." At this time in the early seventies the Old South Jamboree at Walker was in its heyday, and he attended to see both local and nationally known fiddlers who were featured on the shows.

David's musical career began to take focus when a friend, Joe Sanders, introduced him to Cornbread, a Hammond-based "folkgrass" group. He promptly joined them, and they played everything in the key of G to accommodate David's unique tuning. Eventually he learned that the fiddle was tuned wrong, and switched over to mandolin to get used to the standard GDAE tuning. Members included "Red" Weaver on guitar, Michael "Spider" James on washtub bass, and Leo Thomas on washboard. The bluegrass band was completed when—on a trip to Mountain View, Arkansas, for an all-weekend picking on the square—they met David Minor "D minor" Bennett from Little Rock, who played banjo. When Red and Spider began working in Steamboat Springs, Colorado, the rest followed and played in clubs around the ski resort area.

In 1974 they moved to Eureka Springs, Arkansas, establishing a home base there and playing throughout the South at various venues. David describes this group as "a little crazy," with an energetic stage show depicting their free spirit. He points out that they were even "thrown out of spring break at Fort Lauderdale." They recorded one project at a studio in Springfield, Missouri, appropriately entitled *Cornbread*.

In 1976 the group disbanded, and David packed up and headed to Nashville. He played at clubs around town mainly because he had a growing family and did not want to go on the road. Having made one record, he had become enamored with the idea of getting into the studio to do more session work. David notes that his decision to stay off the road hurt his chances: "They didn't want you to make a living doing sessions unless you had served your time on the road." He eventually landed at George Jones's Possum Holler on Printer's Alley, playing in the house band. Jerry Lee Lewis took over the club and gave him a chance to meet and hear many celebrity musicians. This also afforded him the opportunity to meet many of his fiddling heroes, including Kenny Baker, and a chance to play with many "really fine musicians" from the Nashville scene.

Several remembrances from his time in Tennessee include performances at Loretta Lynn's Ranch, the Ernest Tubb Record Shop, and an afternoon show at the Opry House that resulted in a dressing-room jam session trading fiddle tunes with Roy Acuff and Charlie Collins.

"By 1980," he notes, "I was actually playing for a living." Realizing that his dream of session work would probably never materialize, he accepted an offer from a club owner to move to Corpus Christi, Texas, and play at the Yellow Rose in the club's house band, Junction. He recalls, "I put my Sho-Bud amp on a chair the first day I worked there and it stayed on that chair 'til I left two years later."

His stay in Corpus not only brought out the old country and swing sound in his fiddling but also stimulated the inventive, creative side of his musicianship, with the addition of the saxophone to his growing list of instrumental sounds. "I kept hearing all these saxophone solos in the songs we were learning and I said I think I can do that," he commented. After a two-year stay the

David Greely, Brazos Huval, and Steve Riley. Festival Acadiens, 2004. Photo courtesy of David Simpson, LSUE.

club closed; David gigged around Corpus for a while, attempted to start his own band Mama Tried, and did solo work in clubs, singing and playing guitar with an occasional fiddle tune.

Greely moved to San Antonio and continued his role as "Mr. Create-a-Gig" with his innovative spirit doing solo work. Noting the crowds that would line up at Boudreau's Restaurant on the Riverwalk, he approached the owner and contracted to play for waiting patrons. He had previously dabbled in Cajun music and had learned some tunes from the records of Rufus Thibodeaux, Doug Kershaw, and Merlin Fontenot. Jo-El Sonnier had recommended that he get some Balfa Brothers records to learn the music. Upon hearing these recordings for the first time, he notes, "I had an epiphany—I knew what I wanted to do."

Although he could not speak French, David began to learn the lyrics from liner notes on available recordings and sing the words phonetically. Accordion player Blackie Forrestier frequented the club and told him one night, "You know David, what you're singing doesn't make sense." Coupled with an awareness of his family's history, he set out on a mission to learn French and studied the history of the early Cajun people through books such as Barry Ancelet and Elemore Morgan's *The Makers of Cajun Music.*

He worked other restaurants, conventions, and special events around the Texas hill country, recalling, "Sometimes I'd play and sing for eight hours until my fingers felt like clubs." During the day he would do folk music presentations at schools around central Texas, performing for as many as three hundred kids per session, teaching and entertaining with a variety of Irish, mountain, bluegrass, country, and Cajun music.

In 1986 he returned to Denham Springs, putting him back in the bayous of Louisiana where he could learn the music and history of his ancestors firsthand. He continued his "Create-a-Gig" style and strolled the tables for lunch at Mulate's in Baton Rouge and Patout's Restaurant in New Orleans. His musical journey came into sharper focus when longtime friend Joe Sanders, who had introduced him to his first band, took him to Mark Savoy's Music Shop in Eunice, where he met numerous Cajun musicians including Dennis McGee and Steve Riley.

Steve was living in Baton Rouge at the time and would join David at Mulate's for the noontime show. They began playing clubs around town in the evenings. After utilizing several musicians from David's old band, Steve began to add to the group Cajun musicians who could give them the sound they wanted. They began playing on Monday nights at Mulate's, and became the Mamou Playboys band in February 1988. This band included Kevin Barzas on guitar and Michael Chapman on drums. The group was invited to play at the Liberty Theatre and, eventually, Festival Acadiens, where they were heard by Ken Irwin and signed to Rounder Records.

The Mamou Playboys continue today with a worldwide following, featuring David on fiddle, vocals, and sometimes saxophone. They began to supplement their bread-and-butter rural Louisiana dancehall gigs with folk festivals throughout the U.S. and overseas, always remembering that their fans are the basis for their success. The Mamou Playboys have produced twelve recordings that have been well received by their fans, and David produced a solo effort in 1991, *La Talle des Ronces*. He is currently recording a second entitled *Sud du Sud*.

Although David has been influenced by many musicians through the years, his association with Dewey Balfa has had a resounding impact on his career and approach to Cajun music. A 1991 grant from the Louisiana Department of the Arts to study with Balfa brought even more understanding. He states:

> *Sitting with Dewey and listening to him play all alone, I was impressed by the power of his rhythm. Even when he played tenderly, which few Cajun fiddlers did, his time was very even and forceful. He also taught me to listen to detail, and helped me know the difference between what I thought I heard and what I actually heard. I learned that playing the melody was an ingredient, but not the whole dish. The spices were in the details.*

Travel to France and Nova Scotia with the Mamou Playboys has allowed David to further pursue his studies on the history of the Cajuns, especially the Theriots, and the roots of the music we call Cajun today. His efforts in this regard were rewarded in 2004 when he was awarded the Artist Fellowship in Folklife by the Louisiana Department of the Arts. At folk music camps and workshops throughout the country, he teaches the music and history he loves to countless avid fans of traditional Cajun music.

His music career has touched on many fiddle styles, from the bluegrass fiddling of Kenny Baker, Paul Warren, and Curly Ray Cline to the western swing of Johnny Gimble, and finally to the traditional Cajun fiddling of Dewey Balfa and Allen Ardoin. In-depth studies into the styles of Varise Connor and Dennis McGee have brought an even deeper understanding of the sound of Cajun music in the early twentieth century. David has played in almost any venue a fiddler could play, bringing with him the broad knowledge of many genres that has created one of today's most respected and influential Louisiana fiddlers.

Interviews by Ron Yule: David Greely (4-28-2008, 5-7-2008, and 6- 20-2008).

Photo courtesy of Mary Grimsley.

MARY GRIMSLEY

(1944–) Shreveport

In the mid-1970s Mary Lee met Tex Grimsley and began a musical venture that would change the learning of the fiddle in Louisiana. Tex was a seasoned fiddler from the Shreveport area who had played with Arthur Smith and on the Louisiana Hayride, and had already won the Louisiana State Fiddle Championship by the time they met. He introduced her to all the musical fun of the fiddle. The fiddle and love bug had both bitten her at the same time. She recently noted, "I must have fallen in love with the fiddle and the fiddler."

They began to attend fiddle contests all over north Louisiana and east Texas. Over the next few years she would travel as far south as DeRidder, Louisiana, and Center, Texas. They also attended the big contests in Crockett and Athens, Texas. Locally, she attended contests at Blanchard, Shongaloo, Vivian, Haynesville, Zwolle, Coushatta, Fisher, and any others she could find.

Amy Peebles, Crista Goslee, Mary Grimsley, and Amanda Dark. Marthaville, 1989. Photo courtesy of Mary Grimsley.

In 1977 she began entering the Louisiana State Fiddle Contest, and won the Grand Championship in 1988.

Her credentials are impressive, but her major contributions to Louisiana fiddling have been not in playing but in teaching. There was a great need for a fiddle teacher who knew and understood time-honored traditions of fiddling, to teach the instrument and pass on the techniques and love of old fiddle tunes that shaped many pioneers' lives. Although a few taught by ear, many teachers of this instrument taught by classical methods. Students were required to read musical notation and follow the playing techniques of the violinist. Mary was the first teacher in western Louisiana to formally teach using fiddle tunes and ear-training methods on a major scale. She taught fiddling—period! Throughout the 1980s and into the 1990s, her students dotted the winning rosters at fiddle contests and performed at nearly every major festival and celebration in north Louisiana.

She began in 1981 with one student, Paul Owens; by the end of the year she had fifteen. Eager students came to her as if a floodgate had opened. At one time in 1984, she had thirty students taking lessons. She was hauling them to contests and they began to perform as a part of the Red River Ramblers, an old band name that Tex resurrected from his 1940s fiddling days. She made playing fiddle fun, for both the students and their families. They were enjoying playing and performing. She had created a family-fiddling affair. Everyone became involved. Some of the parents learned backup instruments and some even took fiddle lessons so they could become more keenly involved. One student, Amanda Dark, won the State of Louisiana Grand Championship in 1996, and lived in Nashville for a while, playing with many of the top country bands. Paul Owens became the staff fiddler at the Louisiana Hayride.

At the 1985 Louisiana State Championship, seven of her fiddle students entered the contest. Frank Page, the famous KWKH announcer and emcee for the event, thankfully commented, "Thank God for Mary Grimsley." This trend continued until 1992, when Tex's health failed, and her time became very limited. In the mid-1990s, Mary was diagnosed with leukemia and states, "For two years I didn't pick up my fiddle." She said she owes her life to her sister, Carlene Stewart, who gave bone marrow for the transplant that saved her life. Tex's health continued to decline, and he passed away in the fall of 2002.

In the spring of 2003 she began to teach again after an eight-year absence, and now has seven students. She also has become active in giving workshops on playing the fiddle country style. We're glad she's back.

Interviews by Ron Yule: Mary Grimsley (informal undated conversations).

References

Grisham, Dinah. "Mary Grimsley's Students Love Fiddling Around." *Shreveport Journal*, June 9, 1984.

Pick 'N Bow Newsletters. Edy Mathews, editor. Beaumont, Texas.

Southwest Louisiana Fiddlers and Bluegrass Club Newsletters. Ron and Georgia Yule, editors. DeRidder, Louisiana, 1974–76.

Videos: 1985 and 1988 Louisiana State Fiddle Championships, courtesy of Rebel State Park Archives.

Photo courtesy of Susan Roach.

MARCEL "TEX" GRIMSLEY

(1917–2002) Shreveport

From an early age Marcel "Tex" Grimsley seemed destined to become a seasoned performer with talent in all areas of country music. By the late 1940s he wore many hats: fiddler, songwriter, comedian, and violinmaker. He was well versed in each of these areas and loved to perform and demonstrate his musical craft to anyone who was interested throughout his long career.

Originally a Logan, Texas, native, Tex was born in 1917. The family soon moved to Carthage, where at age seven he began to learn the fiddle from his father, Grover, an old-time fiddler. Tex learned quickly and before long was playing around town. Mary Grimsley recalls Tex telling the story that he and Jim Reeves would stand on the corner in Carthage on Saturday and play the guitar and fiddle for money. At the age of ten his mother, Murtis, remarried and the family relocated to Louann, Arkansas. He continued to learn and began playing at country dances and on country shows during his teen years.

Mary also recalls a story from Tex's teenage years. After listening to the Grand Ole Opry for years, he longed to meet Arthur Smith, his fiddling hero. A neighbor was going to Tennessee on vacation and invited Tex along. He wanted to see Arthur Smith, so he agreed to go if they could stop in Arthur's hometown, Dickson, Tennessee, and try to talk to him. When they arrived in Dickson, they did not have to search long to locate him. To their surprise, he was playing on the town square bandstand and invited Tex to get his fiddle and come join them, which he promptly did. To complete the day, Arthur invited them to his house and they continued to play all evening.

After graduating from high school, Tex played at radio stations in east Texas and entered fiddle contests. In 1937 and 1938 he entered the Louisiana State Fair Fiddle Contest, and placed third each year. He was living at Homer at this time. In 1940, while working at radio stations KFRO and KOCA in Kilgore and Longview, he met bandleader Lynn Davis and his wife, Dixie Lee, who later became famous as Molly O'Day. They hired him and he went to Bluefield, West Virginia, and worked as Chief Buddy, "The Indian Fiddler," which was one of his many performing faces.

In West Virginia, his talents as a fiddler, songwriter, fiddlemaker, and comedian were nurtured. He honed his comedic skills and routines during shows. He played on local shows and barn dances and on a daily radio show at WLJS, Beckley, West Virginia, playing with Arthur Smith. Arthur was billed on the show, but periodic bouts with alcohol kept him off the air. Tex had learned his hero's style so well he could fiddle his tunes and no one in the listening audience could tell the difference. He received lots of mail from listeners (400 letters per week) and sold songbooks and autographed pictures. He also played with Molly O'Day, Curly Wray, and Natchee the Indian (Lester Vernon Storer) during this period.

In 1941 Tex entered a fiddle contest in Raleigh, West Virginia, billed as the National Old Time Fiddling Championship, and won first place. Arthur Smith and Natchee the Indian were among the contestants he bested.

Several of his friends from the Shreveport area made the trek to West Virginia and joined him to form a band. Musicians included Sonny Harville, Cliff Grimsley (Tex's brother), and Cliff's wife, Othelle. They played at WLJS until Tex was drafted into the air force. Mary recalls that Tex always regretted leaving his radio show, which he loved.

In 1942 he began his service to the nation. During the service, he played with several bands at local dances and service clubs. He was the manager of the service club and taught administrative procedures to fellow GIs.

Uncle Lynn Davis and His Forty-Niners, early 1940s: Lynn Davis, Tex Grimsley, and James Barker. Front: Dixie Lee. Photo courtesy of Mary Grimsley.

Following World War II, Tex went back to West Virginia and tried to rekindle the radio days of the past, but could not. Times had changed and the listening audience's musical tastes had changed from prewar days. For a while Tex stayed in the West Virginia area, playing with Ernest Tubb, Mother Maybelle Carter, Molly O'Day, and Jim Hall and the Radio Rangers on WMBG, Richmond, Virginia.

In 1946, after a move to Pocatello, Idaho, he worked with a horse show sponsored by MGM Studios, from Hollywood. Don Davis graduated from high school in Shreveport and soon joined him in the summer of 1946. They played as the Hollywood Rangers and appeared on KSEI, Pocatello. Besides Don the group included Joe Smith from Illinois, Kit Nash, and Newell Clark. By fall they had returned to Shreveport.

Tex returned to West Virginia, but things did not work out there. He wound up working across the Midwest, landing in Carbondale, Illinois, where he joined Jim Smith and Don Davis, who had returned to Illinois to play. Don was playing fiddle at the time. Tex played on many stations, including a show at 6:15 a.m. on WCIL in Carbondale with Jack Throckmorton and Bob Moore.

Returning to the Shreveport music scene after ten months, Tex played as the Red River Ramblers and Uncle Tex and the Texas Showboys during this period. He played over KWKH, and in early 1948 his Texas Showboy Band was featured as a part of the Red River Roundup along with the Mercer Brothers, the Bailes Brothers, Scotty and the Rhythm Wranglers, and many other KWKH bands. As a day job he worked as an assistant in the men's clothing department at Sears, Roebuck, and Company, where his boss was Webb Pierce, soon to be a Louisiana Hayride star.

In April 1948 the KWKH management wanted to expand its format to include a "Barn Dance," a type of show gaining popularity in Chicago at WLS, Nashville at WSM, and Alabama at WLAY. Uncle Tex and the Texas Showboys were chosen to kick off the inaugural event, and Tex did it by playing the old fiddle tune "Boil Them Cabbage Down." This would be the Hayride's welcoming ditty for many years. Members of this inaugural band included Don Davis (bass), Sonny Harville (guitar), Bob Murphy (steel), and Tex on fiddle.

Over the years he played with many great artists, including Hank Williams (for six weeks at a club in Longview, Texas), Sunset Carson, Slim Whitman, Webb Pierce, and the Bailes Brothers around Shreveport. In 1949 he co-wrote "I'm Walkin' the Dog" with his brother, Cliff, which was a hit for Webb Pierce. It was one of many that he wrote, including "You Turned a Good Man Down," "You Don't Love Me and the Baby," "Forgive and Forget," "Sorry For You," and "Loved and Lost." Although Tex's recorded output is unknown, he did record several 78s. In 1949 Cliff left the country music business to follow his spiritual conviction to pursue a career in gospel music and ministry. Tex married in 1950 and left the Louisiana Hayride, eventually taking a position as a rocket inspector for Thiokol Chemical Company in central Texas. He did not play professionally again, but did return to Shreveport in 1966.

In the late 1960s, Tex began attending fiddle contests throughout Louisiana and east Texas, winning or placing at nearly all he entered. He was the Grand Champion at the Louisiana State Championship in 1971. In 1977, 1980, 1982, 1985, and 1989 he was crowned the Senior Division State Champion. Tex remarried and from the mid-1970s until his health failed in 1990, he was

Leon Short, Ernest Tubb, Tex Grimsley, and Jimmie Short. WMBG, 1946. Photo courtesy of Louisiana Folklife Center Archive, NSU.

instrumental in promoting the fiddle students his wife, Mary, instructed. He resurrected the Red River Ramblers and they performed at shows and festivals in Fisher (Sawmill Days), Shreveport (Holiday in Dixie and Red River Revel), Natchitoches (Louisiana Folklife Festival), and many more. He not only provided a playing platform for "Mary's Kids," but also helped to organize contests in Fisher and on KWKH so they would have a place to play.

Tex also was a prolific violinmaker and student of the acoustics of the violin, studies he began at the age of fourteen. He learned this art from his uncle, W. A. "Uncle Butch" Spraggins, who had a violin shop in Garland, Texas. During his prewar time in Virginia, his violinmaking skills were honed studying under John Tuttavai, who had migrated from Hungary and was working in the D.C. area as a master violin maker and repairman. Tex continued to make violins wherever he was stationed during World War II, and was featured in several military-base periodicals. After moving back to Shreveport, Tex became one of the major violin repairmen in the area for years. He was a featured folkcraft artist at the Louisiana Folklife Festival in Natchitoches for ten years and was inducted into their Hall of Master Folk Artists in 1982. The sixty-eight violins he made have become collector's items among those collecting Louisiana fiddles, and several professional fiddlers play his instruments. Over the years, he taught violinmaking and repair work to numerous craftsmen including Billy Wester, from Natchitoches, and Joe Leach, from Shreveport.

Tex was proud of his fiddling and loved to show off his skills. When asked how long he had been playing the fiddle he would always reply, "I've been fiddling so long the shadow of my bow arm wore a hole in the floor."

Interviews by Ron Yule: Don Davis (5-12-2005), Troy DeRamus (undated informal conversation), Mary Grimsley (1-2-2004, 5-6-2004, and 7-16-2008), and Billy Wester (undated informal conversation).

References

AF Plant 66 Newsletter. "From Folk Tunes to Rockets." Thiokol Chemical Company, 1957.

Hatley, Don. "Two Notes Higher Than a Gin Whistle: The Sound of the Louisiana Hayride." Louisiana Folklife Archives, Northwestern State University, Natchitoches, Louisiana, July 1, 1981.

O'Neal, Donna. "Tex Grimsley and Friends—Let's Saw a Spell." *Shreveport Journal*, October 16, 1981.

Pierce, Webb. Letter to Tex Grimsley dated October 10, 1952. Louisiana Folklife Center Archives, Northwestern State University, Natchitoches, Louisiana.

"Popular Musician Won to Christ." *Life Tabernacle Newsletter*, November 1957.

Prime, John Andrew. "Hayride Alumni Gather for Taping." *Shreveport Times*, April 7, 1984.

Tucker, Stephen. *Louisiana Saturday Night: A History of Louisiana Country Music.* Dissertation, Tulane University, 1996.

Wenberg, Thomas. *The Violin Makers of the United States*. Mt. Hood Publishing, Mt. Hood, Oregon, 1986.

Photo courtesy of Oran Guidry Jr.

ORAN "DOC" GUIDRY

(1918–1992) Scott

Oran "Doc" Guidry has been described as the "King of the Cajun Fiddlers," but always considered himself to be a blues and jazz instrumentalist playing string band music. With ancestors from Nova Scotia, he was a sixth-generation Acadian from the clan of Pierre Guidry, the patriarch of most Guidrys residing around Lafayette. Doc was born on April 28, 1918, and lived near Scott most of his life.

Doc's father, Clopha, was a front-porch fiddler who played after completion of the daily work on their farm. He also worked at the Lafayette Parish Clerk of Court office. Around the late 1920s Clopha began teaching Nason, Doc's older brother, how to play fiddle, and during the lesson Doc would listen intently. Doc became interested and would take the fiddle out while Clopha was working, teaching himself the tunes he heard at Nason's lessons. When

Nason discovered that Doc was playing on the fiddle he began to beat him up out of jealousy, but, undaunted, Doc persisted. Clopha finally heard the young lad play and quit, giving his copy of a 1624 Maggini violin to Doc. Even though he continued his music studies, Nason gave up the fiddle, taking up the guitar and bass fiddle. Oran Jr., Doc's son, says that Doc also took a correspondence course on playing violin and learned to read music to some extent.

Within two years, at the age of fourteen Doc began playing publicly for dances. Oran Jr. reports that his first band was Joe Fabacher and the Jolly Boys of Lafayette. In a 1991 interview with Shane Bernard, Doc recalled traveling to Dallas around 1934 to record with Joe Fabacher on the Decca label (no record has been found of this in the available literature). The band did record in 1937, but Doc was not listed on any of the credits. At the age of 16, he and Nason joined accordionist Lester Hoffpauir to play at local dances.

In 1936 Doc joined Happy Fats LeBlanc and the Rayne Bo Ramblers, an association that would last throughout Doc's career into the 1970s. Happy Fats came to him and asked him to play the fiddle, and during the course of the conversation asked him his intentions about his future education. Doc told him he wanted to go to college and study medicine. Their first dance was in Morse and when Happy Fats introduced him he introduced him as Doc. The nickname stuck and eventually became so well known around Lafayette that he was listed in the phone directory as Doc Guidry. Few people knew his first name.

Originally the new Rayne Bo Ramblers included Doc and Louis Arceneaux on fiddles, but Arceneaux soon left the group. Doc stayed with Happy Fats for several years, an association that resulted in numerous recordings. During this period he recorded twenty-two sides in New Orleans for the Bluebird label. These sessions occurred on April 2, 1938, and October 23, 1938. Nason played bass fiddle on these sessions. Oran Jr. and A. B. Sonnier note that over the years the Ramblers' exhausting schedule included as many as nine performances per week on numerous radio shows at KROF in Abbeville, KSLO in Opelousas and KVOL in Lafayette, as well as dancehalls from the Showboat in New Iberia to Clem's Dancehall in Abbeville.

On April 1, 1938, one day before the Rayne Bo Ramblers sessions, Doc and Happy Fats played the fiddle and guitar with Joe Werner on eight sides, also for the Bluebird label. Werner had previously recorded with Luderin Darbone's Hackberry Ramblers (Riverside Ramblers) in 1937. One recording, "Wondering," was a hit with the dancehall crowds throughout southwest Louisiana.

Top Row: Jack Richard, Jack LeBlanc, Louis Noel, Felton Hargroder, Raymond Credeur, Edward Jounet, Alvin Seaux, Rufus Thibodeaux, and Berlin Lebleu. Middle Row: Rita Noel, Doc Guidry, Leroy "Happy Fats" Leblanc, and Al Montgomery. Kneeling: Floyd Cormier. KSLO Weekly Amateur Show, ca.1948. Photo courtesy of Hadley Castille.

The Guidrys left the Rayne Bo Ramblers to form Doc and the Sons of the Acadians. A first cousin, Ray Guidry, joined playing tenor banjo. Sidney Guidry, a distant cousin who had been with the Alley Boys of Abbeville and sometimes played between bands, played guitar and sang. This group cut twelve sides for Decca on September 5, 1939. Oran Jr. recalls his daddy telling him this recording was made in Houston, Texas, at the Rice Hotel (cited as Dallas in the Tony Russell's *Country Music Records: A Discography, 1921–1942).*

When the war began, Doc moved to Orange, Texas, to help in the war effort. It is believed that there he met his fiddling hero, Cliff Bruner, and played in the clubs throughout the Golden Triangle.

During 1944, Jimmie Davis was campaigning for the governorship of Louisiana. Doc and his father were at a political rally in Carencro when Jimmy Domengeaux introduced Doc to Davis. Following him to New Iberia, Doc played the first of many campaign rallies for Davis. He subsequently played in the Davis campaigns of 1959 and 1971 (primaries only). In fact, Doc played in several major venues with Davis, playing on the Louisiana Hayride and the Grand Ole Opry several times in the 1950s.

Oran Jr. notes Davis used his father as a representative of the area around Lafayette because of Doc's local popularity. Davis especially liked songs like

"Colinda" and "Big Mamou" and would sing them half in English and half in French. Doc would teach him how to sing the songs phonetically. During the 1944 campaign Doc, like many fiddlers of the era, carried a comedy role in this group, many times wearing red "long johns" under his pants which they would roll up while he was playing to get a laugh. When not on the campaign trail, Doc was playing on radio programs as a member of Happy Fats and the Rayne Bo Ramblers.

After the war, Doc continued to play off and on with his old pal Happy Fats when he needed him, even though Doc had moved to Baton Rouge after the election. He split his time between several bands, including a Baton Rouge–based band headlined by Tony Chatoni. Besides fiddle, Doc played electric mandolin with this blues and jazz–oriented group that included horns. Doc related to his son Oran Jr. that, during his long career, this was his favorite band, mainly due to the high caliber of musicianship among the players.

In 1947 Doc put a group together called the Sons of the South, playing much of the same music he had played with Tony Chatoni. With Curtis DeLoach (drums), Sandy Lormand (guitar), Bradley Stutes (steel guitar), and Jack Richards (tenor sax), for four years Doc continued to play a more pop music style.

From 1948 to 1950 Doc and Happy Fats sponsored a talent show on Saturday mornings at the Rose Theater in Opelousas. It was broadcast over KSLO. Although the band changed personnel several times, Happy Fats carried another fiddler, Ambrose Thibodeaux, Doc's uncle, and Ambrose's son, Merton, who played the bass. At the time, Happy Fats had a recording studio built at his house and they recorded some of their radio shows, which Happy Fats would carry to the radio stations.

Oran Jr. describes Happy Fats as one of Doc's favorite bandleaders. Fats and Doc continued to play off and on after the war, and the incident that highlighted this closeness was described by Oran Jr. Doc had gotten into a fight at a bar and hit a man in the mouth with his left fist, knocking out nine teeth. The man had rotten teeth and Doc subsequently developed an infection and blood poisoning in his hand and could hardly play. When Happy Fats called him about their next show, Doc declined, explaining the situation, even though he desperately needed the money. Happy Fats told him to come on and just give him a "turn around" on each song. Doc never forgot this gesture of goodwill until the day of his death and helped Happy Fats anytime he could, even helping him monetarily toward the end of Fats's life.

Sometime during 1951 Doc began playing six nights a week with another pop-oriented group at the Acadian Lounge. The band, Freddie Rhythm with

Rymes, carried piano, bass, trumpet, and drums in addition to Doc's fiddle and mandolin. Francis "Red" Fabacher—who had played with Doc in the Jolly Playboys of Lafayette in the 1930s, as well as Happy Fats, Harry Choates, and others—returned to play guitar.

In the early fifties Doc played on the Louisiana Hayride several times. On one occasion Happy and Doc appeared with a local singer, Bill Hutto. Happy Fats notes that one rendition of "Jolie Blonde" from Doc brought three encores and several more invitations to appear on the show. As previously noted, he also appeared on the Hayride with Jimmie Davis during this period.

On March 6, 1953, Doc rejoined Davis in Nashville to record "Colinda" on the Decca label, a tune he had recorded with Happy Fats LeBlanc in 1946 on J. D. Miller's Fais Do Do label. Jimmie Davis wrote the English lyrics to the Cajun hit. Other tunes recorded that day were "Big Mamou" and two sides featuring the fiddling of Doc, "Chere Cherie" and an unknown tune.

By 1955 Doc began to scale back and to take other employment, mainly working as a farmer. Besides farming and playing a few shows, he called the Sunday horse races at the Forrest Club, in Breaux Bridge, carrying all the patter of a radio sports announcer.

Although his playing was limited, he continued throughout the fifties and sixties to play with Happy Fats, Doris Matte and the Lake Charles Ramblers, Vin Bruce, and Al Terry, as well as Jimmie Davis in his 1959 campaign. Davis won his second term as governor, and in 1962 helped Doc get a civil service job on the Alcohol, Beverage, and Liquor Control Board. He eventually retired from this position. Over the years, he recorded several albums with Vin Bruce.

In 1963 Doc joined Aldus Roger playing twin and triple fiddles with many fiddlers, including Louis Foreman and Tony Thibodeaux. With the Lafayette Playboys, Doc was on one of the most popular Cajun music television shows of all time on KLFY, Lafayette. During this three-year stint, he also recorded with Aldus.

In 1966, he recorded a solo LP titled *King of the Cajun Fiddlers,* featuring his vast musical talents. The La Louisianne record features titles that read like a panorama of music, with varying styles of fiddling from hoedown to Cajun.

In the early 1970s, Doc moved to Houma and spent most of the rest of his life in Terrebonne Parish. After leaving Scott, he continued to play some with Vin Bruce and at local restaurants like Mulate's. In 1980, he was a part of a government-sponsored trip where they played in California and traveled to entertain in Thailand.

Following World War II, as awareness of the Cajun culture became more prominent, more record buyers began to like Cajun music, but did not understand the French lyrics. With Doc's background he was used as a translator of French lyrics to English. He also served a vice versa function, translating English lyrics into French. He did that throughout his career after his first tour with Jimmie Davis.

Doc never cared to play too far from his Louisiana home but did recall to Oran Jr. that, during one trip to Nashville in the late 1950s, he did get one offer that was very appealing, when Jim Reeves asked him to join him on the road. Doc declined and stayed with Jimmie Davis during his campaign, eventually returning home.

In 1989, Doc fell on the steps in front of his home and broke his wrist. From that time until he passed away in 1992, he seldom played, ending a long and illustrious career as one of south Louisiana's most highly regarded pioneering fiddlers.

Doc has received many accolades over the years, becoming a member of the Louisiana Hall of Fame in 1992 and the Cajun French Music Association Hall of Fame in 1997.

Interviews by Ron Yule: Kevin S. Fontenot (1-30-2007), Oran Guidry Jr. (1-25-2007), Oran Guidry Jr. and A. B. Sonnier (1-29-2007).

Interview by Shane K. Bernard: Doc Guidry, 11-2-1991. Tape in possession of Oran Guidry Jr.

References

Allan, Johnnie. *Memories, Volumes I and II.* Johnnie Allan Publishing, Lafayette, Louisiana, 1995.

Brasseaux, Ryan A., and Kevin S. Fontenot. *Accordions, Fiddles, Two Step and Swing: A Cajun Reader.* Center for Louisiana Studies, Lafayette, 2006.

Broven, John. *South To Louisiana.* Pelican Publishing, Gretna, Louisiana, 1983.

Ferbrache, Lyle. Post-1946 recordings in his collection.

Laird, Tracey E. W. "Country Chameleons: Cajuns on the Louisiana Hayride." www.louisianafolklife.org.

Russell, Tony. *Country Music Records: A Discography, 1921–1942.* Oxford University Press, New York, 2004.

Savoy, Ann Allen. *Cajun Music: A Reflection of a People, Vol. I.* Bluebird Press, 1984.

Yule, Ron. *When the Fiddle Was King.* Fiddle Country Publishing, DeRidder, Louisiana, 2006.

Yule, Ron, et al. *Cajun French Music Association Hall of Fame, Lake Charles Chapter.* Fiddle Country Publishing, DeRidder, Louisiana, 2004.

Photo courtesy of Mary Grimsley.

ELMER LEON "LONNIE" HALL

(1914–1972) Shreveport

Elmer Leon "Lonnie" Hall was one of the premier swing and country fiddlers of the thirties, forties, and fifties around Shreveport. A native of Ben Wheeler, Texas, born December 3, 1914, he came from a very musical family with two brothers who played country and western swing music. One brother, Ramon, played fiddle and guitar; another, John, played guitar. Besides playing in bands, they were known to play the Texas fiddle contest circuit.

Country music historian Cary Ginell writes in the liner notes to *Leon Chappelear, Western Swing Chronicles, Volume 2*:

> *The multi-talented Hall played many instruments but excelled on the fiddle, idolizing jazz violinist, Joe Venuti, as did many early western swing musicians. In 1934 Hall and his brother Ramon . . . were leading a fledgling western swing band in*

> *Tyler known as the Rhythm Rascals, which also included Howard Oliver and guitarist Muryel Campbell.*

Lonnie came to Shreveport in the mid-1930s and landed a job with Leon Chappelear's Lone Star Cowboys on KWKH, an association that would yield his nickname. Beecher Stuckey, a well-known local fiddler, was listening to the radio on Lonnie's first appearance with the Lone Star Cowboys. He tuned into them one morning at 7:30 a.m.: "That was the first morning that Lonnie played with them. Leon Chappelear that had the band introduced him the first morning. He said, 'You're Leon Hall?' and Leon said, 'Yeah.' 'Well, my name's Leon, too.' He said, 'We can't have two Leons here, so we're just gonna call you Lonnie.'" Two of the band members included "Slim" Harbert on bass fiddle and "Skipper" Hawkins, who played tenor banjo and tap-danced on the stage. Beecher recalls they made personal appearances around the Shreveport area, as far south as Coushatta and Mansfield, over into Texas, and north into Arkansas. They played school auditoriums and a few clubs, mainly around Shreveport.

Country historian Kevin Coffey notes in his liner notes to *Leon Chappel, Automatic Mama* that Lonnie, along with other musicians around the Shreveport area, was on the local police force for a while in the late thirties.

Lonnie, who touched on Chappelear's career musically into the 1950s, had an even larger impact on Chappelear's life and career on September 13, 1935, about a month after their Chicago recording sessions. Coffey writes:

> *A month later Chappelear was lying critically injured in a Shreveport hospital. The band had been traveling to a dance that Friday afternoon when twenty-five miles south of Shreveport, at Ninock, their car, driven by Hall, collided with another as it pulled off the road into a filling station. Hall, clarinetist Harvey, and bassist Slim Harbert were only slightly injured, but Chappelear was still unconscious hours later.*

Lonnie received only minor lacerations to the head, but extensive injuries incurred in the accident would plague Chappelear throughout his life. Many thought that Chappelear's music career never had the impetus it had prior to the accident and his potential as an artist was never attained.

Chappelear and Lonnie, who would be associated off and on throughout their lives, were further connected by Lonnie's marriage to Chappelear's niece, Mary Elizabeth. Additionally, Hall was buried behind Chappelear's grave in the Epps Cemetery in Shreveport when he passed away.

Recording in Chicago (August 14, 1935 and August 15, 1935), New Orleans (March 13, 1936), and Dallas (February 14, 1937 and December 12, 1937), Lonnie recorded on seven separate sessions with Chappelear. These sessions resulted in fifty-two sides with Chappelear during this two-year period for the Champion, Decca, and Montgomery Ward labels. One tune recorded on August 14, 1935, "Ben Wheeler Stomp" was written by Lonnie as a takeoff on "Osage Stomp." It instrumentally calls to mind Lonnie's hometown, Ben Wheeler, Texas.

On September 21, 1938, Lonnie recorded seven numbers with Shreveport singer Buddy Jones for Decca Records. It is not known if he was a member of Buddy's band, which periodically played around Shreveport.

By 1937, Lonnie went to work with Bob and Joe Shelton and the Sunshine Boys, also playing locally on KWKH. Beecher recalls that during this period, he traveled with the Sheltons sometimes playing in Dallas/Fort Worth on WBAP and WFAA when they migrated between the two country musical venues. In 1937, he fiddled on numerous cuts recorded in Dallas for the Decca label. These sessions on February 17, 18, and 19, 1937, and December 12, 1937, yielded thirty-nine cuts. The December 12, 1937, session coincided with a session by Leon Chappelear and the Lone Star Cowboys.

As a part of Charles Mitchell's Texans during 1939, Lonnie recorded with Jimmie Davis in Houston on March 5, 1939, and September 3, 1939. Twenty-three sides resulted from these sessions for the Decca label.

By 1941, Lonnie went into the studio with Bill and Norm Nettles and their Nettles Brothers Stringband. This lineup recorded twelve sides during two occasions in Dallas for the Bluebird label (April 3, 1941, and October 8, 1941).

During the 1940s he began playing with Pee Wee King, traveling throughout the United States. Beecher tells the story that Lonnie made extra money with Pee Wee King by helping to pack and move the instruments and equipment while they were on tour. No recordings have been noted with King.

Clyde Brewer recalls that, following World War II around 1945, Lonnie worked in Port Arthur with Moon Mullican and his Showboys appearing on KPAC. He thinks Lonnie may have recorded with him during this period but this has not been confirmed. Lonnie also played with Paul Howard and the Arkansas Cotton Pickers while working out of Shreveport.

Throughout the period after the war Lonnie's travels are sketchy, but it is thought he did surface to record with Chappelear (now named Chappel) in the early 1950s. Kevin Coffey writes in his liner notes to *Leon Chappel, Automatic Mama* on Bear Family Records: "Lonnie may have recorded with Chappelear after the war on Capitol Records. If the bluesy, rustic fiddler from

Moon Mullican and his Showboys, late 1945: Acie Peveto, Reggie Ward, Richard Prine, Cotton Erwin, Lonnie Hall, Steve Inglish, Dean Rasberry, and Moon Mullican. KPAC, Port Arthur, Texas. Photo courtesy of Dean Rasberry Collection/Andrew Brown.

the November '51 session [for Capitol] had possibly been Lonnie Hall, the fiddler on this date [April 3, 1953] almost certainly was Hall, though captured in a far more uptown and jazzy mode."

By 1954 Lonnie was back in Shreveport and off the road, except for a few short trips out with various bands. He got a job working with the local highway department, and his supervisor was Pete Ashby, a fiddle-loving rhythm guitarist. They began to play together, renewing Pete's interest in fiddling. Lonnie began to attend jam sessions and would go to clubs where musicians would gather and pick. Beecher said that besides Lonnie, "Preacher Harkness, who had moved back to the area about that time, would sometime come in and jam." He says, "He and Preacher could really play that twin fiddle stuff. Preacher and Bernie Harkness had a sister that lived down there [Shreveport] . . . she played the guitar and liked the music. She'd invite us over there . . . we'd sit around and play and drink coffee." Lonnie also played with several local country groups at local clubs, and on many occasions played twin fiddle with Beecher. At one time, he traveled to west Texas and played in a club for a while.

Other fiddlers from north Louisiana recall Lonnie's great talent. Pete Ashby said, "He's about the best fiddler I ever heard." Fred Beavers and Bill Kirkpatrick also recall that Lonnie attended many Texas fiddle contests with them but never entered, even though he could play the Texas breakdowns with the best of them. Beecher notes he was mainly a swing fiddler but he was very versatile and could "play good hoedowns." Beecher recalls him playing "Ragtime Annie," "Turkey in the Straw," "Done Gone," and lots of Bob Wills tunes like "Faded Love" and "San Antonio Rose." He says, "I always admired his fiddle playing. He was real polished. He had a good arm and bow action, and a little lick on that bow that many people didn't have. He could just about get a job anywhere." Fred recalls, "He played with the flat part of his fingers, not on the end. His fingers would hang over the fingerboard . . . it was hard to detect his fingers moving." Besides the lefthand style, Fred notes that Lonnie played with a bow that was not under full tension. He told Fred, "Don't play with the bow so tight. Loosen it a little and your playing will be smoother." Lonnie wrote a fiddle tune, which Bill Kirkpatrick calls "Lonnie Hall Breakdown." Bill says it's "something to hear."

Lonnie influenced many of today's fiddlers, including Bill Kirkpatrick, Fred Beavers, Pete Ashby, Beecher Stuckey, and Paul Woodard, to name a few.

Lonnie passed away on September 13, 1972.

Interviews by Ron Yule: Pete Ashby (2-18-2004), Fred Beavers (2-15-2004), Clyde Brewer (5-10-2006), Mary Grimsley (9-30-2004), Bill Kirkpatrick (10-21-2004), and Beecher Stuckey (10-29-2004).

References

Binge, Dagmar Anita. Liner notes. *The Shelton Brothers, Down On the Farm.* Cattle Compact CCD 241, 2001.

———. Liner notes. *The Shelton Brothers, Joe and Bob.* Cattle Compact CCD 258, 2002.

Brown, Andrew. E-mails dated August 4, 2008, and August 6, 2008, about Lonnie Hall's recordings.

Coffey, Kevin. Liner notes. *Leon Chappel, Automatic Mama.* Bear Family Records, 16254AH, 1999.

Ginell, Cary. Liner notes. *Leon Chappelear: Western Swing Chronicles, Volume 2.* Origin Jazz Library, OJL-1001, 2002.

Russell, Tony. *Country Music Records: A Discography, 1921–1942.* Oxford University Press, New York, 2004.

Shreveport Times. "6 Are Injured as Cars Crash South of City." September 14, 1935.

Photo courtesy of Bob Hardin.

PETE HARDIN

(1923–2002) Haynesville

Lawrence Edgar "Pete" Hardin was born in 1921 in Haynesville, the eldest son of nine children born to Jewell and Hugh Hardin, who were a farming family. By the age of eleven or twelve, Pete began learning fiddle from hearing his daddy play old hoedowns like "Leatherbritches" and "Redwing" and waltzes like "Wednesday Night Waltz" on the front porch and around the house after the farming chores were done. This was the beginning of a family band of musicians that played for neighbors and friends around their Haynesville community.

Besides the hoedowns and waltzes, Pete's brother Bob recalls Pete began to listen to the sounds of Spade Cooley and Bob Wills on the radio and a few phonograph records that focused his attention on a different kind of music: western swing. Bob also recalls that several records of Django Reinhardt and Stéphane Grappelli that Pete listened to while he was home were a big

Hardin Brothers, 1950s: Bob, Pete, Bill, Jack, and Dave. Photo courtesy of Bob Hardin.

influence on his playing. He began to emulate the sounds of these fiddlers he heard on record and radio. This would be the style he would develop, a jazz/swing style of playing around the melody.

With so much music in the house, the other eight Hardin children absorbed the sounds they heard and began to learn to play. The four girls, Pauline, Ila Mae, Luthy Ruth, and Louise learned to play the piano from their mother, but did not become as proficient as the boys. Bob notes, "They only learned enough to entertain themselves." The four boys, Bob, Jack, Bill, and Dave all were very interested in music and became band directors and taught in school systems in Arkansas, Texas, and Louisiana. They learned bass, guitar, and all the brass and woodwind instruments associated with the band. Bob says that times were hard and playing music was one of the happier moments in their life. He says, "When we were playing, we forgot our problems." When they would gang up and play on the front porch, the neighbors would hear it and before long they had a yard full of neighbors and friends listening to the music.

Bob also states that Pete was by far the best musician of the bunch, and that the other boys were not as musically talented as Pete. Pete played mainly by ear (he read music a little), but the brothers sought formal training to learn the instruments and the music they wanted to play. He says Pete just picked up the fiddle and played, and that he played music the way he wanted and felt. Bob recalls the family playing at different informal events later in life where

Dave, Bill, Jack, and Bob would be reading the music charts and Pete would be playing by ear, filling in and playing what fit without missing a lick. The Hardin brothers had a band, the Hardin Brothers Quintet, from 1952 until 1975, and played the country club circuit around northwestern Louisiana. They played Latin, pop, jazz, old standards, and some big band music. Pete sat in with them on occasion.

At the age of sixteen or seventeen, Pete walked up to his daddy with fiddle in hand and announced to Hugh, "I'm gonna go play my fiddle," and he walked down the road and left. He had heard bands playing on the radio and wanted to follow in their footsteps. Bob said, "From that time on we only heard from him every six or eight months."

He moved to east Texas and played with several bands as well as playing around Shreveport and on local Shreveport radio stations. He never played with any one band for a long period of time, but played short stints with many bands. Over the years, he played with Pappy Covington, the Rice Brothers, Bob and Joe Shelton and the Sunshine Boys, and many east Texas groups.

Pete served in an army tank division in World War II, and was shell-shocked and burned in combat. He was released from the army hospital and discharged.

In 1949 he played twin fiddle with Troy Beavers and the Southern Swing Boys, playing harmony to Troy's smooth fiddling. Sometime in the 1940s he made one tour with Bob Wills and the Texas Playboys to California, but returned home after a couple weeks. In the late 1940s the Louisiana Hayride was the place to be, and Pete played on the show with both Hank Williams and the Bailes Brothers. Like many of the sidemen that played on the Hayride, he was known to sit in with many more when they needed him.

Pete played music but never depended solely on the music business for a living. He had been to barbering school and was a barber for the tank division during World War II. He made his living from his barbering skills and the clubs that he and his wife, Hilda "Peaches" Hardin, owned around Shreveport. Peaches usually ran the club and Pete handled the music, the bandstand, and the house band that played nightly. Pete played fiddle, saxophone, clarinet, rhythm guitar, lead guitar, bass, mandolin, and piano. Fred Beavers notes, "He would play whatever instrument was needed." Any musician could come by and sit in for a while. Although Peaches could not recall the date, she said the first club they ever owned was the House of Blue Lights on North Market Street.

They are most noted for the Skyway Club on Highway 80, which they operated during the Louisiana Hayride years of the late 1940s and 1950s. This club was frequented by "everybody who was anybody" and wanted to party away from the Louisiana Hayride. Peaches recalls Hank Williams, a young Elvis Presley, Webb Pierce, Slim Whitman, and a host of other Hayride stars visiting the club. She believes Pete met Hank at the club, which led to his playing on the Hayride and at a few local dates with the Drifting Cowboys. She also noted that Hank played at the Skyway with Pete and his house band and that she had sung with both Hank and Elvis at the Skyway Club.

Following the closing of the Skyway, they opened Pete 'n' Peaches Club, also on Highway 80, which followed the same format—she ran the club and he handled the music. She notes he also barbered a lot in the shop he had on the premises.

During his career he also played with Preacher Harkness, Cliff Bruner, Kitty Wells, Red Sovine, Johnny Horton, Ferlin Husky, and many musicians from east Texas and northwest Louisiana.

Except for a couple 45s he cut with Peaches, his only known recordings are with Paul and Hoke Rice and their Rice Brothers Gang. They recorded eleven sides for Decca in Houston on April 6, 1940.

His great musicianship and fiddling talent has been enjoyed not only by his family, but also by many of the fiddlers who recall his ability. North Louisiana fiddlers Paul Woodard, Fred Beavers, and Bill Kirkpatrick quickly recall his improvisational skills, harmony playing, and his vast musical knowledge on the fiddle. Fred recalls hearing him play pop, jazz, and even some classical pieces on fiddle. Bill Kirkpatrick remembers hearing Pete and Troy Beavers playing twin fiddles and each would be playing two parts, producing the sound of four fiddles. His influence has been far-reaching even though he recorded very little and did not play on the road.

Interviews by Ron Yule: Pete Ashby (2-18-2004), Fred Beavers (2-15-2004), Mary Grimsley (8-28-2004), Bob Hardin (8-30-2004), Hilda Hardin (8-29-2004), and Bill Kirkpatrick (10-21-2004).

Reference

Russell, Tony. *Country Music Records: A Discography, 1921–1942*. Oxford University Press, New York, 2004.

Photo courtesy of Jean Harkness.

FELTON "PREACHER" HARKNESS

(1918–1994) Vivian

Many of north Louisiana's current top fiddlers will quickly spout out the name of Felton "Preacher" Harkness when asked about their fiddling heroes. One soon realizes that he was an awesome talent and created music on the fiddle far and above the norm. His influence on Fred Beavers, Paul Woodard, "Preacher" Duncan, or Bill Kirkpatrick, as well as Texas fiddle champion Beecher Stuckey, is well recognized and is noticed in the playing style of the current group of young fiddlers.

Preacher Harkness was born in 1918 and learned to love the sounds of the fiddle at an early age from listening to his mother, Lanora, play around their home, in rural Atlanta, Texas. She used to play at country dances, mainly on a cross-tuned fiddle while Preacher's father, John, beat the fiddlesticks. She also entered contests and won and placed on occasions. Preacher and his family of ten listened to a battery-operated Zenith radio, in the late 1920s and early

Preacher and Bernie Harkness on Channel 12, Shreveport, ca. 1960. Photo courtesy of Jean Harkness.

1930s, to hear the country and swing sounds that were coming over the airwaves. Preacher heard the sounds of the great Texas fiddlers of the era, developing a penchant for the more modern country music sounds. Bernie, Felton's brother, was nine years older and had already learned the fiddle, so he was his main teacher. Felton soon began to play square dances around Atlanta.

By the age of fifteen, Preacher landed his first professional job playing on KFRO in Longview, Texas, for its morning show. He soon joined Bob and Joe Shelton and The Sunshine Boys and began to appear on KWKH in Shreveport, and WFAA in Dallas. The Sheltons, who were regional hits in the country scene, tagged him as the "School Boy Fiddle Player" because of his age. At the same time, Bernie had a fifteen-minute morning radio show on KWKH, so he quit the show and joined the Sheltons and his brother. This began an association that would carry the Harkness brothers through thirty years as Sunshine Boys, off and on. While in Shreveport, the Sunshine Boys appeared at the Municipal Auditorium on Saturday nights as a part of the Saturday Night Roundup where a large group of the KWKH family would play a show at the auditorium and follow it with a dance.

The Sheltons worked from Shreveport to Dallas as well as going into central Louisiana. Crawford Vincent, a Lake Charles area musician and historian, re-

Bob and Joe Shelton and the Sunshine Boys, mid-1930s, KWKH: Slim Harbert, Howard Oliver, Bob Shelton, Joe Shelton, Merle Shelton, and Preacher Harkness. Photo courtesy of Jean Harkness.

calls one of their visits to central Louisiana and the first time he met Preacher. "We were at the Walfus Club, near Oakdale. We'd gone to see the Sunshine Boys. They needed a drummer, so I told them I'd try. The electricity was out that night, so Preacher played the fiddle—the whole dance. He was great." He says he was one of the best he ever heard.

On September 18 and 19, 1938, Preacher recorded eighteen sides with the Sheltons in San Antonio for the Decca label, including "Let a Smile Be Your Umbrella," "Lost Woman," "Mandy," "She's Somebody's Darling Once More," "Knot Hole Blues," "Ace in the Hole," "That's No Way to Treat the Man You Love," "You Can't Fool a Fool All the Time," "Meet Me Somewhere in Your Dreams," and "That's Why I'm Jealous of You."

Although the dates are not known, Crawford recalls that Preacher played with the Jubileers, a Port Arthur western swing band, mainly in the Golden Triangle area in southeast Texas. He also played with Ray Shaver and the Western Swing Kings.

One stint carried him into Arkansas as a part of the Hot Springs Medicine Show. He recalled in a *Shreveport Times* article that they had "once toured the area in a mule drawn covered wagon." This musical journey is described in part by Tracey Laird in *Shreveport's KWKH: A City and Its Radio Station in the Evolution of Country Music and Rock and Roll*. She notes in an interview

Kneeling left: Bernie Harkness, Joe Shelton. Kneeling right: Preacher Harkness. On rail: unidentified, Slim Harbert, Jimmie Davis, unidentified, and Sleepy Brown. Late 1940s at Robert Taylor and Barbara Stanwyck's ranch in Palm Springs, California. Photo courtesy of Jean Harkness.

with trumpet player Sleepy Brown that, in 1939, Preacher joined Smokey and Bunny's Medicine Show and toured Arkansas selling what Sleepy calls a foul-tasting laxative, Satanic Medicine. While in Hot Springs, Sleepy sold ads for the show and purchased a radio. Sleepy recalls that when they could, they listened to the sounds of Joe Venuti, the virtuoso jazz and improvisational violinist who was one of Preacher's favorites.

When Preacher was nineteen he developed rheumatic fever, and the after-effects of this illness caused him to flunk the army's rigorous physical exam. In 1943, needing work and wanting to help with the war effort, he moved to California and went to work in the shipyards in Long Beach. Following a Bob Wills concert in Long Beach one night, he met the legendary country figure. He auditioned the next morning and was invited to a rehearsal. After taking a "ride" on one of the tunes, Bob liked what he heard and hired him for one hundred dollars a week. He toured up and down the West Coast for a while, before returning home.

After leaving Wills, he rejoined Bob and Joe Shelton and the Sunshine Boys, and by 1947 he was with San Angelo–based Lowell McManes. He and Bernie then landed a job with Jimmie Davis. He toured with Davis all over the country and, while back in California, played to large crowds of dancers at the

Staples Club, a nightclub run by Davis in Palm Springs. Jean Harkness notes that via this job he met Frank Sinatra and Barbara Stanwyck. He appeared with Davis and recorded on the soundtrack of a movie from this period, *Mississippi Rhythm*.

He left California and Davis, and played with the Southernaires, a western swing band that played at the Southern Club in Lawton, Oklahoma. As the house band, they backed many of the top acts that came through touring: Jimmy Dickens, Hank Williams, Tex Ritter, and other Nashville acts. During this period, he also played with Lefty Frizzell, a stint that included appearances on the Grand Ole Opry. From 1958 to 1962 he and his brother, Bernie, reunited with the Sheltons and appeared on the Jones Junction TV Variety Show on KSLA and later KTBS in Shreveport. The band included Bob and Joe Shelton, Slim Harbert, Mallie Ann Harbert, Louis Wheeler, plus Preacher, and Bernie. His wife, Jean, recalls they would do a routine with the fiddle when they played "Listen to the Mockingbird." Bob would act like he was trying to take the fiddle from Preacher and in the midst of the fuss one would bow while the other noted the fiddle, and vice versa. Preacher's mother, Lanora, even got in on the act and appeared on the show several times. When local sideman Sonny Harville replaced Slim Harbert, the opportunity was provided to play some twin fiddle pieces on the show.

In the sixties Preacher joined the house band at the Reo Palm Isle in Longview for several years and played with Paul Howard, a former Louisiana Hayride entertainer, on shows from Texas City, Texas, to Hot Springs, Arkansas. Bernie was again a part of this band and they appeared with Howard during the sixties and seventies on a limited basis, when Paul would line up a few shows.

In 1960 Preacher remarried, and he and Jean had a daughter, Caroline. Caroline was a good musician, having perfect pitch like her famous father, and learned the fiddle, piano, and guitar as well as singing lead and harmony. Following graduation from high school, she obtained her degree from Northeast Louisiana University, studying broadcast journalism. After three years on KWKH, she moved to Nashville and currently does vocals on demos as well as working at her regular job. During his career, Preacher penned several songs; one, "Same Ole Room, Day by Day," was recorded by Caroline.

From 1966 to 1979, Preacher limited his playing and stayed off the road most of the time. He even turned down a job with Hank Thompson as one of his Brazos Valley Boys. During this time, he worked in a garment factory in Vivian.

In 1986, he had open-heart surgery and went into a "depressed state" in which he would not play fiddle and did very little. Jean credits one of his former students, Beecher Stuckey, for bringing him back. Beecher showed up at the front door one day and talked Preacher into playing again. The neck on Preacher's fiddle had come unglued and Beecher had it repaired by a New Boston, Texas, violin repairman. Preacher began playing again and continued until his death in 1994. During his last years, he attended and played at many of the Bob Wills Reunions and entered a few contests. In 1993 he won the Louisiana State Fair Fiddle Contest.

Preacher was posthumously inducted into the Cowtown Society of Western Music's Hall of Fame in 2003. The Fort Worth–based group recognized him as an "American Swing Hero." In the liner notes to the *Texas Fiddle Collection*, Johnny Gimble praised Preacher's musical skills by commenting, "Preacher mastered the whole instrument with a command of jazz, double stops, and strong melody." Joe Holley, the left-handed hot fiddler in the Playboys of the thirties and forties, stated, "Preacher was the best harmony man ever." Preacher is beloved by many of the fiddlers from all over the area who will attest to the fact that he was one of the best they ever heard.

Interviews by Ron Yule: Fred Beavers (6-14-2003), Preacher Duncan (5-12-2003), Kevin S. Fontenot (11-22-2005), Tillman Franks (1-21-2004), Jean Harkness (2-18-2004), Bill Kirkpatrick (7-15-2003), Beecher Stuckey (7-29-2004), Crawford Vincent (7-16-2003), and Paul Woodard (6-14-2003).

References

Binge, Dagmar Anita. Liner notes. *The Shelton Brothers, Down on the Farm.* Cattle Compact CCD 241, 2001.

———. Liner notes. *The Shelton Brothers, Joe and Bob.* Cattle Compact CCD 258, 2002.

Boyd, Jean A. *The Jazz of the Southwest: An Oral History of Western Swing.* University of Texas Press, Austin, 1998.

Burton, Larry. "Fiddlin' Around, Shreveport." *Shreveport Times*, Shreveport, Louisiana, 1991.

Gimble, Johnny, and Paul F. Wells. "Texas Fiddling and Texas Fiddlers: A Short History." Liner notes, *The Texas Fiddle Collection.* CMH-LP 9027, 1981.

"Harkness Inducted into Hall of Fame." *Caddo Citizen*, May 29, 2003.

Laird, Tracey E. W. *Louisiana Hayride: Radio and Roots Music Along the Red River.* Oxford University Press, New York, 2005.

———. *Shreveport's KWKH: A City and Its Radio Station in the Evolution of Country Music and Rock-and-Roll.* Dissertation, University of Michigan, Ann Arbor, 2000.

Russell, Tony. *Country Music Records: A Discography, 1921–1942.* Oxford University Press, New York, 2004.

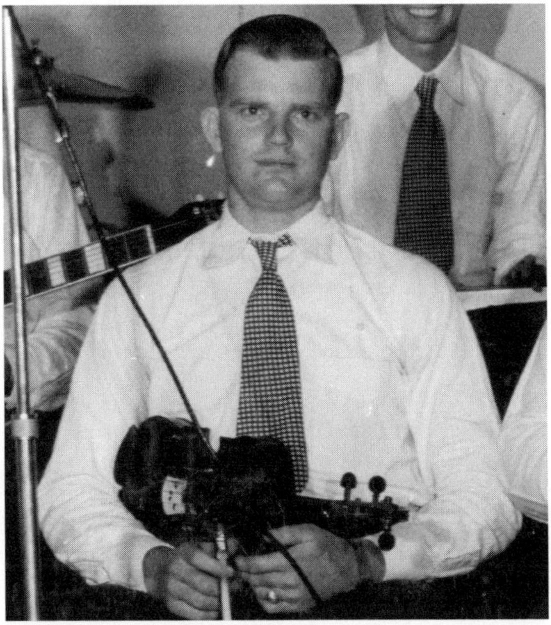

Photo courtesy of Eddie Friday Collection.

BOB HENDERSON

(1925–1996) Gonzales

Robert (Bob) Henderson was born in 1925, in Forney, Texas, a hotspot for fiddling with many notable fiddlers hailing from the area. His father, William "BB" Henderson, was an old-time fiddler who played for country dances in the area. BB's stepfather, Baker (first name not remembered), was a fiddler, too; however, no one in the family can recall anything about his playing. After moving from west Texas in the early part of the century, BB settled near Forney and worked a 130-acre farm "on the halves" for Joe Hughes, who happened to be a famous Texas fiddler and an early recording artist. BB also played every instrument from five-string banjo to pump organ.

Hoeing and picking cotton and corn was the order of the daytime, and at night, it was music. Letha Rogers, Bob's older sister, describes their existence: "That's the way we entertained ourselves. When we were young, we were poor as church mice, and we picked cotton all day long . . . or chopped corn or whatever we had to do on the farm. And then at night—of course we lived way out in the country and we didn't have any way to go . . . but mules and a wagon. So we entertained ourselves. We had an old cement storm house in the front yard and it had a big square cement platform. [RY: "A stage?"] That's what we played out like it was. And we'd get out on that after we'd come in from the field and had our supper and everything . . . and we would play 'til all hours of the night. I would fiddle and Lowell and Robert would play the guitars. Then Robert would fiddle . . . the neighbors always talked about how they could always hear us down there playing. It was a way of life." Two brothers (Terry and Jim) and a sister (Edna) also played but Letha says, "very little."

She describes Robert as a hard worker. "Robert could pick more cotton, oh that guy could pick cotton. Robert and I picked thirty-nine bales one year, just the two of us. I tell you, we got to the field before we could see and didn't get home until we couldn't see. Daddy raised six of the hardest-working kids, but I always said he didn't drive us; he led us. My daddy was a worker too." Later she notes, "The hotter it got, the more Robert and I could pick. Robert and I picked the cotton and Daddy and Lowell picked the corn."

Saturday nights were anticipated with much excitement because there would be a dance somewhere. If the Hendersons didn't host one, someone in the neighborhood would invite everyone over. "My father, he played for country dances." She added that when they were young they played for country dances but could not recall if they ever made any money playing at these dances. She does recall that they did not go by horse, mule, or wagon but someone usually came by and picked them up in an automobile to carry them to the dance. She states, "They had them in their homes. That's the way they entertained themselves back in those days." When they were kids they would go along and play with their father either playing the fiddle or guitar. Laughing, she explained, "Sometimes we'd have knockdown drag outs, but it was lots of fun." Someone usually got out of line at the dances but they had too much fun to let that get in the way.

Square dancing was also popular at these dances. Letha notes they always had a square dance at every dance. They would usually mix it up with couples dancing.

Before they got electricity (ca. 1930), she remembers their first radio. "We had a little ole outfit. It had 'rabbit ears.' It had a crystal and a little wire and you punched it around 'til you found good reception, if you could. And that's the kind of radio we had. We didn't have anything." After they got electricity, Letha only remembers one radio in the house.

Smiley Bennett (bass fiddle), Matt Bennett (guitar in middle), Bob Henderson (fiddle on right), Louis Peck (guitar 2nd row behind Matt), and Joe Carlino (piano). Club 20, Highway 1, Alexandria, 1951. Photo courtesy of Eddie Friday Collection.

Bob was a formidable foe at fiddle contests in the area. Letha remembers playing at numerous contests, even as far away as Terrell, Athens, and Gilmer. They played many contests around Dallas and the local area, and she recalls one local contest where she surprised everyone. "It was the 4th of July and they had a big contest out at Fair Park and we played. That I distinctly remember, because I won over Robert and I don't know how I ever did it . . . and that really got him too." Contestants at many of these contests were their neighbors Joe Hughes and the Solomons, Ervin, Vernon, and Norman. Letha recalls, "I always thought that Ervin was the best fiddler, breakdown fiddler, that I ever heard in my life . . . I could just listen to Mr. Solomon fiddle all night long, he was just terrific." Bob spent a lot of time with the Solomons and learned many of the techniques of Texas-style fiddling from his association with them. He expressed to Louisiana fiddlers Ray Brandin and Curry Perkins in the 1980s that he had learned the Texas-contest style of fiddling from his association with the Solomons.

Letha recalls, "We lived on Mr. Joe Hughes' place and he was a fiddler. He'd come down to the house and we'd make music. In fact, I think he encouraged us kids more than my father did. . . . They were having a contest at Gilmer, Texas, and he was gonna fiddle in the contest and Robert and Lowell were

Jelly Elliott and the Singing Cowboys, 1953. Back row: Sleepy Ebert, Jimmy Carpenter, Slim Watts. Front: Bob Henderson, Jelly Elliott, Abe Manuel. Courtesy of Letha Rogers.

just real young . . . They were in their early teens. So he wanted them to accompany him while he fiddled. We were poorer than church mice so after he left and Robert and Lowell . . . They wondered what in the world they would wear [laugh] to go. As it happened I had some white domestic that I was gonna make some sheets out of so I made those two kids a white shirt, each . . . All through the years, Robert would laugh and tell about how they went to that fiddling contest with Mr. Joe with their flour sack shirts. That was so funny. To him it was."

By the early 1940s, the family played a few dances in several clubs around Dallas. "Then Robert, Lowell, and I and another fellow from Kemp, Texas, his name was Richard Payne. . . . He played the bass fiddle. We had a band and we played for nightclubs after we grew up, of course." One she recalls was Danceland, on the southwest highway. This was the only one she could remember, but she notes the family band did not do this very long.

Letha says, "I quit playing when I married. Robert took off and we disbanded our band. Robert left and wound up in Louisiana. . . . I remember he was on the Fort Worth station, I don't remember the call letters at that time, but he was with Hank Thompson." She does not remember the date. The years after Bob left home are not well documented but he was known to play with bands in Fort Worth, Amarillo, Beaumont, Alexandria, and throughout central Louisiana.

Several musicians from the period remember Bob playing around central Louisiana from 1948 until 1953. Ed Johnson recalls that, during 1948 and 1949, he played with a band around Glenmora at the USO Club, an unknown club in Turkey Creek, and the Golden Slipper in Woodworth. The band included Jimmy Johnson, (electric guitar and fiddle), Happy McNichol (drums), Pete Singley (upright bass) and Bob (fiddle and guitar). Ed also recalls that Johnny Porter, who had played with Hank Williams for a short while, played with the group. Dates are unknown, but he played with the Roy Conn Orchestra at clubs around Alexandria, and in 1951 he played with Matt and Smiley Bennett at Club 20 on Highway 1.

Eddie Friday also recalled that during this period Bob lived on Lee Street Extension in Alexandria and had a disc recorder on which he made his own recordings.

In July 1952 Bob recorded on two sessions with Lefty Frizzell. One session was in Dallas and the other was recorded at J. D. Miller's in Crowley. Andrew Brown notes that none of these were issued. No one recalls how long he stayed with Frizzell. One central Louisiana stint in 1952 and 1953 was with Jelly Elliott. He was a part of the two bands Elliott was promoting at the time. Elliott had been chosen to be the spokesman for the U.S. Forestry Service's forest fire prevention campaign and Bob was a part of that band, which was known as the 3 Knotheads. One poster from 1952 shows Bob along with Slim Watts and Deacon Anderson as members of this promotional group. Elliott also appeared with Elliott's Singing Cowboys, who played at local clubs, school shows, parish fairs, and on KSYL and KALB. The 1953 band included Slim Watts, Jimmy Carpenter, Abe Manuel, Sleepy Ebert, and Elliott. They also played throughout the state and into east Texas.

Besides playing with Hank Thompson, Letha Rogers recalls that he played with Bob Wills and George Jones, but she could not recall the dates. "Pee Wee" Whitewing, a former steel guitarist with Hank Thompson, remembers Bob when he met him in the early 1950s. On one occasion when Hank Thompson and the Brazos Valley Boys were traveling from Oklahoma City into south Louisiana, Bob hitched a ride back to his home in the Alexandria area. He does recall that Bob did not play with Thompson while he himself was a member, from 1952 until 1955.

In 1960 Bob left the road and opened the Music Box, a club in Gonzalez, Louisiana. Starting from scratch, he built a club and dancehall that became known throughout Louisiana, had multiple bandstands, and would accommodate as many as two thousand people. Playing whatever instrument was needed, whether it was fiddle, piano, drums, guitar, or any other country instrument, he helped with the entertainment. Top-billed acts included Willie Nelson, Ace Cannon, George Jones, Conway Twitty, Charlie Rich, Fats Domino, Jerry Lee Lewis, Boots Randolph, Ernest Tubb, Mickey Gilley, and Loretta Lynn, to name a few.

In 1982, in an effort to entertain the "older folks," Bob started Sunday afternoon "Senior Citizen Dances" at the Music Box. These lasted until his death in 1996.

Bob recorded with several unnamed Louisiana musicians, recording "Hadacol Boogie," "A Million Tears," "Over the Waves," and "Hen Pecked Blues" on the Louisiana record label sometime in the 1960s. In the early 1970s, several 45s issued on the Houston-based Guide label influenced numerous fiddlers in the south central part of Louisiana. Cuts were "Carroll County Blues," "Chere Tout Tout," "Jole Blon," and "Poor Hobo."

Bob's musical talent and legacy are being carried on by two of his children. Robert Jr. plays a multitude of instruments and travels and records with many country and gospel acts based in the Baton Rouge area. Daughter Tareva Henderson is a country artist who has been on *Nashville Now* and other television and country shows in Nashville.

Bob not only was one of the finest fiddlers who graced Louisiana stages, but a great musician and band member who could fill in anywhere and do his job well. A tribute to Bob in the *Gonzalez Weekly* following his death in 1996 sums it up best: "Bob the Fiddler, Bob the Singer, Bob the Entertainer, Bob the Friend . . . we all loved him for our own special reasons."

Interviews by Ron Yule: Ray Brandin (6-10-2005), Eddie Friday (6-20-2005), Bob Henderson Jr. (7-4-2005), Ed Johnson (6-21-2005), Curry Perkins (6-25-2005), Letha Rogers (7-5-2005, 7-12-2005, and 8-5-2005), and "Pee Wee" Whitewing (6-20-2005).

References

Brown, Andrew. E-mails dated 8-5-2008, re: Henderson recordings with Lefty Frizzell and private recordings on the Louisiana label.

Cooper, Daniel. *Lefty Frizzell: The Honky-tonk Life of Country Music's Greatest Singer.* Little, Brown and Company, 1995.

Hevey, Kimberly. "The Music Box Legacy." *The Advocate*, Baton Rouge, Louisiana, January 10, 1997.

"Tribute to Robert E. 'Bob' Henderson." *Gonzalez Weekly*, Gonzalez, Louisiana, November 1, 1996.

U.S. Forestry Service promotional poster, 1952.

Yule, Ron. "The Louisiana State Championship—1974". *Louisiana Folklife*, Louisiana Folklife Center, Volumes 26–27.

THE 1974 LOUISIANA STATE CHAMPIONSHIP

The following segment comes from my remembrances of the 1974 Louisiana State Championship at Boyce, which were published in Louisiana Folklife, Volumes 26 and 27. It is used with the permission of the Louisiana Folklife Center, NSU Box 3663, Northwestern State University, Natchitoches, Louisiana 71497. Copies of this issue, dedicated to the history of the Louisiana State Championship, can be obtained at the above address.

. . . Then came the announcement. Needless to say, neither Wilfred [Luttrell] nor I made the finals; our names were not on Troy DeRamus' list. This is what we expected, but we did have hope—until the announcement of the finalists. We were out. The "ins" were Ray Beebe, J. W. Smith, Hank Strickland, Jewel Lasyone, and Bob Henderson. These were the top five—the finalists.

Now the heat was on. They all rushed to practice. That was, all except Bob Henderson. We were kneeled by the front door talking. He asked me "What should I play?" I loved his fiddling and had bought both of his 45-RPM records. One had recordings of "Chere Tout Tout" and "Carroll County Blues." The other had "Poor Hobo" and "Jole Blon." I suggested that he play "Jole Blon." I knew I liked it and figured a panel of judges might like it too. I recall Jewel, in a light blue striped coat, walking around outside, practicing nervously. He was going to be hard to beat. I didn't know anything about J. W. Smith, but I knew Hank and Ray were repeat winners at local contests and Hank was the defending champ.

The finals started and I don't recall what J. W. played.

Ray played "Ragtime Annie" and "Ranger's Waltz" and did a great job. His son, Mike, was his accompanist. The crowd responded to their hometown boy. He was the Old Barn's house band fiddler and they let him know how much they liked him and his playing.

Hank played "Sugar in the Gourd" and announced that he was playing "Over the Waves" for his second tune. That was his show tune, and he gave it a whirl. He started and played it through twice with Mike Beebe's guitar accompaniment. The guitar dropped out and he then played a round unaccompanied. He played two, three, and four string chords, performed fancy bowings, plucked the strings, and played many classically oriented movements. The crowd responded accordingly. They cheered and cheered.

Jewel Lasyone played as he always did. When the finals came and the pressure was on, he always did his best. He never faltered a bit. He played "50 Year Ago Waltz" with all its many chords and played it well. When he finished he turned away from the mike and cross-tuned his fiddle to ready himself to play the "Black Mountain Rag." This was probably the most popular song played in the contests of the early 1970s. Warren Ferrier, Tex Grimsley, Hank Strickland, Ray Beebe, and Doug Lee all frequently played and won with this tune at contests. Jewel had made it a showpiece, his most requested number. It had the rhythm and ring only a cross-tuned fiddle could have. Jewel played it as only he could. The crowd responded accordingly. They cheered and cheered.

Bob Henderson stepped up, and showing his versatility, played an old tune with a Texas style arrangement he had learned from the Solomon family in Texas. His rendition of "Arkansas Traveler" was a tour-de-force. When he went into the 3rd position and played it, I knew he was after the money. The contest was getting tighter and tighter and closer and closer.

I do not recall that any fiddler had played a Cajun number during the contest, but they were fixing to hear one. They announced "Jole Blon" would be his next tune, and he tore into it, putting all the good stuff in it. It had drones, 3rd position slides, and at the end he played the crying version like Harry Choates had done on many of his recordings. The crowd stood and screamed and cheered. It was a rare sight. (It was one of two times that I've seen a contestant get a standing ovation after a performance at a fiddle contest.)

Bob won the State Championship.

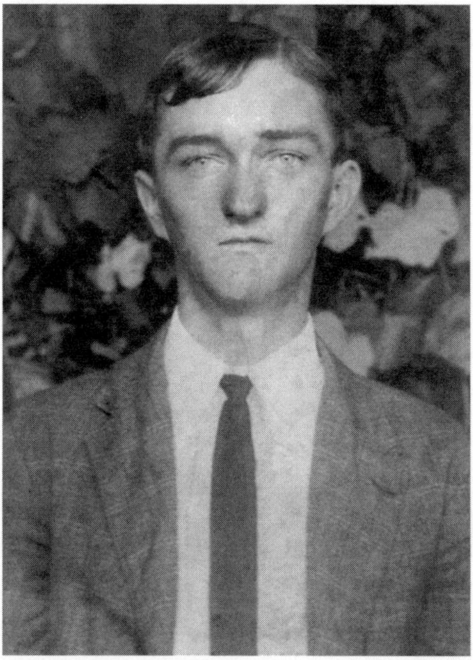

Photo courtesy of Lillian Fallin.

SEAB HOOD

(1899–1938) Hilly

In the 1920s and 1930s, fiddlers and fiddling contests could be found in fairly large numbers. A few of these local fiddlers obtained highly touted reputations as formidable opponents. The Hood family of Hilly, nine miles north of Arcadia, was well known, traveling and playing throughout the region. Stories of their fiddling feats have been noted as far south as Bienville and Caldwell Parish, Ruston on the east, and west to Shreveport and into Texas on occasion. They loved playing the fiddle so much they were known to travel to Arkansas to play and enter contests.

Of all the Joseph S. Hood family fiddlers, four in all, Seab (1899–1938) was regarded as the best. His arrangements and playing of tunes were well known, and other members of the family learned from him. Three of his brothers, Claude B. "Slick" (1893–1943), W. C. "Buck" (1898–1956), and Reid (1892–1963),

Front: Seab Hood, _____ Harrison, Mutt Hood. Others unidentified. 1920s. Photo courtesy of Paul Woodard.

played, as did three cousins: Almer B. "Sip" (1897–1972), Gilbert "Mutt" (1907–1977), and Calvin "Tissue" (1895–1974). Seab learned to play from his father, Joseph S., and other fiddlers he met at country dances and fiddle contests through out north Louisiana.

Besides the normal social functions such as country dances and house parties, Seab was known to serenade throughout the area. Lillian Hood Fallin, Seab's daughter, remembers musicians coming to their home many times for music sessions in the 1930s. Seab was also known to play in Ruston as well as at weekly get-togethers held upstairs at the Arcadia City Hall in the 1930s.

The Hoods, and especially Seab, loved entering fiddle contests. His prowess at contests earned him a reputation among the family as well as local and regional fiddlers. By 1929 Seab made his first trek to Shreveport to enter the Louisiana State Fair Contest and won second place in the younger division, being beaten by noted contest fiddler, H. C. Wilkerson of Shreveport. He won the below-fifty division in 1931, getting the nod over two members of the Old Fiddlers Club, Baron Hollingsworth and Bill Richardson, who placed and won in this contest several times from 1928 to 1938. In 1934 he again placed second in the under-fifty division. It is not known how many times he entered the contest, but after the cancellation of the 1932 and 1933 contests, he requested gate tickets for himself and his brothers for the 1935 event, when over fifty fiddlers entered the competition.

Lester Hood, a nephew, recalls Seab winning a bull (which he named Gandy) as his prize at a contest in Athens. On another occasion he won parts for his truck. Pearl (Templeton) Hood, who played the violin in school, recalls entering a local contest in Lisbon, Louisiana, where Seab Hood won first; Henry Welch, the one-handed fiddler from Dodson, won second; and she won third. Many times merchants in the area would have fiddle contests to draw customers, and Seab would enter and win goods such as a bucket of syrup or a sack of flour.

Lester Hood recalls there was a competition among the family: "One of them won the contest in Shreveport one year, and Uncle Seab thought he was supposed to be the only one to win. He was the top man when fiddling comes. I remember some of them laughing when Sip won the contest one year. Uncle Seab said, 'The only reason he won it was because he played my piece.'"

Lester recalls Seab's love for the fiddle:

> *He went up into Arkansas. He went all over the country. Anywhere he could hear of any fiddling goin' on. He loved it.*
>
> *Uncle Seab lived that. He ran that sawmill. He'd come home. The sawmill was across the road down in front of the house. He'd come home for dinner and when he walked up the steps. They had a dogtrot hall down there. Had a chair sitting there. It was never moved. And the first thing he did was pick up that fiddle and sit down there and play a few tunes . . . while Aunt Gertha was getting dinner ready. Then he'd eat and go back by and he'd sit down there and play the fiddle a little more and go back to work. . . . He lived by that.*
>
> *Uncle Seab was a live wire. He went in a hurry all his life. Workin', playin' the fiddle.*
>
> *Seab was very independent and resourceful. He ran a sawmill, a gristmill, and farmed the family land, sometimes having tenants farm some of his property. He even employed some of the family members in his sawmill operation for a while. . . .*
>
> *Uncle Seab had a sawmill and a gristmill. He ran the sawmill all week and the gristmill on Saturday morning. I'd ask, "Uncle Seab, where'd you get that bull?" "Oh, I won him. His name is Gandy. I won him up at Athens, at the fiddlers' contest." You know they'd have fiddlers' contests, different ones would contribute something . . . for the prize. And this registered bull was the prize up at Athens. . . . And the binders on his log truck. "Uncle Seab where'd you get those binders?" "At a fiddlers' contest." And that happened all the time. . . . They'd have those contests*

and some merchant in the little town, wherever it was, would contribute something for a prize.

Mr. Reynolds, the band director over at Tech [Louisiana Tech at Ruston] would come out and listen to him. He tried to get Uncle Seab to get into other kinds of music.

There were six of those boys. [Burl] was the only one that didn't play anything. That worried Uncle Seab real bad, so he went by Elton Whitaker's [pawnshop] over there. He checked with them to see what they had. He found a pretty banjo over there, and he bought that banjo. He came home that night. As soon as they ate supper he wanted to go and take this banjo to Burl. So they got the family together and they went down there after supper to carry this banjo to Burl, the youngest boy, cause he couldn't do anything but whistle, and he COULD do that. They carried it down there and Uncle Seab presented him with this banjo. . . . It worried him that he couldn't play . . . and [Burl] said "I don't want that thing." Boy that hurt Uncle Seab's feelings. So he started trying to pay him to try it. Just strike a little tune. Just try it. After a little while, he pulled a hundred-dollar bill out of his pocket. He always had money cause he ran the sawmill, and he offered him a hundred dollars just to try it. Uncle Burl said, "Sha, I can't play one of those things." That was the end of that.

I was up there one time when he came back from Monroe with a new fiddle . . . he'd bought it at Hunt-Whitaker's in Monroe . . . That's a pawn shop over there. He give a tremendous amount, I didn't even know people had that kind of money. . . . He gave several hundred dollars for this fiddle, and sat down in that little chair I's telling you about and fiddled on it just a few minutes and went back in there and got a paste board box with these clamps and stuff in it, fiddle fixin' stuff and took that fiddle all to pieces. Boy, my jaw teeth like to fell out. He went out there by the chimney and got some windowpanes that were broken and started to work on that fiddle. He did all he knew to do and then he took it over to this ole German fiddle maker at Gibsland and he did the other part he wanted done to it. Supposedly it was a fine fiddle.

Lester also recalls that Seab even liked working on fiddles. He was known to visit and collaborate with Julius Shradieck, a violin maker who had been trained in New York and lived in Gibsland in the twenties, thirties, and forties.

Seab died of a cerebral hemorrhage in 1938. None of the Hood children pursued the fiddle.

Interviews by Ron Yule: Fred Beavers (1-15-2005), Lillian Fallin (2-05-2005), Lester Hood (1-10-2005 and 1-20-2005), and Milton Hood (1-10-2005).

References

Shreveport Journal. "Old Fiddlers at Fair Draw Large Crowd Thursday." November 7, 1929.

———. "Two Shreveport Fiddlers Win at La. Fair Contest." November 8, 1929.

———. "Tom Sawyer Wins Fiddlers' Contest at Fair Thursday." October 25, 1935.

———. "Old Fiddlers Claim Spotlight at Fair." October 29, 1936.

Shreveport Times. "Old Fiddlers to Play Today." November 7, 1929.

———. "Shreveport Old Fiddlers Winners in Two Classes in Annual Contest at State Fair Grounds on Thursday." November 8, 1929.

———. "Old Fiddlers Contest at Fair Has 35 Entries." October 29, 1930.

———. "Old Fiddlers Hold Contest." October 30, 1930.

———. "Winners in State Fair Contest." October 30, 1931.

———. "S. R. Patterson, H. C. Wilkerson, Best Fiddlers." October 26, 1934.

———. "Fiddlers Have Their Day at State's Fair." October 29, 1937.

Letters from Dr, Joseph E. Richardson to J. S. Hood dated October 25, 1931; October 17, 1935; and July 24, 1936. From the collection of Lillian Hood Fallin.

Letter from Julius Shradieck, Maker of Artist Violins, Gibsland, Louisiana, dated May 29, 1933. From the personal collection of Lillian Hood Fallin.

Photo courtesy of Jewel Johnson, wife of Dobber Johnson.

DOUGLAS "DOBBER" JOHNSON

(1930–1995) Shreveport

Douglas "Dobber" Johnson, who received his nickname early on because he liked to play with "dirt dobbers," started learning to play the fiddle by ear when he was six on a homemade cigar-box fiddle. His early learning efforts came from hearing fiddlers on Shreveport radio stations and Saturday night broadcasts of the Grand Ole Opry. Within a few years his father bought him a fiddle from Sears and Roebuck.

He developed fast, and by the age of ten his father began taking him to KWKH, where he was eventually asked to play with Bob and Joe Shelton and the Sunshine Boys. "Preacher" Duncan, a local Shreveport fiddler, recalls that in the early 1940s KWKH hosted talent shows and the winners were allowed to play for periods of time with the Sunshine Boys. He thinks Dobber was a part of their program that was featured on Saturday mornings. During this period Dobber also played with Hershel Boyett and Harry Todd of Cedar Grove, on

Jimmy Day, Dobber Johnson, unidentified, Tibby Edwards, unidentified, Don Davis, Frank Page, and Horace Logan. Louisiana Hayride, 1954. Photo courtesy of Jewel Johnson, wife of Dobber Johnson.

a KWKH morning show with Hal Burns. They also played at parties, school shows, and other gigs around north Louisiana. He played on radio with other groups and played at clubs around town when not with a regular band. He also toured with Harmie Smith and the Ozark Mountaineers on shows and tours in Texas and Arkansas, as well as Shreveport.

Following his graduation from Fair Park High School in Shreveport, he began to pursue music on a full-time basis. On May 3, 1947, Dobber, Tillman Franks, and Felton Pruitt were hired by radioman Dick Hart to move to Little Rock, Arkansas, and play with Les Gibbs and the Arkansas Cottonpickers. They appeared on radio station KARK and played local shows in central Arkansas. They were promised a minimum of forty dollars per week, a nice paycheck for the young upstart fiddler. The promised salary never materialized, with the band not being paid for weeks at a time. Tillman recalls in *I Was There When It Happened*, "Like Felton said one time, he didn't even have enough money to buy a bus ticket to get out of town." By the end of July, they packed and headed back to Shreveport. On a positive note, Dobber met his future wife Jewel, who was from nearby England, Arkansas.

Like several other Shreveport acts, Hank Locklin and the Rocky Mountain Boys left KWKH to move to Houston. Dobber and Pruitt joined the band, appearing on radio stations KLEE and KTHT. The shows were sponsored by the Laird brothers, Elmer and Elmo, who separately owned car lots and promoted

Dobber Johnson, Hershel Boyett, and Harry Todd. Cedar Grove, 1943. Photo courtesy of Harry Todd.

their businesses over the airwaves. The Rocky Mountain Boys also worked clubs in the Houston area. In early 1948 Dobber returned to central Arkansas, where he worked for the Arkansas Power and Light Company and married Jewel in June.

In the fall of 1949 he returned to Shreveport to work with the Kansas Southern Railroad, a position from which he eventually retired as a locomotive superintendent. He began to attend the Louisiana Hayride and, with his musical connection to musicians like Tillman Franks and Felton Pruitt, he was asked to join the Louisiana Hayride staff band in November of that year. He continued with the KWKH Louisiana Hayride staff band, playing his last Hayride performance on the last show broadcast from the Municipal Auditorium in Shreveport. His career on the Hayride included broadcasts on the CBS Network and the Armed Services Network overseas.

While on the Hayride he played with many stars, including Webb Pierce, Faron Young, Red Sovine, Hank Williams, Jim Reeves, Nat Stuckey, Jim Ed Brown, Johnny Cash, Elvis Presley, Johnny Horton, Jimmy Newman, the Wilburn Brothers, Billy Walker, Bill Carlisle, Mel Tillis, Slim Whitman, and Claude King.

Many times fiddlers are called on to perform comedy, and Dobber was no exception. On one Hayride show while Dobber was playing a fiddle tune, June Carter walked out and began to roll up Dobber's britches, exposing his skinny legs. This drew a giant laugh and uproar from the crowd. They continued this act to get a laugh over the years. Dobber and Buddy Attaway, who was limber and "trick fiddled," became the focus of the comedy act as other performers began rolling up their britches legs.

Dobber also recorded with many of these stars at their first sessions; he is a legendary fiddler among those in the Shreveport area. Dobber's only known early solo effort came in 1958. Andrew Brown recalls one cut on an early Starday EP of various artists which features Dobber and the Louisiana Bluegrass Boys on a fiddle instrumental, "Pickin' Cotton." Following his Louisiana Hayride days, he continued to record when asked, but he never recorded a full album that featured his fine instrumental fiddling. Finally, around 1990 he recorded an album of his own, *Dobber Johnson—Hayride Legend,* that featured numerous old fiddle tunes he loved to play and showcased the beautiful "Five String Waltz," a tune he authored. He used Bobbie Primm and the Desperadoes as his accompanying musicians.

In 1984 and 1985 several events brought attention to Dobber and other Hayride legends. The 1984 Louisiana Hayride reunion show, "Cradle of the Stars," aired on PBS television and told the story of the Hayride, the stars and staff band, and the Hayride's impact on Louisiana country music. Also in 1984, several of the Louisiana Hayride staff band played at the World's Fair in New Orleans. Billed as the Hayride Stringband, the group included Dobber, Bill Kirkpatrick, Mike Kirkpatrick, and former Hank Williams bassist Lum York. In 1985 Dobber received a Certificate of Appreciation from the Smithsonian Festival of American Folklife in Washington, D.C., for his contributions to country music. The Hayride Stringband made the trip.

Dobber was primarily noted as being a country and western fiddler but was equally adept at other styles that influenced the Shreveport audiences in the forties and fifties. Like many fiddlers of the forties, fifties, and sixties, he was comfortable playing western swing and even big band music. Following the changes in music of the mid-1950s, he adapted and backed Elvis Presley as well as other more modern groups. When bluegrass acts would appear on the Hayride without their regular fiddler or would need one, Dobber would fill in and do a fine job. He played with both Buzz Busby and the Bayou Boys and Jimmy Martin and the Sunny Mountain Boys during many of their appearances

Louisiana Hayride. Dobber Johnson, Coach Floyd, Charlie Walker, and Felton Pruitt. Photo courtesy of Jewel Johnson, wife of Dobber Johnson.

on the Louisiana Hayride in the mid-to-late 1950s. He recorded on several of Buzz Busby's 45s on the Jiffy and Carol labels in 1956 which were cut at the KRUS radio studio in Ruston. Personnel included Buzz Busby (mandolin), Charlie Waller (guitar), Dobber Johnson (fiddle), Don Stover (banjo), and Lee Cole (bass fiddle). Tunes included "Just Me and the Jukebox," "Cold and Windy," "Whose Red Wagon," and "That Guy's Gotta Go."

Although he had many opportunities to go on the road with some of the stars, he chose to work for the railroad and play music as a second job. Jewel recalls Hank Williams asked him to go on the road with him several times, and even went so far as to announce he was joining the Drifting Cowboys from the stage. He summed up his feelings in the liner notes to his album: "I guess I'm the luckiest person I know of. I've had the opportunity to use a God given talent to make many friends in a musical career, and to then have a career in railroading. Not many people can do the things they are happy doing, but I've been able to do it twice."

Dobber entered and won many fiddle contests in the Shreveport area and as far south as Fisher. He was the Louisiana State Champion in Division IV at the Marthaville contests in 1988 and 1989.

Dobber also played mandolin and began learning the piano in the later part of his life. He continued to perform musically and played with a local country and western band, Bobby Primm and the Desperadoes.

When someone talks of the Louisiana Hayride, after Hank, Elvis, and Webb's names are mentioned, the name of Dobber Johnson soon comes up. He was a Hayride legend, the fiddler who backed 'em all up.

Dobber passed away on February 13, 1995.

Interviews by Ron Yule: Fred Beavers (2-7-2005), Andrew Brown (9-21-2008), Don Davis (2-4-2005), Tillman Franks (2-9-2004), Jewel Johnson and Jan Lea (8-14-2008), Bill Kirkpatrick (2-4-2005), and Harry Todd (7-13-2005).

References

Busbice, Wayne F., and Patricia Busbice. *Uncovering the Secrets of a Southern Family.* Author-House, Bloomington, Indiana, 2007.

Franks, Tillman. *I Was There When It Happened.* Sweet Dreams Publishing, Many, Louisiana, 2000.

Johnson, Dobber. Liner notes. *Dobber Johnson—Hayride Legend.* LP, ca. 1990.

Laird, Tracey, E. W. *Louisiana Hayride: Radio and Roots Music Along the Red River.* Oxford University Press, New York, 2005.

Prime, John Andrew. "Hayride Alumni Gather for Taping." *Shreveport Times*, April 7, 1984.

———. "Hayride Veterans Lead Hometown Delegation to D.C." *The Shreveport Times*, June 23, 1985.

Strickland, Rhonda. "Buzz Busby: A Lonesome Road." *Bluegrass Unlimited*, November 1986, Manassas, Virginia, 1996.

Photo by author.

AL JORDAN

(1932–) Calhoun

Al Jordan (b. 1932) is one of the premier bluegrass and country fiddlers in north Louisiana and has played with many groups on the festival circuit and at shows throughout Louisiana, Texas, Oklahoma, Arkansas, and Mississippi. He is exceptional at backup and harmony fiddling and sings all parts in duets and trios, making him a very valuable asset to any country or bluegrass band.

From the time Al was a child, he heard the strains of fiddle and guitar from his father, Albert Jordan, and an uncle, Charlie Walker. They played the fiddle and guitar at the country dances, socials, and get-togethers around Calhoun. Al's older brother, Addis "Pee Wee" Jordan, learned fiddle at an early age and Al remembers him playing around the house. Al finally got a fiddle and began learning at the age of ten. His sister, Pauline, played guitar, so they began playing around the house.

Pee Wee, five years older than Al, soon left home and began playing professionally. Initially he joined Jelly Elliott in El Dorado, Arkansas, then left to play with Buster Dobson, traveling all over the country. He eventually landed a job with Bob and Joe Shelton and the Sunshine Boys, playing on KWKH. Although he had become very competent in the swing style of fiddling, he tired of the road, and by 1949 he had returned home and quit playing.

When Pee Wee left home, Al turned to the radio to learn many of the tunes and techniques he had begun to play on fiddle. One of Al's primary sources for fiddling on the radio was the Grand Ole Opry, where he listened to his favorite fiddlers; Benny Martin, Chubby Wise, Georgia Slim, and Howdy Forrester. He heard them weekly and picked up on the styles of these legendary fiddlers.

Al also began to pick up on the new style of hillbilly music, bluegrass—Bill Monroe and the Bluegrass Boys as well as Flatt and Scruggs and the Foggy Mountain Boys. He had been playing with a friend, Buzz Busby from nearby Eros, as early as 1948, and they were constantly walking to each other's homes to play and pick. Buzz not only played mandolin but also sang in the bluegrass style, which offered Al a chance to learn the backup style of a bluegrass fiddler as well as the harmony and high lonesome singing of bluegrass bands on the radio. In the very early 1950s Buzz moved to the Washington, D.C., area to pursue his famous career, but Al would play with him when he returned to north Louisiana.

After Buzz left, Al began seeking other venues to play. One of the first stars Al performed with was Jerry Lee Lewis when he first started in the eastern Mississippi River Delta areas of Louisiana. Al notes that he met him in a church at Sterlington, and Jerry invited him to join him when he played at the Ouachita Valley Jamboree in Monroe. He not only played with Lewis but also joined many of the other local pickers and his family's own country group to play spots on the Saturday night show.

In 1955 Buzz Busby and the Bayou Boys, on their second audition, were invited to join the Louisiana Hayride as members. When Buzz auditioned for the Louisiana Hayride, he called Al and paid him to come to the Hayride to perform with him. This began a routine of playing on the Hayride with the Bayou Boys while Buzz was a member.

As time permitted, Al played at shows and with various country and bluegrass groups in the late 1950s and early 1960s. In the mid-sixties Dennis Lucas and Travis Stewart formed the Southern Bluegrass Boys, and Al played with them at school shows and churches in north and central Louisiana. Al has

Louisiana Grass, late 1980s. Front: Terry Barbin, Marty Kutz, and Joe Spence. Rear: J. C. Henderson, Don Wiley, and Al Jordan. Photo courtesy of Joe Spence.

played with a Who's Who of Louisiana bluegrass pioneers over the years: the Southern Bluegrass Boys (Travis Stewart, Dennis Lucas, Gene Alford, Floyd Jasper, J. D. Yarbrough, and Joe Spence); the Dicksons (Larry and Jackie Dickson, Clyde Baum, and Dick Alexander); the Bluegrass Riders (Pappy Booth, Calvin Free, George Mercer, Carl Franklin, and Ralph Tucker); Bill Grant and Delia Bell; the Southland Bluegrass; Don Wiley and The Louisiana Grass; and even some Lewis Family shows.

In the 1980s, after intermittently attending bluegrass festivals and shows during the late 1970s, Al joined Don Wiley and the Louisiana Grass. Don, a Jonesville native, had appeared on radio and television regionally, playing country and western. He changed his style to bluegrass and with Al (fiddle), Joe Spence (mandolin), Terry Barbin (banjo), and "Catfish" Henderson (guitar) they played throughout Texas, Oklahoma, Louisiana, Arkansas, Missouri, Alabama, and Mississippi. For the next ten-plus years they played at festivals, churches, school shows, and radio and television.

It could almost be said that Al was the staff fiddler at nearly every bluegrass festival he attended from the early seventies until the early nineties. He played with everybody, and could adapt to their arrangements and even sing harmony if they needed. In the early 1990s, at the Mt. Holly Bluegrass Festival near Magnolia, Arkansas, Al showed up, paid at the gate, and walked in just to see what was going on and to jam and pick under the trees. Bill Grant, who always used a pickup band, saw him standing around talking and asked him to sit in with them on their show, and he did, like he had played with them every night. Before long he was playing with two groups in a row, with occasional relief when the Revelators or Twice as Nice took the stage. Greg Edwards and Ron Yule did a twin-fiddle arrangement of "What a Friend We Have in Jesus" during the Revelators show, and Al came back to the stage and played a beautiful third part. Al does it all with ease.

Al is as comfortable playing forties and fifties country as bluegrass. Willard Cox, who remembers him from the Louisiana Hayride and local shows, once commented, "Al is as good a country fiddler as you'd ever want to hear." David Booth recalls playing fiddle tunes with Al when he was beginning to learn the guitar, and playing a few bluegrass standards while he and his father "Pappy" were at Al's house. Fred Beavers recalls that he plays swing, rock and roll, and country equally well.

Two of Al's favorite show tunes are "Going Home" and "Tragic Romance." You can always count on him to belt these out when he gets on a festival stage. He sings and plays them with his whole being, from the bottom of his toes. He is one of the pioneer bluegrass and country fiddlers of the last half of the twentieth century in Louisiana.

Interviews by Ron Yule: Fred Beavers (2-3-2005), David Booth (6-6-2006), Al Jordan (8-15-2004), and Joe Spence (5-3-2007).

Photo courtesy of Kay family.

JACK KAY

(1929–1971) Leesville

The area west of Leesville, in Vernon Parish, has produced a wealth of fiddle talent. From this geographical location came the Holts, the Bracks, and the Kays, all well known in the annals of fiddling in western Louisiana. Each family has its place in the history of early country music in dance halls, churches, and on radio and stage.

The most influential of these fiddlers was Jack Kay, a towering figure of a fiddler who was not satisfied playing locally, but set his sights on playing with the many country stars of the time. His travels would lead him to Nashville and the Grand Ole Opry stage by his early twenties.

He came from a long line of fiddlers stretching back into the mid-1800s. His grandfathers, George Washington Kay and David Billingsley, were country fiddlers who played at the socials and country dances of their era. Jack's father, Moss, followed in their footsteps, playing at dances and winning fiddle contests in the Vernon Parish area. They were all breakdown fiddlers and played tunes like "Arkansas Traveler," "8th of January," and numerous old-time reels and tunes common to the area. Lynn, Jack's brother, tells the story: "Daddy drove a school bus and could not afford the gas to drive the ten miles back home, so he'd stay in town all day. He would take his fiddle and play during the day. Sometimes his friends came by and they played together. They'd fill the bus." Besides Jack, brother A. B. and sister Geraldine played the guitar.

Jack took up the fiddle as a kid, learned from Moss, and began to play country dances around Leesville, Evans, and Cottonwood. He played the tunes of his forefathers but, like many fiddlers of the era, was beginning to hear country music on radio and phonograph. He especially liked the western swing sounds of the Texas bands, Bob Wills and the Texas Playboys and Cliff Bruner and the Texas Wanderers. By his early teens he was hanging out at the honky tonks and joints around Leesville.

In 1944, at the age of 15, he joined the merchant marines, sailing and working out of Port Arthur along the Gulf Coast and as far as the Bahamas and South America.

Following World War II he gravitated to Beaumont, to seek his fortune in the world of country music and with the legendary bands of western swing that were playing in southeast Texas clubs. He played with Lefty Frizzell, Cliff Bruner and the Texas Wanderers, Ray Keemo and the Radio Ranch Boys, the Beaumont Squarenaders, and finally Moon Mullican. Although he held various jobs during the day, his main income was from playing in clubs and on KFDM in Beaumont. In the late 1940s these bands were playing venues from Lake Charles to Houston and beyond. Jack's touch on the fiddle was becoming known to everyone in the Golden Triangle and as far north as Shreveport.

In April 1948 the Louisiana Hayride opened in Shreveport and took the country music world by storm, broadcasting nationwide and attracting many good country musicians from Louisiana and Texas. Jack played with the Bailes Brothers and other bands on the Hayride and at local shows during the week. Webb Pierce had met Jack in the clubs around Leesville when he was in the army at Camp Polk during the war. He sent for Jack, finally offering him a permanent job with his show, and Jack made the weekend trek from Beaumont to Shreveport. Lynn, Jack's brother, recalls he was paying Jack $150 per week plus road expenses. Teddy and Doyle Wilburn, Pierce, and Jack all moved to Nashville together. While with Pierce he twin fiddled with one of the most innovative and improvisational country fiddlers of the time, Dale

Jack Kay, Charlie Dauzat, and Hermon Lasyone. Jack Kay Show, KALB-TV, Alexandria, 1963. Photo courtesy of Hermon Lasyone Collection.

Potter. Mastern Brack recalls playing with Jack in clubs around Leesville in the 1960s. Jack reminisced about his days in Nashville and told him that, after a show, he and Dale Potter would stay up all night practicing and arranging some of their classic breaks for Webb Pierce shows. Their fiddling can be seen and heard on the Classic Country videos from the 1950s television shows, still available through some country music outlets. Jack's fiddlin' can be heard on most Webb Pierce LPs of the 1950s. While with Pierce he was in some movies, but no one can recall the titles. Much in demand, he played brief stints with Ernest Tubb, Hank Snow, Lefty Frizzell, Jimmy C. Newman, Porter Wagoner, and many other Opry stars.

His recordings with Pierce began in March 1953 and spanned into the 1960s, according to Eddie Friday. He recalls that even after Jack had left the road, Webb would send him plane tickets to fly to recording sessions and shows. The discography accompanying the Bear Family Records box set, *Webb Pierce, Wondering Boy, 1951–1958*, indicates Jack recorded at least forty sides with Pierce during that period. By 1959 Pierce's recordings began to limit the

Webb Pierce and his Wonderers, 1950s. Standing: Doyle Wilburn, Webb Pierce, and Jack Kay. Kneeling: both unidentified. Photo courtesy of Kay family.

use of the fiddle, and Jack appeared on fewer sessions. Studio musicians began to replace recording artists' road bands at sessions. Tommy Vaden, another Nashville fiddler, notes that by that time recording sessions were being held without the presence of the singing artist.

By the late fifties demand for fiddle in a country band was dwindling, and Jack was tiring of the Nashville scene. He moved back to the Leesville area and worked club dates in Leesville and Alexandria. He played at the Lion's Club, the Nut Club, the Wig-Wam, the Welcome Club, the Pecan Club, the Hayride Club, and dances at the K.C. Hall in Zwolle, as well as other clubs around Leesville, with Billy Lewis, Kenneth Midkiff, Junior Booth, James Jeter, Jim Brack, Jimmy Jeans, Frank Leone, and Leo Mitchell. He twin fiddled with fiddlers Mastern Brack, Slouch Holt, Eddie Friday, and Kenneth Cryer. Webb invited Jack, along with Lewis, Midkiff, Mastern Brack, and Booth, to play on some of the Opry Tour of Stars shows, at the Municipal Auditorium in Shreveport and other cities.

Country music abounded on local radio and television in the early 1960s, and Jack was a major force in the central Louisiana music scene. Besides playing on Leesville's KLLA, he traveled to Alexandria and played on KALB. He even fronted his own television show for a while on Sunday morning on KALB, using the talents of local musicians like Charlie Dauzat, the Moses Sisters, and Hermon Lasyone. The Clark Brothers Quartet was featured on the gospel portion of each Sunday morning show. In the mid-1960s he moved to Alexandria, worked for the Rapides Parish Sheriff Department, and played music at the Cotton Gin, Highway 112 Club, Dubé Hall, and other central Louisiana clubs.

Like many musicians of the time, he played for politicians Earl and Gillis Long, fronting their stumping on the campaign trail. He worked these and other central and west central Louisiana gigs, from Hessmer to Leesville, with other noted musicians Eddie Friday, Ambrose Williamson, Don Wiley, Troy DeRamus, Jay Chevalier, Charlie Pollard, Hank Fisher, Eddie Raxsdale, and Hermon Lasyone. He also occasionally made trips to south Louisiana and played with Jimmy C. Newman.

Jack was highly regarded among fiddlers and musicians for his natural talent and ability with the fiddle and was especially well known for his classic breaks on western swing numbers. Many local musicians talk of his breaks, which would be "way out there." Kenneth Midkiff and others have noted that not only did they not know what he was going to play on a break, but that neither did Jack, saying, "He would just take off." He was also noted for his great double-stop harmony playing, a skill he probably learned and honed with the legendary Dale Potter while they were with Webb Pierce.

Several homemade recordings exist of his playing with the Moses Sisters and other local Alexandria musicians.

Jack passed away in 1971.

Interviews: Mastern Brack (11-25-2003), Bill Clark (9-10-2004), Eddie Friday (3-4-2005), James Jeter (10-22-2002), Kenneth Midkiff (7-9-2004), Lynn Kay (11-2-2002, 6-21-2003, 7-9-2004, and 3-2-2005), and Hermon Lasyone (06-24-2003).

Reference

Kitsinger, Otto, and Richard Weize. Liner notes and discography. *Webb Pierce, The Wondering Boy (1951–1958)*. Bear Family Records, 1990.

Photo courtesy of Doug Kershaw.

DOUG KERSHAW

(1936–) Lake Arthur

Doug Kershaw is one of the most recognized Cajun entertainers in the world. He was born on January 24, 1936, in Tiel Ridge, on a houseboat. His mother, Rita, played guitar and fiddle; his father, Jack, played accordion; and his older brothers played various instruments, including fiddle, guitar, and accordion. He started playing the fiddle when he was five years old, when his uncle Abel, an accordion player on his father's side, made him a cigar box fiddle. Although he learned mainly from local fiddlers and fiddlers who passed by the house, he came from a long line of excellent musicians on his mother's side, the Broussards. His great-great grandfather Nicholas had been a popular country dance fiddler, playing with Savan, another talented cousin, around Creole. His grandfather Albert played fiddle at country dances all over the country with his brother, Charles, and Theo Young. All were well-known fiddlers in southwest Louisiana. One cousin, Carrol Broussard, played and recorded with

Harry Choates in the late 1940s. Although his main instrument is fiddle, like his ancestors Doug is a multi-instrumentalist and plays nearly thirty different instruments.

His father died when he was seven and the family moved to nearby Lake Arthur. Times were hard for the family, and Doug began working at a young age as a shoeshine boy in Lake Arthur. This launched his music career when he used the fiddle to lure and entertain potential customers. If they stopped to listen to the fiddle, he wanted to shine their shoes.

By the age of nine he made his debut onstage, at the famous Bucket of Blood in Lake Arthur. Soon he joined his mother and a local musician named Zenis LaCombe as the White Shirt Band at dancehalls around Lake Arthur.

At the age of eleven, Doug joined his brothers, Nelson "Pee Wee" and Rusty, in the Continental Playboys, a band Pee Wee had formed. Pee Wee was also multi-talented and played fiddle, guitar, and accordion. In the Continental Playboys Pee Wee played accordion, Rusty played guitar, and Doug the fiddle.

They started playing at bars around Lake Arthur and graduated to playing in the Lake Charles/Sulphur area. Crawford Vincent played drums with them at the Silver Star and notes they mainly played country music. He said Doug was a showman even back then, and danced around the bandstand. He was beginning to earn his title, "The Ragin' Cajun."

Rusty and Doug eventually left the Continental Playboys and struck out on their own. As before, they followed no musical labels. They played country and rock and roll as well as Cajun music. Doug notes his versatility, in an article in *Fiddler Magazine* by Michael Simmons, when he states that he still loves to play "Stardust," a big band hit. Before long Rusty and Doug landed a spot on KPLC television in Lake Charles. In 1953 they met record producer J. D. Miller from Crowley, and after recording "So Lovely Baby," a song Doug had written, they traveled to Nashville and re-recorded it for Wesley Rose's Hickory Records. It reached #14 on the country charts in 1955.

That same year, Rusty and Doug joined the Louisiana Hayride, the popular Shreveport country music radio show broadcast on KWKH. They played around some of the great stars like Elvis Presley, Jim Reeves, and Slim Whitman. They eventually landed in Wheeling, West Virginia, at WWVA and the Wheeling Jamboree. They continued touring, writing, and recording and finally got a hit with Felice and Boudleaux Bryant's "Hey, Sheriff." Later that year they joined the Grand Ole Opry.

In 1959, Rusty and Doug were both drafted and served two years in the military.

Doug Kershaw, Pee Wee, and Rusty Kershaw. 1950s. Photo courtesy of Ervin Lejeune.

In 1961, a few weeks after being discharged, Doug began to write songs of his bayou roots and upbringing in Louisiana. This move would bring him more notoriety than any songwriting venture he had done before. Many of the songs he wrote included memories of Tiel Ridge and Lake Arthur and his family. "Louisiana Man" made it to #10 on the country charts. Others over the years included "Dans La Louisianne," "Cajun Joe," "Spanish Moss," "My Uncle Abel," and "Faisdodo." Soon they recorded more Cajun tunes like "Diggy Liggy Lo" and "Jole Blon." In 1964, Doug and Rusty split up. After struggling in the 1960s with MGM and Mercury Records, Doug finally got a break when he recorded *The Cajun Way* for Warner Brothers. It got him an appearance on the *Johnny Cash Show*, a national television show. Bob Dylan and Joni Mitchell, who were very hot acts at the time, also appeared with him. Following this success he then began playing all over the world, attaining national and international success.

His fifty-year career has included playing on the Louisiana Hayride, the Wheeling Jamboree, and the Grand Ole Opry. He has had all the country success he could ask for. He has expanded his career further by sharing the stage

Rusty and Doug Kershaw, 1956. Photo courtesy of Andrew Brown.

with rock, folk, and country superstars all over the world, and continues to draw big crowds while performing in Branson and other venues.

He is known as the "Ragin' Cajun" and his show personifies that. No matter what his antics on the stage, he is still a good fiddler. His recording of "Jole Blon" on *The Cajun Way* is an excellent example of his Harry Choates–oriented fiddle style. His recordings of "Louisiana Man" and "Diggy Liggy Lo" became popular because of his tasteful Cajun fiddling. He also plays traditional fiddle music as can be noted on his recordings of fiddle tunes like Bill Monroe's "Uncle Pen," "Orange Blossom Special," and "Eighth of January." Over the years he has come back to the bayou land to resurrect these sounds and play and record with other local Cajun musicians like Leo Abshire, Michael Doucet, and Hadley Castille. In 2001 he recorded several French tunes on *Sweet Home Louisiana*, a CD he produced that included "Johnny Can't Dance," D. L. Menard's "Back Door," and a re-recording of "Jole Blon."

Doug and Pam Kershaw were married on June 21, 1975, at the Astrodome in Houston, and Doug gave a concert after the game that night. Doug has five sons (Douglas, Victor, Zachary, Tyler and Eli (Elijah), all of whom are musically talented like their father. Son Tyler often plays the drums in Doug's band.

His influence is far-reaching. People love Doug as an entertainer, but many fiddlers love him for his rhythmic, enthusiastic playing. His influence has been one of spreading Cajun fiddling to the masses and helping many young fiddlers find excitement and fun in Cajun music. Although his "Ragin' Cajun" show is rhythmically intense, Doug's intricate noting and melodious sound are ever-present in his fiddling. When he plays the bayou songs of Louisiana, you can hear overtones of Iry Lejeune, Harry Choates, or Will Kegley playing in his soul and feel his heartfelt love of the music of his ancestors, the Kershaws and the Broussards.

Interviews by Ron Yule: Leo Abshire (undated conversation), Gordon Broussard (4-12-2005), and Hadley Castille (undated conversation).

References

Humphrey, Mark. "Doug Kershaw." *Frets Magazine* vol. 3, no. 10 (October 1981).

Kershaw, Doug. *Cajun Sweet Home Louisiana*. International Music Series, CD, 2001.

———. *Louisiana Man: The Doug Kershaw Songbook.* Collier Books, New York, 1971.

———. E-mails dated 7-1-2007 and 9-22-2007.

Simmons, Michael. "Doug Kershaw: The Real Deal in Cajun Fiddle." *Fiddler Magazine* 10, no. 10 (Spring 2003).

Photo courtesy of Susan Roach.

BILL KIRKPATRICK

(1928–) Shreveport

Following in the tradition of other north Louisiana fiddlers, Bill Kirkpatrick has made many contributions to fiddling in Louisiana country music annals. For more than sixty years he has played at everything from house parties to the stages of the Louisiana Hayride and modern fiddle contests. Born on May 8, 1928, near Homer, Bill began to like the sound of the fiddle early on. His first instrument was a cornstalk fiddle made by an uncle. Bill laughingly describes its tone: "It made a bunch of noise." His brother Pete tried to play a real fiddle but did not succeed, so he gave Bill his fiddle around the age of six.

He was soon hanging around the Beavers clan (Jeff, Coy, Lewis and John) who lived between Homer and Haynesville, attending their many sessions on the front porch, in the yard, and in the living room. Other influences included the W. E. Caston siblings who lived and played around Haynesville: John Caston, Van Caston, and Fleecy Caston Philyaw. By his teens he was playing with the Thomas Philyaw Band and Dr. J. E. Richardson of Shreveport and attending fiddle contests at fairs and festivals in northwest Louisiana. During this formative period, Bill listened to the fiddlers he heard on the radio, trying to pick up on their sound.

Around the age of fifteen, he played with an unnamed Texas singer around Haynesville at dances. He also played with the school band, on both guitar and bass fiddle.

In 1945 his family moved to Bossier City, and that gave him access to new musical adventures. Within a year he began going to local radio stations KRMD and KTBS, meeting musicians, and playing with bands on early-morning radio shows. One band he worked with was Scotty and the Rhythm Wranglers, a group he would work with for the next couple years. After his move to Shreveport, he joined Fleecy Philyaw, Dr. Richardson, Bill Harper, and all the local fiddlers for jam sessions at the museum and fairgrounds. He also played at some minstrel shows with Paul and Hoke Rice.

Bill played the warm-up show on the opening night of the Louisiana Hayride and recalls it vividly. He states, "I played 'Ragtime Annie' on the show for Scotty and the Rhythm Wranglers and Tex Grimsley played his first song next." He added, "The Hayride started out as a local show and changed as they got other acts." He notes that Scotty and the Rhythm Wranglers never made it onto the main Hayride show because of the musicians union's involvement in the stage show production. After getting his union card, he joined Cousin Emmy on the Hayride stage playing bass fiddle, guitar, and fiddle.

After being drafted he began playing in the U.S. Army Band, with several different groups. He recalls playing in the hillbilly band with a Lake Charles musician, Pee Wee Calhoun, who had previously played with Leon McAuliffe. He recalls one show at the University of Arkansas in Fayetteville, while stationed at Fort Chafee: "They had this 105-piece band playing all that sweet music. Well, those people in Arkansas didn't know what that was. So, we got up and went out there and I played the fiddle and sang a couple songs and played that 'Orange Blossom Special' and they nearly tore the stadium down." They then began to play all the shows plus playing the clubs on the base.

Following his stint in the army, he played bass fiddle with the Milt Chapman Orchestra for sixteen years, playing fiddle mainly around the house. They played at all the big clubs around Shreveport/Bossier City: the Crystal Ballroom at the Washington Youree Hotel, American Legion, and Club Coronado in Bossier. This was an eleven-piece ensemble and played big band music, much like the Glenn Miller Orchestra. He also recalls playing with

Mike and Bill Kirkpatrick at the 2004 Louisiana State Fiddle Championship, Natchitoches. Photo courtesy of Peter Jones and the North Louisiana Regional Folklife Program.

Vaughn Monroe and Hoagy Carmichael when they performed in Shreveport, as well as in several Broadway-style productions: *South Pacific* and *Peter Pan* starring Mary Martin. He recalls playing at these dances with Chapman. "We'd go off and play for those big dances. We'd get a little money . . . eleven dollars, that was a lot of money back then. . . . I remember that's what we got on the Hayride, eleven dollars a night."

Bill quit playing in the orchestra and returned to playing fiddle music, jamming with Lonnie Hall and eventually playing with Tex and Mary Grimsley. This led to entering fiddle contests around east Texas and Shreveport. He won many times and was a perennial winner at the Zwolle Hot Tamale Contest from 1977 to 1985. He has placed numerous times in the state fiddle contests at Marthaville and Natchitoches, was the Louisiana State Champion fiddler in Division IV in 1984, and runner-up for the Grand Championship in 2006.

Bill, Dobber Johnson, Lum York, and Mike Kirkpatrick, appeared as the Louisiana Hayride String Band at the 1984 World's Fair in New Orleans. In 1985, he and Dobber Johnson were invited to play at the Festival of American Folklife on the National Mall in Washington.

The highlight of any Bill Kirkpatrick performance, whether on stage or at a contest, is "The Last Fiddler's Waltz," a beautiful waltz he penned early in his career and copyrighted in 1985. Younger fiddlers like David DeRamus have learned and played this song at contests.

His superb fiddling and rhythm guitar style have influenced many of the younger fiddlers around Shreveport, including DeRamus, Karen Lawrence, Lauren Morgan, and Randall Stevens. He continues to influence any fiddler who hears his blues, swing, hoedown, and waltz tunes. His son Mike, who now resides in Shreveport, is following in his father's footsteps and playing the guitar and fiddle.

Interview by Ron Yule: Bill Kirkpatrick (3-5-2007).

Photo by author.

KENNIE LAMB

(1930–2007) Baton Rouge

Kennie Lamb is one of the memorable fiddle figures from the Baton Rouge area. He moved to the area in 1967 and eventually started a fiddle shop, formed a bluegrass group, and organized a bluegrass club that booked many national acts, most with a focus on good fiddling.

Kennie was born in Maryland in 1930, and began listening to country music as a child in Severna Park, Maryland. By the late 1940s, he developed an interest in playing country fiddle from hearing local fiddler Pee Wee Herron on WDBJ, Roanoke, Virginia. Pee Wee had played with the Florence Brothers when Lester Flatt was a member of the band.

He began playing locally with many groups in the "beer joints," as he puts it, eventually joining the military. While stationed in Germany (1952–53), Kennie played with the USAREUR Grand Ole Opry shows, appearing all over the country with the U.S. Army Band.

When he returned to the States, he continued playing off and on with local bands while working at jobs around Baltimore. In the late 1950s he moved to Virginia, where he lived for six years until his move to Gonzalez, Louisiana, as the manager of a meatpacking establishment. Eventually he moved to Baton Rouge and started his own business as a meat broker.

Due to work commitments, Kennie had quit playing for a while; when he moved to Gonzalez he met Lum York, a bassist who had played with country acts including Hank Williams and Lefty Frizzell, and Lou Millet, who had been the front man for Lefty Frizzell around 1952. He jammed on many occasions with them and other local musicians at the Old South Jamboree at Walker. Most of his playing time was spent informally jamming with the country and bluegrass musicians in the area.

By 1977, Kennie formed his first bluegrass group, Virginia Pride. Members included Jimmy Stewart (banjo and fiddle), Chuck Nation (fiddle), Glen Carter (guitar), and Steve Stewart (bass). One unique feature of this group was that three members could play the fiddle, and on many occasions the group would play instrumentals using three fiddles. Although the group was short-lived, Kennie recalls they played shows at Luke Thompson's Folsom Bluegrass Festival and the Watermelon Festival, as well as other festivals in the area. Kennie notes that the pay for playing bluegrass in the area was so low they decided to disband.

Around 1985 Kennie, along with fellow bluegrass musicians Jim Nation, Glen Carter, Adolphus Warren, and Johnny Rushing, formed the Louisiana Bluegrass Association. The stage shows featured the Cox Family, Warrior River Boys, Rushing Brothers, Colyell Mountain Boys, Glen Carter, plus many other entertainers and local bluegrass groups. Kennie's love for fiddling brought a focus on the fiddle with the booking of fiddlers like former Bluegrass Boys Chubby Wise and Jack Youngblood; world champion fiddler Frazier Moss; and old-time fiddler and entertainer John Hartford. The club was very successful, but due to the decreasing popularity of bluegrass in the area the show and the club were disbanded around 1990.

Although Kennie was an excellent fiddler and influenced several local fiddlers with his old-time country style, his main impact on the music came from his skills as a repairman and trader of music instruments, especially fiddles. Almost every Florida Parishes fiddler knew Kennie Lamb, having traded or purchased a fiddle, had a fiddle repaired, or a violin appraised by him. His contacts were not only local, but included violin centers throughout the United States.

Drawing of Kennie Lamb with the John Hartford violin by Barnes and Lamb. Photo courtesy of Jim Nation (artist unknown).

Kennie recalls his first efforts at violin making:

> *I could always carve. When I was a kid I'd carve guns out of wood. When I started playing my fiddle I became more interested in it and wanted to know how they were made. So, around 1947, I sat down and through trial and error tried to copy an old fiddle . . . I was about 20 years old. My wife and I lived in a little apartment, and I used to cook my wood on her stove [laugh].*

By the early 1950s, Kennie had learned enough to perform repair work for Walker's Music Store in Baltimore. Continuing to learn the skills necessary to work on these delicate instruments, he informally trained with Baltimore-based violinmaker Nicholas Vasich. Also, during his military service in Germany, he had traveled throughout the country with the USAREUR Grand Ole Opry Shows, which had given him the opportunity to visit German violinmakers' shops in Mittenwald as well as the major violin centers of Europe. He said, "I picked up a lot of pointers in Germany."

Eventually he opened his own repair shop south of Baltimore, where he also made violins. He began trading fiddles at this time—or as he puts it, "I was always looking for that one famous fiddle." Through his many travels he continued to trade on a small scale, but around 1977 he increased his operation and began trading and making on a larger, more professional scale. Kennie does not know how many fiddles he has made but knows it is in excess of 250.

During his career in Louisiana, Kennie has kept his acquaintances and business ties to East Coast violin shops. Through these associations Kennie became acquainted with East Coast luthier Mac Barnes, and around 1983 they began producing violins and other stringed instruments together. The "Duiffoprugcar-Vuillaume" style fiddles produced by French makers of the 1800s had become popular among fiddlers in the 1970s due to the fact Vassar Clements began playing one. They began to focus their attention on producing reproductions of these ornate violins. These violins were very recognizable with their carved scrolls, inlaid writing in Latin around the sides, and village and castle marquetry scenes inlaid on the back. Kennie and Mac began making these fiddles and putting them in the hands of some of the country's finest fiddlers. Kennie and Mac even appeared on the Grand Ole Opry in Nashville to present a violin they made for Roy Acuff for his fiftieth anniversary on the Opry. Others stars who received these prized instruments included Ramona Jones, Bobby Hicks, Chubby Wise, Frazier Moss, John Hartford, and Tommy Williams. They were unique in that they usually featured a scroll carved with the head of the performer and inlays and paintings featuring the many highlights of the artist's career on the garlands and back table.

Due to complications resulting from diabetes, Kennie lost most of his vision and ceased repairing and making instruments in 2002. He continued to trade on a small scale until he passed away in 2007.

Interviews by Ron Yule: Kennie Lamb (9-19-2006 and 10-12-2006).

References

Forrester, H. H. *Bluegrass Music and Feliciana Grass.* Unpublished work in the possession of Jim Rushing, 1988.

Gruhn, George. "An Interview with Kennie Lamb." *Bluegrass Unlimited* (April 1989).

Nation, Jim. *A History of the Louisiana Bluegrass Association.* Unpublished manuscript in possession of the author, 1987.

The Advocate. "Fiddles." Baton Rouge, Louisiana, March 10, 1989.

Wenberg, Thomas. *The Violin Makers of the United States.* Mt. Hood Publishing, Mt. Hood, Oregon, 1986.

Photo courtesy of Creola Linzay.

JEWEL LASYONE

(1933–1984) Verda

Jewel Lasyone came from a family rich in fiddle tradition. His uncle, Alfred, and father, Orelius "Reel," began playing at a young age, learning from their father, "Uncle Buck," who was a noted fiddler in the Verda and Colfax areas of Grant Parish. Reel played breakdowns and waltzes at country dances and house parties in the area. Alfred's son, Hermon, also fiddled and played right alongside Jewel at country dances, square dances, clubs, and on radio and television for years.

Jewel, born in 1933, started playing mandolin at age four, learning from his father. Reel would later recall that Jewel would lay flat in the bed and play mandolin when he was a kid. It would be four more years before he would take up the instrument that commanded his musical attention the rest of his life. Jewel's brother, J. B., learned guitar and accompanied the Lasyone fiddlers (Alfred, Reel, Jewel, and Hermon) at country dances.

Jewel Lasyone, Hank Strickland, Hermon Lasyone, Kenny Guillot, and Mel Hinkley. Old Barn Dance, Alexandria, 1949. Photo courtesy of Hermon Lasyone Collection.

Jewel began performing at C.C.C. camps (he would play for the workers and they would pass a cup around to get him a little money) and for soldiers who came around the area before and during World War II.

In 1949 Jewel played at the Old Barn Dance in Alexandria, when his cousin Hermon had to sneak him in the back door. He joined some of central Louisiana's best fiddlers: Hank Strickland, Ray Beebe, Eddie Friday, Winston Salard, and Charlie Walding. Playing mainly square dance music, he played on KSYL, broadcasting from the barn. He also played on KALB with various bands.

In 1953 he joined the navy and served overseas in Japan. His fiddle was never far away. He had brought the old Sears and Roebuck fiddle he had owned since he was eight, and played it when he could.

After the service he returned to playing on KALB, this time with the J. W. Thompson Band. The band included Eddie Friday and Hermon Lasyone.

He married in 1959 and moved to Shreveport in 1962. After laying the fiddle aside for a few years, he and his wife, Creola, attended the Keithville Jamboree in 1965, a weekly country and western show. Being around the music again

Jewel Lasyone with David Booth and Ernie Maples. Old Barn, 1978. Photo courtesy of Creola Linzay.

rekindled his interest in the fiddle, so the next week he brought his fiddle and began to play with various groups on the stage show.

He began to attend local shows and a few jam sessions, playing mainly country and western. Until the late 1960s, Jewel had played the hoedown and waltz numbers of his country dance heritage and the popular country songs he heard on the radio. He soon discovered the sounds of bluegrass fiddle and headed in a new direction with his music.

His first encounter with bluegrass came in 1969 while attending the North Caddo Hayride in Vivian. Creola says they went in and sat in the audience and before long Jewel disappeared behind the stage. She waited, but he did not come back. Soon he walked out on the stage with his first bluegrass band: Harrell Bell (guitar), J. W. Alexander (mandolin), Carl Franklin (bass), and Andy Lord (banjo). Jewel's son, Tim, soon learned the bass and replaced Carl Franklin. In 1974 he attended his first bluegrass festival, at Fern Lodge in Bossier City, and followed that by going to the Red River Bluegrass Festival in Coushatta in 1975. The Lasyones then became a fixture at bluegrass festivals in Louisiana, Arkansas, Texas, and Mississippi.

He spent most of the last ten years of his life playing bluegrass. Much in demand as a sideman, he had a long list of bands to his credit. At festivals and shows he played with Steve and Stacy and the Deep South, the Sullivan Family, Clyde Baum, Tom Uhr and the Shady Grove Ramblers, Delia Bell and Bill Grant, Chubby Wise, and Mac Wiseman. He also appeared with Shoji Tabuchi on some of his shows around Shreveport and they became good friends. Shoji taught him "Danny Boy" and Jewel showed him how to cross-tune the fiddle and play "Black Mountain Rag." He also appeared on the Louisiana Hayride in Bossier City. By 1980 he was booking festivals as a single act and had surrounded himself with some of the best pickers in the country.

Over the years, he played with many country and bluegrass bands, but in the last few years of his life he fronted his own band. They appeared mainly at bluegrass festivals and played styles ranging from Cajun to country to bluegrass. They recorded two LPs while he was playing the bluegrass festival circuit, *Cajun Grass* and *Traveling On*. Featured on these albums were Jewel's friends Greg Edwards (banjo), Ernie Maples (bass), and David Booth (guitar), and his son, Tim (mandolin).

In the 1970s Jewel won or placed in many contests throughout Louisiana. His biggest wins were the 1977 and 1978 Louisiana State Fiddle Contest, at the Old Barn in Boyce. Other wins included the Poke Salad Festival at Blanchard, Pecan Festival at Colfax, Louisiana State Fair, Fourth of July Festival in Montgomery, Holiday in Dixie at Shreveport, and the festival in Greenwood. In almost any contest he could be counted on to play his favorite tune, "Black Mountain Rag," to win the championship. It was one of many he would be remembered for. He also wrote numerous fiddle tunes in his latter years, which he recorded and played at shows and contests. One of his most requested compositions was "Maggie's Waltz." Creola related that he had been working on the tune for some time when all of a sudden, in the middle of the night, he jumped out of bed and finished the composition.

His musical talent has been passed on to his family. Tim plays mandolin, guitar, and fiddles a little. His grandson, Cody, plays banjo, mandolin, and guitar and his granddaughter, Emily, played fiddle for a while.

Jewel passed away in 1984, having influenced numerous young fiddlers and musicians such as John Johnson, and providing early bluegrass audiences with some fine, pure bluegrass fiddle. Ernie Maples in his liner notes to *Travelin' On*:

> *How does one describe Jewel's fiddling? If one listens to him play, he can hear a little Chubby Wise, a bit of Paul Warren, and a taste of South Louisiana Cajun, but mostly he hears music that is uniquely Jewel Lasyone's. On this album Jewel brings*

> *you familiar breakdowns, sacred tunes, and waltzes, mixed with new tunes that he wrote especially for this album—all done in his own inimitable style.*

Tom Uhr of the Shady Grove Ramblers notes in the liner notes to Jewel's first LP, *Cajun Grass*:

> *It was then [at Shady Dell Acres] that I first heard the "sweet" fiddling of Jewel Lasyone. It was about three in the morning, and he was pulling a super smooth bow. I ambled over to him, and I sat quietly to watch this man put his heart and soul into that fiddle. Every time you watch Jewel play, you will see a man who looks at ease, is having a good time, and is playing smoothly on any thing he plays.*

Interviews by Ron Yule: J. C. Daniels (undated informal conversation) and Creola Linzay (4-16-2004).

References

Maples, Ernie. Liner notes. *Travelin On, Jewel Lasyone*. Southern Star Records, SS337, 1982.

Uhr, Tom. Liner notes. *Jewel Lasyone, Cajun Grass*. Southern Star Records, SS-336, 1980.

Photo courtesy of Leblanc family.

FLOYD LEBLANC

(1924–1975) Mermentau

Floyd LeBlanc was born on September 17, 1924, in Mermentau, Louisiana. Born into a musical family, his musical career began at an early age. His father, Lessin, played French accordion and fiddle and his mother, Merillia, played rhythm guitar and sang. In the early 1930s the family moved to Cypress Point, where Floyd and his brother, Steve, began making homemade instruments from cigar boxes, screen wire, and boards because their parents could not afford real instruments. These homemade instruments brought frustration to their mother, who later recalled to family members that she could not keep screen wire in the doors because they would continually remove it to make strings for their musical instruments. Their interest was finally noted and their parents bought a fiddle for five dollars and a guitar for four dollars. Floyd was influenced first by his father's fiddling and second by Hackberry Rambler fiddler Luderin Darbone, who was popular in the area at the time. The brothers

Oklahoma Tornadoes, ca. 1946–47: Dudley Champagne (drums), unidentified (steel guitar), Floyd Leblanc (guitar), Iry Lejeune (accordion), Ben Oldag (bass), Bennie Hess (guitar), and Virgel Bozman (guitar). Photo courtesy of Ervin Lejeune.

learned to play quickly, and a month or so later were asked to play a dance. Floyd was only fourteen at the time, and he and Steve soon became popular local favorites, playing house and barn dances.

With the advent of World War II, they both joined the military but continued to play music while serving their country. While stationed in San Antonio, Floyd met Virgel Bozman, and they started a band called the Oklahoma Tornadoes, playing both French and country music. Joe, Floyd's son and also a musician, noted they played the "Highway 90 Strip" from New Orleans to Houston and as far north as Oklahoma. They became very popular and much in demand. During this time, they recorded "Grinding for You Darling," "Just a Year Ago Today," and "La Prison" for Gold Star Records in Houston.

While playing at a dancehall in New Orleans in late 1946 or early 1947, Floyd met the legendary accordionist Iry Lejeune, who was playing at a nearby club. They became musical buddies, and soon after returning to southwest Louisiana they were playing at the Pine Grove Club, in Evangeline, when Floyd invited Iry to record with them in Houston. Floyd had made an effort to get a contract and record with Bill Quinn at Gold Star, the same company that had recorded and distributed Harry Choates's "Jole Blon," but he had not recorded with Quinn at that time. As luck would have it, Jimmy Bryant and Bennie Hess (a member of the Oklahoma Tornadoes at the time) separated from

Pee Wee Lyons, unidentified, Riley Clark, Floyd Leblanc, and unidentified. KIKS, Sulphur, 1950s. Photo courtesy of Floyd Leblanc family.

Quinn and formed the Opera label, so Floyd carried Iry to Houston and the Oklahoma Tornadoes recorded "Love Bridge Waltz" and "Evangeline Special" on their new label. This turned out to be a major event in Cajun music. The public fell in love with Iry's playing, which led to the effort to bring the accordion back into Cajun recordings and to the prominence it had enjoyed in the pre–string band era of the late 1920s and early 1930s. Iry became one of the most influential figures and accordion players in Cajun music history.

Several tunes were recorded by the Oklahoma Tornadoes on the Opera label, one with Bennie Hess and the Nation's Playboys: "Drink-Drink-Drink" and "You Ain't Cheatin' on Me Now." Andrew Brown notes that the Nation's Playboys and the Oklahoma Tornadoes were probably the same band at this point, and that Floyd is probably playing electric guitar on Hess's "Drink-Drink-Drink."

The Oklahoma Tornado band was well-known, and Floyd. Virgel, and Iry Lejeune made a trek to Nashville in 1947 to seek their fortune. Iry returned home after a couple weeks, but Floyd played with several bands while there, including Ernest Tubb's Texas Troubadours, and played in numerous jam sessions with many of the stars on a nightly basis. The Tornadoes' stay in Nashville was also short-lived.

Upon his return, Floyd continued to record and play around southwest Louisiana, but in 1950 quit playing for a while. He went into private business, opening Floyd's Net Shop on Fontenot Road (then the Gulf Highway) in Lake Charles. He worked as a carpenter and fished commercially during this period.

Floyd's talent was well-known around Lake Charles and the offers continued for him to return and play dances, both country and Cajun. By the mid-fifties he relented, and began playing with Sidney Brown and the Traveler Playboys. In the sixties Floyd played at clubs and local shows with the bands of Doris Matte, Bobby Leger, Robert Bertrand, Jo-El Sonnier, and Joe Bonsall. He played at KIKS in Sulphur, and played with Doris Matte on KPLC-TV's "Saturday Night Down South."

Floyd cut numerous sides for various labels. He never recorded as a solo artist with Bill Quinn at Gold Star, but began to do so with Opera Records in 1947. He cut such songs as "Louisiana Waltz," "Hackberry Two Step," "You Mustn't Cry," "LaGrange Waltz," "Brow Bridge Waltz" (*sic*, "Breaux Bridge Waltz"), "Unis Two Step" (*sic*, "Eunice Two Step"), and "Over the Waves." In 1949, he also recorded on other labels such as (Virgel Bozman's) O.T., cutting "Orphan's Waltz" and "Louisiana Stomp." The latter was reissued on the Khoury label a few years later. He also recorded at J. D. Miller's Studio in the late 1960s, with tunes produced on Cajun Classics and later reissued on the Flyright label: "Roseland Two Step," "Tolan Waltz," "Louisiana Stomp," "Floyd's Waltz," and "Jolie Blond."

He also recorded on two LPs in the 1960s with Joe Bonsall and the Orange Playboys, prior to teaming up with longtime friend Oday Boudreaux, who had a recording studio. They recorded "Cher Bassette" and "The Lake Arthur Waltz" around 1966 or 1967. At the time of Floyd's death, he and Oday were making an album, which was never completed. Crawford Vincent notes that Floyd wanted to make an LP that would be a tribute to Luderin Darbone, but never did because Luderin explained that he could not make a tribute album of his music until he was dead.

Floyd passed away on November 8, 1975, in Lake Charles.

Interviews by Ron Yule: Jeanne Farque (4-12-2007), Joe LeBlanc (3-22-2003 and 8-23-2004), Arthur Leger (4-9-2003), and Crawford Vincent (6-15-2004).

References

Brown, Andrew. E-mail dated 9-21-2008, re: history of Oklahoma Tornadoes and Floyd Leblanc's recordings.

Cajun Music City News. Leon Marcinac, editor. Westlake, Louisiana, vol. 3, no. 3; vol. 4, no. 4.

Ferbrache, Lyle. Notes from Floyd LeBlanc CD, private collection of Floyd's early recordings, Milpitas, California.

Opera Records recording contracts. In possession of the Floyd LeBlanc family.

Savoy, Ann Allen. *Cajun Music: A Reflection of a People, Volume I*. Bluebird Press, Eunice, Louisiana, 1984.

Yule, Ron. *Iry Lejeune: Wailin' the Blues Cajun Style*. Fiddle Country Publishing, DeRidder, Louisiana, 2007.

Yule, Ron, et al. Cajun French Music Association Hall of Fame, Lake Charles Chapter. Fiddle Country Publishing, DeRidder, Louisiana, 2004.

Photo courtesy of John Leleux.

LIONEL LELEUX

(1912–1996) Leleux

Lionel Leleux was born on October 12, 1912, in Vermillion Parish, in Leleux, a town named for his grandfather. His father, Pierre, was a farmer in the early part of his life but mainly owned and operated PB's Grocery in Leleux until his death in 1965. He played some fiddle but never pursued the instrument the way Lionel did.

Throughout Lionel's life his trade was barbering, a skill he began learning at the age of fourteen while cutting his family's and friends' hair. At eighteen he received his license, and he always said it was a job he never liked.

His passion was fiddles: playing, repairing, and making. He noted that his love for the fiddle has been with him all his life; even as a child he tried to teethe on his father's fiddle, leaving marks on the instrument. Lionel began playing early, and by the age of eleven had raised enough money working on the farm and caring for the horses and mules to buy a fiddle for four dollars

Display at the CFMA Hall of Fame, Eunice, showing Lionel Leleux's violinmaking wood and tools. This display was used at the many workshops he attended throughout the United States. Photo courtesy of Dave Simpson, LSU-E.

and fifty cents. Besides his father, some of the first music Lionel learned was from listening to music at his Grandfather Ernest Leleux's Dancehall across the road from his house. He would listen to one of his favorite fiddlers, Bascom Mouton, from his front porch because he was too young to attend the dances in person.

As with most fiddlers of the era, Lionel played country and house dances, many times with Nathan Abshire. He also was known to associate with Lawrence Walker and Leo Soileau through his uncle's dancehall, although he never played formally in their bands in the early years. By the early thirties, he was playing with Happy Fats and the Rayne-Bo Ramblers, using an automobile-powered generator to run the PA system.

Around 1934 Lionel met his wife at a dance. After they married and had their first child, he quit playing for dances and began to barber for a living. John Leleux, Lionel's son, notes that his sister was born on December 6, 1935, and December 5, 1935, was Lionel's last dance for years to come. In fact, Happy Fats had spent the night at the Leleux's on the 5th and Lionel told him the next day he was quitting. He would not renew public performance on the fiddle until the early 1950s.

Bascom Mouton and Lionel Leleux.
Photo courtesy of John Leleux.

By the early 1950s, Lionel began playing around the area with his son, John (rhythm guitar), and other musicians. Their first shows were at Adolph Martinez's Dancehall in Morse. This brought Lionel back into the music; he soon began to play with Joe Falcon and his Silver Bell Stringband of Crowley. In 1963 the band was recorded by Valerie Post at the Triangle Club (Scott, Louisiana), and this recording is available on Arhoolie Records.

Following Joe's death in 1965, Lionel played with various people, including the legendary Angelas Lejeune. During this period he played with Lawrence Walker and the Wandering Aces, sometimes playing on KATC television in Lafayette. He stayed with Walker until Walker's death from a heart attack in 1968.

Shortly thereafter, Scott accordionist Don Montoucet began to play with the remaining Wandering Aces, U. J. Guidry, Sim Schexneyder, and Lionel. They eventually changed their name to the Mulate Playboys when they began playing at the now famous restaurant. Don recalls they played everywhere, traveling to France, Russia, Canada (seven times), and all over the United

States. One LP was released around 1985, which Don says was produced by a company in England. They played together for twenty-eight years until Lionel's death.

Lionel played as a trio with Eddie Lejeune and the Morse Playboys, featuring Hubert Maitre on guitar. One album was produced in 1991 from this group, *It's in the Blood* on the Rounder label.

In 1974 he, along with many other Cajun musicians, played the Tribute to Cajun Music held at Blackham Coliseum in Lafayette. Lionel always felt he had an obligation to be the best musician he could, with a responsible attitude toward his job. This, and his desire to promote the Cajun music he loved, is demonstrated in Barry Ancelet's "The Cajun Music Festival: Genesis and Legacy," from *Accordions, Fiddles, Two-Step and Swing.* Amid terrible weather conditions, Lionel was one of the first to arrive at the coliseum. Barry describes the scene:

> *To make things worse, the afternoon of the concert the skies opened, dumping nearly a foot of rain on most of South Louisiana, accompanied by a spectacular display of lightning. At that point we weren't even sure that the musicians would come. After all, no one was being paid a cent, not even travel money. The concert was scheduled to start at seven-thirty. By four o'clock the sound system was set up and ready. Fiddler Lionel Leleux had arrived early, pants rolled above his knees and instrument case held high and dry.*

Lionel joined friends Marc Savoy, Varise Conner, and Don Montoucet and demonstrated the band sound of the old house dance days.

Soon thereafter, he began performing with various groups and demonstrating his violin-making skills at festivals and workshops throughout the United States and Europe. Trips included tours to the 1976 Festival of American Folklife at the Smithsonian and to Nova Scotia in 1978.

Another aspect of Lionel's association with the fiddle was his early dreams of making a violin. Many who knew and studied with him refer to him as the "King of the Louisiana Fiddlemakers." Violin making seemed almost to haunt him throughout his early life; in 1925 he began repairing bows, following it up in 1927 when a neighbor brought him a fiddle that needed repair. During the early years his tools were primitive and homemade, but in 1932 he began to buy tools with the little money he could scrape together.

Although he did not play publicly during the late thirties and forties, Lionel continued to pursue his passion for luthiery. After numerous hours of study, he began to make violins in the early 1940s, pursuing a skill that would be his legacy in Louisiana country music.

Lionel had a passion for repairing or making violins with traditional methods handed down through the ages. He selected only the best woods, parts, and varnish, no matter what the project. With the patience of Job, he meticulously addressed every violin repair. Time was not an enemy—as many have commented on the length of time he would take to repair an instrument. His patience and attention to detail are best noted by his studies on violin making and violin varnish. In a March 11, 1973, interview with Alton Broussard for the *Lafayette Advertiser*, he comments on violin making:

> *The art of fiddlemaking requires—precision and control. . . . In a sense it's like tempering steel. Each part is an individual unit of the instrument yet it must blend with the other parts for best tonal quality. That requires considerable experience. . . . You can't just do some hokus pocus and a violin comes out—no! . . . You have to love that wood. Me I prefer to do that [make violins] than eat.*

Over the years he repaired violins at a shop in his home, for fiddlers from the Midwest and Nashville as well as locally for Louisiana fiddlers. The twenty-plus violins he made are played by musicians from Illinois, Virginia, Louisiana, and Tennessee. Each is an impeccable work of art, lauded not only by players but by other violin makers as well. He also constructed several bows.

He was not a highly educated man in terms of formal schooling; but through perseverance, Lionel taught himself the necessary skills to ply this craft. After conquering the many details of violin making from his math and geometrical studies, he began to address violin varnish with the same enthusiasm and study ethic.

His rare skills as a fiddler, repairman, and fiddlemaker were an asset to Louisiana Cajun and country music. Unselfishly, he taught his skills to several apprentices and students in both luthiery and fiddling through grants, studies, and workshops.

Lionel passed away in 1996.

Interviews by Ron Yule: Fred Beavers (undated informal conversation), John Leleux (2-26-2006), Don Montoucet (2-26-2007), and Ken and Buford Smith (undated informal conversation).

References

Allan, Johnny. *Memories.* JADFEL Publishing, Lafayette, Louisiana, 1995.

Ancelet, Barry, and Elemore Morgan Jr. *The Makers of Cajun Music.* University of Texas Press, Austin, 1984.

Ancelet, Barry. "The Cajun Music Festival: Genesis and Legacy." Brasseaux, Ryan A., and Kevin S. Fontenot. *Accordions, Fiddles, Two Step, and Swing: A Cajun Reader.* Center for Louisiana Studies, Lafayette, 2006.

Broussard, Alton. "Skilled Hand Carves Violin from Native Wood." *Advertiser*, Lafayette, Louisiana, March 11, 1973.

Post, Lauren. Liner notes. *Joe Falcon: Cajun Pioneer*. Arhoolie CD 459, 1997.

Strachwitz, Chris. Additional liner notes. *Joe Falcon: Cajun Pioneer*. Arhoolie CD 459, 1997.

Photo courtesy of the Lewing family.

AUD LEWING

(1899–1972) Many

If ever there was a legendary figure in west central Louisiana old-time country fiddling, Aud Lewing could be that figure.

> *"Mighty fine!"*
> *"He played different songs than anyone else."*
> *"He was a showman!"*
> *"He made fire breathe from his fiddle!"*
> *"He commanded the attention of anyone who ever heard him play."*

These are comments from fiddle fans who heard him play. Anyone who heard him never forgot him; his playing at country dances, fiddle contests, around a pot-bellied stove, or on the front porch was the stuff legends are made from.

Many people who knew Aud and played with him have related that his enthusiasm during a performance was almost legendary. Many talk of how he would holler, dance, and sing while he played. He usually played with the bow overly tightened to where the bow was bent outward like a hunting bow and the hair taut. According to R. L. Springer, from Pollock, he would "whip it," creating great rhythm and danceability. Many, including R. L., thought he was the best fiddler in the country.

The Lewings were of Irish descent and migrated to the area via the Mississippi River from the Midwest around the early 1800s, settling south of Many in what is now known as the Lewing Settlement.

Aud inherited his musical talent from both sides of the family. His father, Bluford, was a fiddler; his mother, Mary Elizabeth, came from a family of rural country musicians, the Stricklands. Besides his father's teaching, Aud, born February 11, 1899, learned the fiddle at age six by watching other fiddlers play at house parties and reunions in the area around Many. Aud was almost obsessed with the fiddle, and some family members recall he seemed to always have it in his hands. His sister recalled that he played so much when he was a kid that he wore a hole in his trousers on the inside right knee from keeping rhythm with his knees while he played.

Fiddling was a family affair in Aud's youth. His father taught him numerous tunes—many he could not recall the titles of. His brother, Lester, learned rhythm guitar in his youth and accompanied him at house parties. His cousin, Hank Strickland, and his musical family played with him on many occasions at country dances and parties around Many and in the Lewing Settlement in the 1930s. These gatherings featured not only fiddle and guitar but jug and trumpet playing as well. Delores Barber and Jerome Hammons, Aud's niece and nephew, recall the many Friday night pickings at homes throughout the Lewing Settlement during the forties, fifties, and sixties, with Jerome recalling, "Every Friday night someone had one." They recalled local musicians who attended: Lester and Aud Lewing, Harold Hayes, Steve Mitchell, Ray Court, Lambert Peterson, Jimmy Ray Hayes, and Vic Anders.

Pollock fiddler Robert L. Springer recalled him playing at their Kisatchie home with his father, Joe Springer, in the 1930s. It is apparent from comments on the Springer tapes that Aud learned several tunes from Joe and was influenced in part by his association with him, as was Robert.

Aud played all the old-time tunes, but was especially noted for "Listen to the Mockingbird," "Sally Goodin," "Black Mountain Rag," and "The Fox Chase." Luckily, Mr. Springer preserved some of this music on tape and a list

Aud and Lester Lewing. Many Theater, 1967, following the Toledo Fall Festival fiddle contest. Photo courtesy of Lewing family.

of some of the tunes is noted at the end of the article. R. L. Springer and Ken Halbrook both recalled Aud staying with Mr. Springer for about a week, on one occasion, at his Pollock home on Pollock Cemetery Road, and the group had jam sessions every night. Troy DeRamus, who attended several of these sessions, noted that Aud would carry the whole jam session with his enthusiasm and music. Troy noted that he did not need an accompanist to keep rhythm for him.

Aud was quite the entertainer during these sessions. Comments preceding the tunes from some of these tapes:

> *Well, I'm coming out again with the "Wednesday Night Waltz." Y'all listen to this, will yah. I'm going to try to play it here. I got Robert Springer here with me and he's enjoying himself too. And I am too, you know I am. 'Cause I wouldn't be fiddlin' if I wasn't enjoying myself. My dog's out here fightin', out here but I don't think we'll pay him no mind. The "Wednesday Night Waltz," Here we go now.*
>
> *"Orange Blossom Special." Good people listen to this. Dog's are fightin' . . . we're drinkin' coffee and cold drinks. Ain't that a happy life. [plays E chord on fiddle] Listen to that ole fiddle.*

Aud was always very limber, and his showmanship on the fiddle was demonstrated when he played behind his back, between his legs, over his head, and would even get on the floor, arch his back, and play the fiddle under his back. Jerome recalls that Aud was quite the ladies' man and one of his favorite tricks was to pick out the prettiest girl in the room, put his arms around her, and play the fiddle behind her back, the whole time never touching her.

Tom Petty, whose grandfather was a front porch fiddler, recalled Aud would walk to Many nearly every Saturday morning and play at the drug store. Old-timers and children alike would gather just to hear him sit and play the old tunes.

Jerome said Aud won many contests, including the one in Athens, Texas. He won the Sabine Parish Fair fiddle contest numerous times, and in 1946 won the Beauregard Parish Fair fiddle contest. He entered many contests held at local theatres like the Many Theater in Many, Taylor Theater in Pleasant Hill, and the Lee Theater in Leesville. In 1967 he won the contest at the Toledo Bend Festival held at the Many Theater. A. F. Ott Jr. recalls Aud winning the Taylor Theatre contest on many occasions. One of Ott's father's great thrills was occasionally beating Aud in these Saturday evening contests. Several have noted that he placed in the Lee Theater Louisiana State Championship Contest in Leesville in 1947.

Aud passed away on December 26, 1972.

Interviews by Ron Yule: This article is almost completely from undated conversations about fiddling in which I remember details of conversations about Aud Lewing with Troy DeRamus, Ken Halbrook, James Jeter, A. F. Ott Jr., Tom Petty, James Springer, and R. L. Springer. Delores Barber (8-4-2008) and Jerome Hammons (10-9-2003 and 8-4-2008).

References

Beauregard News. "175 Register for Old Folks Day at Fair." October 18, 1946.

Springer, R. L. Cassette tapes of Aud's playing around 1971–72.

Yule, Ron. *When the Fiddle Was King.* Fiddle Country Publishing, DeRidder, Louisiana, 2006.

Following is a list of some of the tunes played by Aud on the R. L. Springer tapes made at jam sessions around Pollock with Ken Holbrook, Lester Lewing, R. L. Springer, Vernon Cogdill, and Milton Trammel ca. 1970–71:

"Sally Johnson," "Natchez Under the Hill," "Boil 'em Cabbage Down," "Joe Springer Special," "Leatherbritches," "Aud's Blues," "8th of January," "Billy in the Lowground," "Black Mountain Rag," "Nashville Tennessee Rag," "The Fox Chase," "Fire on the Mountain," "Arkansas Traveler," "Orange Blossom Special," "Aud's Waltz in E," "Ole Joe Clark," "Over the Waves," "Lone Star Rag," "Blues in B♭," "Sugar in the Gourd," "The Waltz You Saved for Me," "Sugarfoot Rag," "Fisher's Hornpipe," "Wild Horse at Stoney Point," "Ida Red," "Ragtime Annie," "Listen to the Mockingbird," "Spanish Two-Step," "Down Yonder," "Sally Goodin," "Cindy," "Cotton Eyed Joe," "Cacklin' Hen," "Salt River," "Great Big Taters in the Sandyland," and numerous other unnamed blues, waltz, and breakdown tunes.

Photo courtesy of Hermon Lasyone Collection.

ABE MANUEL SR.

(1926–2003) Lake Charles

The Abe Manuel story is a tale not only of a respected musician and fiddler, but of a talented musical family and its torch-carrying legacy. Abe grew up playing with family, played with family during his early country music career, and finished his career playing country music with his own gifted sons, Little Joe and Abe Jr.

Abe Sr. (b. 1926) learned to play fiddle from hearing his father, an accordion player, as a youth in the Basile area of Evangeline Parish. He learned guitar at age eight and later fiddle. He had a brother, Joe Adam Manuel, who played fiddle, banjo, and guitar. Both played with some of the legendary fiddlers and country stars of the forties and fifties. Both were mainstays in the band of Harry Choates, toured with him, and appeared on many recordings with him, playing various instruments. Joe was also a vocalist on several of the famous Gold Star recordings for Choates, including "Basile Waltz" and "Allons a Lafayette." Abe would go on to play with many country giants before settling in to play with his own family band later in life.

Abe played Cajun music (on guitar) with his family and friends around Basile and Oberlin for years, and at some point in his youth took up the fiddle. He had been around fiddling all his life and took to it with ease. In the early 1940s he played with Leo Soileau at the Avalon Club in Basile, followed by playing with various bands and country musicians during the 1940s, including Chuck Guillory, Carrol Broussard, Harry Choates, Ralph Richardson, "Pee Wee" Maples, and Ferrell "Benny" Frugé. Carrol Broussard, who played steel guitar with Harry Choates for a couple years, recalls that Abe filled in on fiddle for Harry when he "went off to get cured." This stint lasted for three or four weeks.

His travels with Hank Williams Sr. were memorable. In the *Daily News Journal* he is quoted as saying:

> *[W]orking with Hank Williams was something else, particularly the night in 1948 when he kicked out the front windshield of my Buick after we'd finished playing a date down in Louisiana. Hank had been drinking. He kicked out my window, but he never let liquor cause him to not finish a song or performance. If he showed up, he did the songs right. He also recalls, Lefty Frizzell was class and could always pack a house.*

Although the dates are not known, he periodically played on KWKH Shreveport "in the Louisiana Hayride days," as his wife, Dorothy puts it. He played with many of the stars as a sideman on the Hayride stage as well as in the many pickup bands that played at local clubs. During this period he began to play with other country giants like Jim Reeves and Carl Smith, on both guitar and fiddle.

Abe and Joe had briefly formed the Rockola Playboys in 1949. In the early fifties Abe was playing at dances all over Louisiana and Texas. In 1950 he performed around Corpus Christi, Texas, clubs as Sandy Austin, apparently his stage name at the time. Steel guitarist Carrol Broussard, who played with Manuel during much of this period, recalls: "He used the name Sandy Austin while he was in Corpus Christi. When his brother Joe joined him, they went under the names Sandy and Joe Austin. When they left the area they didn't use the name anymore.... No one ever said why they called themselves that." Labeled as the Fiddle (*sic*, Fiddlin') Frenchman and his Cajuns, he cut two sides for the O.T. label, "Madame Saustain" and "Scrambled Eggs." He also

Rockola Playboys, 1949: Abe Manuel, unidentified, unidentified, Joe Manuel. Photo courtesy of Hermon Lasyone Collection.

performed with Adolph Hofner and his Pearl Wranglers in central Texas in 1951.

Following his stay in south Texas he began to play with Lefty Frizzell in late 1951, working out of Beaumont and appearing around the country from California to Canada to the Opry. They began as a two-man traveling show, using a pickup band on tour shows and the staff band on the Opry. Manuel, who helped with the sales of souvenir items on the road, recalls that the Canadian tour was horrendous. In 1953 he played with Jelly Elliott and his Singing Cowboys on KALB, in Alexandria as well as venues around central Louisiana.

By 1954 he was back in southwest Louisiana fronting his own band, Abe Manuel and the Louisiana Hillbillies. The band that appeared on the now-defunct KTAG television included Bradley Stutes, Dottie and Abe, Amos Comeaux, and Wiley Barkdull. During this period he recorded several songs for J. D. Miller in Crowley on Miller's Feature label.

In 1957 the Manuels were living in Grand Chenier and, like many Gulf Coast residents, suffered the wrath of Hurricane Audrey. Abe Sr. was working as a bridge tender, and prior to the storm left Dottie and the children (Tim, age two, Maureen, one, and Dollie, who had been born two days before) to go to the bridge where he worked.

Carroll Broussard, Pee Wee Maples, Abe Manuel, George Duhon, Joe Manuel, and Benny Frugé. Aransas Pass, Texas, ca. 1950. Photo courtesy of Hermon Lasyone Collection.

The winds from Audrey were fierce, but the tidal wave that ripped through Cameron Parish separated the family and caused some agonizing and anxious moments. With the house afloat and the water rising, they cut a hole in the roof and escaped to sit and wait for rescue. After thirty-six hours of separation and worry, Abe, Dottie, and the children were reunited. Sadly, over twenty-five of their cousins and loved ones perished, including Dottie's great-great grandmother, who drowned in her wheelchair at age ninety-six.

In the early 1960s, Abe and Dottie joined with Rufus Thibodeaux, Carrol Broussard, and others and recorded their famous "Tribute to Harry Choates" at J. D. Miller's studio in Crowley. Abe provided the vocals for the monumental band, which showcased Rufus's powerful and creative Cajun fiddling. Abe continued to play locally, appearing on KPLC television on the Saturday Night Down South shows and at local honky tonks like the Moulin Rouge, Bamboo Club, and the Silver Star. This band included Dorothy (guitar), Hermon Lasyone (bass fiddle), and Glen Croker (steel). Guitarist Kenneth Midkiff recalls working numerous local shows around Calcasieu and Cameron Parishes in the 1960s, sponsored by KIKS DJs Eddie Roberts and Curt Maddox. These shows included Abe and Rufus Thibodeaux playing twin fiddles. They also worked many shows with country acts when they came through town, including Jimmy C. Newman and Rufus Thibodeaux.

Julio "Steve" Stefanni (drums), Abe Manuel (fiddle), Lefty Frizzell, Melvin Twilligar (bass), and Pee Wee Whitewing (steel guitar). Tracy Gardens, San Jose, CA, 1952. Photo courtesy of Pee Wee Whitewing.

Abe's versatility emerged in the late 1960s when he played bluegrass at jam sessions with banjoist "Red" Corbin, I. K. Green, and other local bluegrass musicians. They played a few local shows and appeared at Shakey's Pizza Parlors in the area.

In the 1970s the band format changed; he not only had Dorothy playing guitar, but also began to include his talented sons. He returned to work the Shakey's Pizza Parlors in the area with a band that consisted of Abe (fiddle), Dorothy (guitar), Abe Jr. (piano and vocals), and Little Joe (lead guitar). They eventually worked for Shakey's Pizza Parlors in the Houston area, before Abe retired and moved to Milton, Tennessee, in the Nashville area.

In 1988 Abe started a restaurant and country store in Milton, which operated for thirteen years. They put on shows with the family at the restaurant as entertainment for the customers. Their music provided a perfect backdrop for an eatery that served the Louisiana cuisine of the Manuel's home state. Folks came from as far away as Europe to eat at the restaurant and listen to the music.

Little Joe started playing guitar and banjo at the age of five, and began the fiddle under his daddy's tutelage at nine. After the gigs at Shakey's, he moved on to Nashville and played and recorded with many of the stars of country music. He has played with Jimmy C. Newman, T. G. Sheppard, Ricky Skaggs, Freddie Powers, and Lynn Anderson, to name a few.

Abe Jr. learned piano at an early age (five), and in 1978 took up the fiddle, learning at the same time as his friend, Johnny Carpenter (fiddler with Tracy

Byrd). He also has played drums with Mickey Gilley in Houston, and with Bob and Eddie Curtis in New Orleans. After moving to Nashville he played with Jimmy C. Newman (with his brother), and in 1992 he worked with Merle Haggard. He has now moved back to southwest Louisiana and is living in Creole and playing with Moe-D and other local groups, recording locally with groups and occasionally going out with Merle Haggard when he needs him.

Abe Sr.'s complete recorded output is not known, although it is known that he recorded with numerous acts as well as on his own. Four sides were cut with Harry Choates in 1946: "Basile Waltz," "Jole Blon," "Port Arthur Waltz," and "Allons a Lafayette." Besides the one 78 r.p.m. recorded on Virgel Bozman's O.T. label under the name of Sandy Austin, four sides were issued on the Feature label: "Country Gentleman," "Country Girl," "Hippy Tiyo," and "I've Got Your Heart Locked Up." A later 45 r.p.m. on Tribute featured "French Wedding March" and "Country Gentleman." Dot, as Tit Cajun Belle, recorded "La Valse de Cajun" and "Amour, Amour" at Goldband Studios in Lake Charles.

Abe Sr. was the consummate country picker of the mid-twentieth-century. He could do it all and enjoyed the fun of making music as an unnoticed sideman while many big changes came to country music. He also was a great showman who would pull out all stops to entertain the crowd. One stunt he did with the fiddle was to loosen the bow, thread the fiddle between the hair and the bow stick, consequently playing four strings at one time, and play tunes like "Orange Blossom Special" and "When You and I Were Young Maggie."

Abe passed away on June 9, 2003.

Interviews by Ron Yule: Carrol Broussard (9-21-2004 and 9-18-2008), Andrew Brown (9-19-2008), Red Corbin (9-19-2008), Lyle Ferbrache (6-6-2006 and 9-18-2008), Dorothy Manuel (2-3-2003), Kenneth Midkiff (9-30-2008), Ralph Richardson (4-17-2005), and Crawford Vincent (10-10-2003).

References

Brown, Andrew. Booklet accompanying *Devil in the Bayou*. Bear Family CD, BCD 16355 BH, 2002.

Brown, Andrew. E-mails dated 9-22-2008, re: Interviews with Abe Manuel Sr. and his recordings.

Cooper, Daniel. *Lefty Frizzell: The Honky-tonk Life of Country Music's Greatest Singer.* Little, Brown and Company, 1995.

Ferbrache, Lyle. E-mails dated 9-15-2008 concerning the recording history of Abe Manuel Sr.

Whipple, Dan. *Daily News Journal*, Murfreesboro, Tennessee. Undated article in possession of Dorothy Manuel.

Photo courtesy of Billy McGee.

DENNIS MCGEE

(1893–1989) Eunice

Dennis McGee is one of the most revered fiddlers in Louisiana music history. Born on January 26, 1893, he studied and learned the fiddle from nineteenth-century fiddlers and lived long enough (ninety-six years) to pass on to today's younger fiddlers these tunes and earlier, now-extinct dance and fiddle styles . He was one of the first Louisianans to record extensively, not only with a fiddle band but also with an accordionist, either Amédé Ardoin or Angelas Lejeune. Extensively interviewed and studied, he lived to be a part of the festival scene that arose in the 1970s, giving listeners and musicians alike a window into the south Louisiana music of a century ago.

Dennis was born in Bayou Marron to John McGee, of Irish descent, and Amelia LaFleur, of French and Seminole Indian ancestry. Dennis first began learning from his father, his first tune being "Valse de Pop." In his youth he went to live with his grandmother, where he was surrounded by fiddle players. As with many other rural fiddlers, music was a family affair with Dennis—listening to the playing of his uncles, Ulysses and Joseph McGee, and a cousin, Oscar McGee.

After working with a cousin, Ben Courville, on his farm, he moved and began living with another cousin, Theodore McGee. This was a positive move for Dennis's musical career. Theodore took him to Ville Platte to buy a fiddle, and within six months he was attracting the attention of neighbors who would come to hear him play. Besides house dances, he began playing dances in Ville Platte, sometime twice weekly for a dollar a night. At these early-twentieth-century dances, Dennis would play square dances as well as two-steps, waltzes, and reels. Dennis even provided accompaniment for silent films at theaters in Mamou and Eunice.

Dennis's learning experiences were heightened during this period. His association with longtime fiddler Sady Courville began when he would visit neighbors to play music. Besides meeting Sady, Dennis began learning old tunes from Sady's father, Eraste, and uncle, Arville Courville, who had played as a fiddle duet at dances for years. They were one of Dennis's most important links to the music of the 1800s. Their repertoire included contradanses, gigues, galops, reels, mazurkas, polkas, and cotillions—eighteenth- and nineteenth-century styles not used in today's Cajun music—done as fiddle duets. He also heard nearly one-hundred-year-old fiddler Gustave Ardoin, another link to the previous tradition.

One friendship that would have a big effect on Dennis' career was his introduction (around 1921) to black accordionist Amédé Ardoin, while both were tenant farmers on Oscar Comeaux's farms. Comeaux would have them play at house dances throughout the area. They played dances together because of their camaraderie and the fact that Ardoin, who had had trouble at white dances, felt safer with McGee by his side. After moving to Eunice to work on another farm, they continued playing music together. During and following their recordings in New Orleans and San Antonio, they remained friends until Ardoin's death in 1941.

Dennis continued to play dances and worked at a multitude of jobs, including farming and barbering. He married his third wife, Sady Courville's sister Gladys, in 1927. Playing dances was a necessity because of the hard times of the late 1920s. He played many times as a solo act, others with Sady Courville, and many times with Leo Soileau, who would join them to play as three fiddles. Sady would play the tin whistle on many of these three-fiddle sessions.

Sady Courville and Dennis McGee. Photo courtesy of Billy McGee.

Sady and Dennis appeared on KWKH in Shreveport in 1927 as a part of a promotional campaign for Cajun music by a local Eunice man, Mr. Marks. This was a pioneering event in Louisiana country music. One year later they were approached by Sady's employer, a local storeowner, to record in New Orleans. following the lead of other Cajun artists. In March 1929 they recorded eight sides for the Vocalion label at the St. Charles Hotel. Courville has noted that his name was not included on the record label because he was afraid his friends would laugh at him. Only one song came out with his name on the label. The others said "second fiddle." Sady retired from playing that year.

The next session in New Orleans was with another friend of Dennis who played house dances, Angelas Lejeune. They had even been known to play at dances in China, Texas, an all-night ride from Eunice. Angelas entered a three-day accordion contest in Opelousas in late September 1929, in which a part of the judging involved the playing of street dances. Accompanied by Dennis and second fiddler Ernest Frugé, Angelas won first place. He was approached about recording in New Orleans, and the trio joined Opelousas native Abe Boudreaux for the trip. On September 30, 1929, this trio recorded six sides for the Brunswick label. Dennis, using Ernest on second fiddle, returned to the

Dennis McGee. Festival Acadiens, Lafayette, 1980. Photo courtesy of Calvin Ardoin.

studio on October 2, 1929, and recorded eight more sides for Vocalion. To add to this exhausting schedule of traveling and recording, McGee returned one more time in the early part of December with accordionist Amédé Ardoin. They recorded six sides for Columbia on December 9, 1929.

In mid-November 1930, the duo of McGee and Frugé returned to New Orleans to record ten more sides for Brunswick. The same trip yielded the second session with Ardoin for Brunswick; ten sides were recorded with Ardoin, but Frugé did not participate.

It would be 1934 before Ardoin and McGee would return to the studio. Traveling to San Antonio, they recorded six songs for Bluebird on August 8, 1934, and made their final recordings on December 22 of that year. This final duo session was again held in New Orleans and yielded twelve cuts for the Decca label.

This collection of recordings is invaluable to scholars and students of early Cajun music. They contain a wealth of stylistic information and are probably the earliest link to Cajun music as it was in the 1800s. The recordings with Frugé contain vocals by Dennis and two by announcer/caller Walter Coquille. Dennis's vocals also give an insight into the vocal style of the period.

Billy McGee. Photo by author.

McGee's recording career was over until the 1970s, but he continued to play dances throughout an area spanning from Lake Charles into Texas. Many times he was gone for weeks, causing hardships for his family. In the late 1940s he made an attempt to move to Port Arthur, Texas, where work did not pan out, and after playing music there for a while, moved back to Eunice and worked as a farmer on Louis Savoy's farms.

Dennis quit playing in clubs and for dances around 1954 to devote more time to his family life. He did not play again in public until 1970.

Dennis's musical life can almost be divided into two separate careers. In the 1970s musicologists, music historians, scholars, and fiddlers realized that Dennis McGee was a unique musical figure. Much like fiddler Eck Robertson, Dennis was a living connection to fiddling and country music of the 1800s. Historians Richard Spottswood, Barry Ancelet, Gerard Dole, Marc and Ann Savoy, and Will Spires, to name a few, began to study and honor his place in Louisiana's rich musical history. He rejoined with his brother-in-law, Sady Courville, and several albums and numerous tapes of tunes and stories of the early years were released. Louisiana's rich Cajun musical history was coming alive. These old-timers began performing at festivals and venues throughout the nation. Young fiddlers like Michael Doucet, Al Berard, Faren Serrate, Dennis Stroughmatt, Tina Pilione, and David Greely, to name a few, studied the music of McGee and included his songs, licks, and style in their repertoires. The trend continues today: younger fiddlers attend workshops by Dennis's disciples, carrying the rich tradition of Dennis McGee's music to another generation of fiddlers. As long as there is Cajun music, the music will probably begin with a history of Dennis McGee. He is known as the "Dean of Cajun Music."

Interviews by Ron Yule: Billy McGee (7-13-2007 and 8-1-2007).

References

Ancelet, Barry, and Elemore Morgan Jr. *Cajun and Creole Music Makers.* University Press of Mississippi, Jackson, Mississippi, 1999.

Brasseaux, Ryan. *Bayou Boogie: The Americanization of Cajun Music.* Thesis, Louisiana State University, Baton Rouge, 2004.

Crowley Signal. "Angelas Lejeune Wins Accordion Contest." October 1, 1929.

Daigle, Brenda. "Acadian Fiddler Dennis McGee and Acadian Dances." *Accordions, Fiddles, Two Step, and Swing: A Cajun Reader.* Ryan A. Brasseaux and Kevin S. Fontenot, editors. Center for Louisiana Studies, Lafayette, 2006.

Daigle, Pierre. *Love, Tears, and Laughter: The Story of the Acadians.* Acadian Publishing, Church Point, Louisiana, 1972.

Ray, Gayleen. "Dennis McGee, Dean of Cajun Music." *Daily Reveille*, February 12, 1987.

Russell, Tony. *Country Music Records: A Discography, 1921–1942.* Oxford University Press, New York, 2004.

Savoy, Ann. *Cajun Music: A Reflection of a People.* Bluebird Press, Eunice, Louisiana, 1984.

———. Liner notes. *The Complete Early Recordings of Dennis McGee: 1929–1930.* Yazoo 2012, 1994.

Sweetman, Ron. "Recording Activity in New Orleans in the 1920s." www.bluesworld.com/NODiscog.html

THE LIFE AND TIMES OF DENNIS MCGEE

By Billy McGee

Editor's note: In 2002, Billy McGee, Dennis McGee's son, sat down and wrote the following account of his father from his and other family members' perspectives. He notes these accounts are as concise as possible and confined to the experiences of the immediate family members.

As a young boy growing up, it was indeed a curiosity touching the personal life of Dennis McGee regarding the fiddle. No fiddle player has ever expressed himself so thoroughly and so comprehensively as did Dennis when he played. His playing exemplified the past while living in the present and the present became the past while being articulated.

With unequaled vividness and unsurpassed emotional power, he played with a style that would enhance the passing of an era as well as the birth pangs of a new style that in some instances was an insult to his techniques—even though nostalgia is perhaps the dominant emotion in his playing, and much of the very best of it could be described as elegance in a mournful manner.

To his family, in his later years, he was an amiable person of a kindly disposition. To others he was "the man who never took his armor off," especially in his earlier years. Some people found him peevish (hard to please), self-righteous, and as he grew older and his health deteriorated, perhaps a little vindictive, even though he was knocking on a century. Though Dennis had a difficult life, no one questioned his integrity. It was set at the highest-toned trust. He was the most noble man I have ever known. I say this with the utmost respect—only because I think I knew my dad better than anyone.

His life's work includes some fifty-three recordings he was involved in as far as we know. He had a reputation for modesty, yet his complex character would shed a field of colors everywhere. It is well documented that he was not a good Dad: at times early on he loved to play cards, and at the same time didn't provide for his family at the early stages of his life. Throughout his career he was very unpredictable. He did not have the start of a typical boy. He had no education—was bounced from family to family for several years, was abused physically and mentally. It is a wonder he grew up not knowing which way to turn. Yet his success came while excelling in a second career after years in the first, a career that was extremely supportive of the latter. He and Mom were living by their wits and nearly starving in the process because of his changing of jobs so often at first.

It seems as though during his late life he would dedicate himself to making the promise of opportunity with his unique style of playing through his own desires and will. As a fiddle player, his success was not only a result of his talents, but a determination to succeed with an abundance of hard work. I believe that this was an absolute tribute to his success as he perceived these opportunities early, and he capitalized upon them brilliantly.

Dennis was charming with both small and large groups. In major appearances, he seemed a bit cranky because of his independence, and at times dull because of his imperfect oratory. Nevertheless, he contributed substantially throughout most of his life to keep the vibrancy of his music alive.

I cannot think of any other fiddle player who was a match during his time, taking and making his superb talent into a major reputation. His fans were from all over the state of Louisiana, the United States, and abroad. One Saturday morning at Marc Savoy's, I was introduced to a fan of his and he was from Australia.

In his methods of composing a song, he once told me many years ago, the melody should be satisfactory to me. Sometimes he would make changes, but fundamentally it would remain the same. He would concentrate his methods to grow in a natural way and try to remain in that one direction. He would permit the material to develop by itself in a clear form, and quite often in a most unusual way as one could tell by his techniques. He seemed very intense to me when he sat down to play one of his songs. This preoccupation was also reflected in his composition, which became in a way, natural.

At the early age of seventeen he was playing well enough to play dances in and around the neighborhoods. The local fiddle players adopted him as one of their own. Some of the songs he developed were taken by other musicians, named different and he didn't get the credit he deserved.

He liked to think that his music was as "melodious as the birds singing," he once said in his broken English. Some of his songs to me were sort of witty even though there was some technical quality to them. I can't ever think of one time in his life that he gave a recital. He knew absolutely nothing of atonal music, yet he could tell you how many notes a fiddle (violin) had.

For years, many fiddle players believed that Dennis was not a very good fiddle player. One such fiddle player once said, "Dennis makes good notes, but he can't play." Others have said other things like, "He can't even tune a fiddle," but yet, his seven tuning methods to play different songs was one of his trademarks besides his exceptional low stroking, which has never been attempted except by me. Many fiddlers studied the unique tuning methods he so expressly used. The more his music grew, the more people appreciated it and the more they loved him and his music.

Slowly, gradually, his music won the respect and the tribute of young and old and yes, some of the same ones who criticized him. It took years for him to be accepted, though even up to the time of his death, he enjoyed that frequency of performing that a fiddle player of his formidable stature so richly deserved. As his style became more and more inclusive and compressed, his music gained in intensity and acidity and was found by some of his peers too severe, too complex.

Probably the two most influential people in his life would be, to my better judgment, his father and the people who took him at about 13–14 years of age. His enthusiasm was easily fired when an uncle he was living with in Ville Platte purchased and gave him a fiddle at the age of 15. The reason why I say his Dad was influential is because when he was a little boy his father, John McGee, would play and Daddy would tap his feet on the floor. He loved to hear his Dad play "La Valse a Pop," and it's certain from his memories, he never forgot it. It became one of his favorite songs. In 1951–1952, Grandpa John was on his deathbed in Palmetto, Louisiana, and sent word to Dad to come and to bring his fiddle. We recall later that grandpa asked Daddy to play "La Valse a Pop"; Daddy had to stop playing because the two of them began crying. It was just a short time after that Grandpa John McGee passed away. Papa was in his later 50s then —we were too young to understand anything about emotions or feelings. A son who was abandoned by his father at the age of just two years old might have. Even after Grandpa's second marriage, we're not certain how long Papa stayed with his father and stepmother. Nevertheless, Papa had some treasured memories of his past with his father only because he would talk about them. I can only remember a few things about Grandpa John. He was a rough, crude individual who didn't care too much about being pestered by us young-ins. When he would come and visit us on Cane Street (in Eunice), he would stay a few days and then leave—he was never too much for words. There is one real item that sticks in my memory of my Grandfather—he was constantly cutting on his nails with a pocketknife.

Dennis was probably one of the most, if not the most famous fiddle players of our time and has become legendary. His biography reveals the main facets and all the possible phases you could imagine. He was absolutely a man of many roles, moods, and ideas as far as his music was concerned, and yet an inspiration to many people in regards to his unique style of playing. His continued inventiveness and creativity are seen in the words and music of his songs, but his music reflected a style not copied by any one fiddler.

He seemed, I imagine as a young boy, to instinctively know or deftly seek out a song's needs. Even though he could not supply it right then and there, he would make a mental note of it, he once told me.

Over the years, Dennis gained much acclaim and received many honors. He was one of the pioneers among Cajun fiddlers. He was also one of the first to make recordings of Cajun music, and he has traveled all over America giving concerts and talking about the Cajun music he played. There's a 1981 Humanitarian of the Year Award on his wall at home from the Eunice Lions Club. Two years later, he received a special award for providing "pure Cajun music" to the generations with him and those to come. The University of Southwestern Louisiana took note of his contribution to Cajun music in 1982 when they named him the "Dean of Cajun Music" at Festival Acadiens. He appeared on several tour shows with Kris Kristofferson as well.

Born around the small farming community of Chataignier, he has been playing the fiddle for over 75 years in the traditional Cajun form—simply because he loves it.

At the age of 93, Dennis was one of the last of the old timers of pure Cajun music. Before him, there were others. But afterwards, there are but a few who may be able to play the fiddle quite as he does, tap his feet, and sing from the heart—pure Cajun music of love and trials and triumphs of a people exiled.

He was considered as one of the last living links to the culture's musical past.

Photo courtesy of Chuck Nation.

CHARLES "CHUCK" NATION

(1953–) Denham Springs

Charles "Chuck" Nation was born in 1953 in Chickamauga, Georgia, and lived in the hills of northern Georgia until his teens, when the family moved to Louisiana. Following in the footsteps of his father, Jim, he was a natural musician who took to all the instruments in a bluegrass setting with great ease.

Although he played all the bluegrass instruments, Jim had specialized in banjo with a north Georgia group, the Deep River Boys. Chuck heard bluegrass music from the time he was a toddler and learned to play guitar, fiddle, banjo, and mandolin. He notes, "I'd been listening to it all my life so I knew what to do."

By the age of nine he began playing guitar, his favorite instrument, backing his father at gatherings, contests, and shows. He notes:

> *My dad taught me my first guitar chords. I remember some mornings, as he was getting ready for work, he shaved and whistled "When You and I Were Young Maggie" while I practiced rhythm on an old guitar. I accompanied his banjo playing so often that I soon memorized the basics of banjo and just picked it up and started playing it, once I could get my hands on one.*

Chuck especially enjoyed playing rhythm guitar to the fiddle tunes Jim and a fellow Georgia fiddler, Wally Bryson, would play at these events. Besides his father, Chuck credits Wally as a major influence on his fiddling in the early years. Wally had been a consistent winner at regional fiddle contests and was a past Georgia state fiddle champion.

In 1968 the Nations moved to Denham Springs, and Chuck became in demand as a bluegrass sideman. He began playing with Luke Thompson and the Green Valley Cut Ups, playing with legendary banjo player Allen Shelton. With Luke and other local Florida Parish musicians, he picked on radio, television, and at festivals at the Old South Jamboree and Folsom. He was already listening to the sounds of "Bluegrass Boy" Kenny Baker, but another former "Bluegrass Boy," Byron Berline was stationed at Fort Polk. Since Byron traveled throughout the state playing with the Southern Bluegrass Boys, Chuck was exposed to his inimitable style during this period.

By 1972 Chuck had played with most of the bluegrass pickers in the area and was improving his skills on fiddle, picking up fiddle licks from another transplanted fiddler, Kennie Lamb. He credits Kennie with showing him how to "pull the tone out of his fiddle."

On his many travels with the Green Valley Cut Ups, he landed in Bean Blossom, Indiana, at Bill Monroe's 1972 festival. He met and picked with the Bluegrass Alliance, a Kentucky-based band. They asked him to go on the road with them, and for the next two years he toured with them, playing guitar and singing. Chuck states that he has played at nearly every major bluegrass festival in the United States and was offered the opportunity to play with every bluegrass picker that was playing at the time. His fiddling skills were further honed from listening to the many great fiddlers at the festivals and jam sessions. He recalls playing with Tony Rice, Sam Bush, and others around the eastern Kentucky area where he was living.

After two years on the bluegrass circuit, a friend who had converted to Christianity ministered to him, and had a major effect on the way Chuck looked at life. He soon decided to leave the road, attend Bible college, and study for the ministry.

Green Valley Cut Ups, 1968: Chuck Nation, Luke Thompson, and Allen Shelton. Photo courtesy of Luke Thompson.

The latter part of the 1970s was spent studying for his bachelor's degree at Tennessee Temple University in Chattanooga, Tennessee. His earnings at the weekend contests so popular in the 1970s in the mid-South area gave him the money to get through college. He traveled to every contest within reason and entered fiddle, guitar, mandolin, and banjo contests, hoping to win enough living-expenses money to continue his studies.

In 1978 Chuck returned to Louisiana a Baptist minister; he continued to play, but on a more limited basis. He joined Kennie Lamb in Virginia Pride, continued to play in his father's group, the Deep River Boys, and picked with others as time permitted from his ministerial duties. He stayed in Louisiana until 1985 and recalls playing over the years with other Louisiana-based pickers like Johnny and Jim Rushing and Dennie Blount. He joined numerous pickers to play at the 1984 World's Fair, even playing some Cajun music. He says he enjoyed all the musicians and his tour at the fair, especially the diversity of the music played.

In 1984 Louisiana moved its state fiddle championship from the Old Barn in Boyce to Rebel State Park in Marthaville. Chuck won the inaugural Marthaville event, defeating fiddlers Waylon Thibodeaux, Bill Kirkpatrick, and

Deep River Boys: Chuck Nation, Jim Nation, Gordon Jones, Glen Carter, and Steve Stewart. New Orleans World's Fair, 1984. Photo courtesy of Chuck Nation.

former and future state champions Fred Beavers, Curry Perkins, John Johnson, Mary Grimsley, Tex Grimsley, and Ron Yule. His playing was so impressive that Curry Perkins still recalls the tunes he played in the finals: "Cotton Patch Rag" and "Yellow Rose Waltz."

In 1985 Chuck and his family moved to Georgia, where he began ministering in a Baptist church. Although on a limited basis, Chuck continued playing and began to incorporate his family into his music on some occasions. He and his wife, Susan, still sing duets in church. Their children play music but have opted to play other styles than bluegrass.

Chuck readily admits that his favorite instrument is guitar, but he has excelled on all the instruments of the bluegrass band. Chuck cites Jim Nation, Allen Shelton, Gary Davis, Garland Shuping, Jim Smoak, Barry Palmer, and Charles Wood as influences on his banjo playing. Sam Bush is his favorite mandolin player and he enjoys the playing of all the major flatpickers in bluegrass circles: Don Reno, Doc Watson, Dan Crary, and Tony Rice.

In 2006 Chuck completed his first solo CD, *One Man Band*, on which he plays all the instruments including guitar, bass, banjo, mandolin, and fiddle. It showcases his very unique talent. The CD as well as other productions are available from him at www.chucknation.net.

Although fiddle is not his major instrument, his impact on fiddling in Louisiana during his relatively short eighteen-year stay was monumental. Pickers and fans alike still remember his presence with the fiddle and recall his wonderful touch and versatility.

Interviews by Ron Yule: Chuck Nation (10-5-2006 and 7-16-2007).

References

Forrester, H. H. Jr. *Bluegrass Music and Feliciana Grass.* Unpublished work in possession of Jim Rushing, 1988.

Nation, Chuck. Liner notes. *One Man Band.* Murrayville, Georgia, 2006.

Seelinger, Terry A. *Folklife in the Florida Parishes: Don't Give Up Your Day Job: Country Music.* Louisiana Division of the Arts, 1989.

Thompson, Luke. *50 Years of Bluegrass Music with Luke Thompson and the Green Valley Cutups.* CD, Baton Rouge, Louisiana, 2004.

Photo courtesy of Patterson Family.

SANFORD REAMEY PATTERSON

(1881–1939) Shreveport

Reamey, as Sanford Patterson was known, was one of the premier fiddlers in Shreveport in the early part of the century. He was born on October 3, 1880, and became an awesome musical talent, having been trained in classical violin technique as a youth. He moved to Shreveport from Malvern, Arkansas, and played in local orchestras. During the silent movie era, he played in movie houses, playing the background music for the picture show. He once related to Murray Richardson that he memorized as much as forty sheets of music so he could play and watch the movie at the same time. His wife, Clara, often accompanied him on the piano.

The *Shreveport Journal* notes, "Mr. Patterson has been playing the fiddle all his life and delights in the old time tunes." Being a former concert violinist, he played with superb intonation and a beautiful tone. The *Shreveport Times*, October 26, 1934, describes his playing after he won the 1934 contest:

"By laying down a barrage of high notes, trills, and fast runs, S. R. Patterson, . . . emerged victorious at the Louisiana State Fair grounds Thursday afternoon."

According to Murray, he used his expertise on the violin to play harmony to other fiddlers. The usual method of playing duets on country fiddle tunes at the time was to play rhythmic bowings and chords on the second fiddle while the first fiddle played the melody. He played harmony on the fiddle like modern fiddlers do when they twin fiddle. Murray notes, "He knew what notes would go with each tune."

Recalling conversations with Mr. Patterson, Murray said, "He played anything because he had the music. He didn't use the music to play it [the old-time tunes], he memorized everything . . . he told me that he used the old-time tunes for bowing exercises. . . . If he had to switch he'd rather switch to a different violin than to switch his bow . . . the bow weighed exactly right and he was used to it. He could always play better as long as he had the same bow." Reamey told Murray, "Sheet music is just the basic recipe. You take the basic recipe and season it to your own taste to play." Murray adds, "He'd throw in grace notes and slurs, whatever."

He was a member of the famous Old Fiddlers Club of North Louisiana that performed on radios station WGAQ, KWKH, KRMD, and KTBS in the 1920s and 1930s. As a member of the club, he attended jam sessions at the home of Dr. J. E. Richardson, played concerts with the group, and played for square dances in the area.

Reamey started entering the Louisiana State Fair Fiddle Contest in 1927, when he was nearing the age of fifty. Over the next eight years he won eight ribbons, including seven first-place prizes. In 1928 he teamed with Bill Richardson and won the doubles. Two years later he again won the doubles competition teamed with the famous John W. Daniel. He won first place in the contest in 1927, 1928, 1930, 1934, and 1937. He was such a crackerjack fiddler that he dropped out and judged on several occasions, to give someone else a chance to win. Murray noted that he was such an awesome fiddler that no one wanted to compete against him. This was especially true in the doubles competitions. He could do things other fiddlers could not do. His reputation was such that Murray recalls hearing fiddlers comment, "If we'd known that fella's goin' to be here we wouldn't have come."

Of his three children, two were gunsmiths. When Reamey began to lose his hearing later in life, he turned from playing and teaching the violin for his livelihood, and began to work as a locksmith and gunsmith with his son J. W.

"Pat" Patterson. His son's shop, City Cycle and Gun Shop, was on Barksdale Avenue in Bossier City. Murray did not remember whether he had acquired his locksmithing skill early in life or whether he was trained by his son. Another son, Rex, also was a gunsmith.

Some of the tunes he played included "Leatherbritches," "Rochester Hornpipe," "Turkey in the Straw," "Fisher's Hornpipe," and "Eighth of January." Murray notes he could play them all.

Reamey passed away on October 13, 1939.

Interviews: Nicole Matthews (3-2-2005), Steve Patterson (8-4-2008), and Murray Richardson (9-4-2004, 9-8-2004, and 3-3-2005).

References

City Directory, Shreveport, Louisiana. Selected years. R. L. Polk and Co., Dallas, Texas.

Haynesville News. "Old Fiddler's Contest Attracts Interest Here Last Thurs." November 28, 1928.

Shreveport Journal. "Patterson Wins '27 Old Fiddlers Contest at Fair." November 4, 1927.

———. "Heavy Rain Fails to Dampen Ardor of Fiddlers Entered in State Fair Contest Thursday." November 2, 1928.

———. "Fiddlers' Contest Winners." November 2, 1928.

———. "Two Shreveport Fiddlers Win at La. Fair Contest." November 8, 1929.

———. "Local Man Wins In Old Fiddlers' Contest at Fair." October 31, 1930.

———. "Winners in Old Fiddlers Contest." October 25, 1934.

———. "S. R. Patterson is Winner of Old Fiddler's Meet." October 25, 1934.

———. "Tom Sawyer Wins Fiddlers' Contest at Fair Thursday." October 25, 1935.

———. "Old Fiddlers Claim Spotlight at Fair." October 29, 1936.

———. "One-Armed Fiddler Wins Contest at Louisiana Fair." October 30, 1936.

———. "Winners of Fiddle Contests." October 31, 1936.

———. "S. R. Patterson of Shreveport Winner of Fiddling Honor." October 29, 1937.

———. "Winners in Fiddle Contest at State Fair." October 28, 1938.

Shreveport Times. "Shreveport Old Fiddlers Winners in Two Classes in Annual Contest at State Fair Grounds on Thursday." November 8, 1929.

———. "Old Fiddlers Contest at Fair Has 35 Entries." October 29, 1930.

———. "S. R. Patterson, H. C. Wilkerson, Best Fiddlers." October 26, 1934.

———. "Champion Fiddlers' in Contest Thursday / Tom Sawyer Best Fiddler at Fair Here." October 25, 1935.

———. "Fiddlers Have Their Day at State's Fair." October 29, 1937.

———. "Old Fiddlers Have Their Day at State Fair / Gibsland Man Best Fiddler." October 28, 1938.

Wendland, Barbara. E-mail dated 8-18-2008.

Yule, Ron. *When the Fiddle Was King*. Fiddle Country Publishing, DeRidder, Louisiana, 2006.

Photo courtesy of Brenda Perkins.

CURRY PERKINS

(1970–) Reeves

If you travel down the Bel Fire Tower Road between Ragley and Reeves, make the turn on Burnett Road, trek through the swamp, and pass a few sheep, you will probably begin to hear the sound of a fiddle echoing off the pine trees. You may think you are in Ireland or Texas or Kentucky, but you are not. You are hearing the strains of Curry Perkins's fiddle, and he can do it all. And if you drive a little farther you will probably catch him sitting on a stump or on the porch of Dempsey's old-time workshop, learning a new tune. To be around the homestead is a return to the days of "good ole country." You will think, it can't get any better than this. Dempsey and Brenda, Curry's parents, have both been inducted into the Northwestern University Hall of Master Folk Artists; Brenda for her wool felting and weaving, and Dempsey for his white oak basket making and wood turning. This is the environment in which Curry

Curry Perkins and John Leblanc in Dempsey Perkins's shop. Photo courtesy of Brenda Perkins.

learned to fiddle: the country way. Life at the Perkins farm continues as usual even though Dempsey passed away in 2005.

Curry's interest in fiddling stems from listening to an eight-track tape of Scotty Stoneman while riding in the family car. He remembers being captivated by the sound of the instrument even at a young age. No fiddle teachers were available, so his original lessons were from Gerald Zamost, a violinist who was living on Bundicks Lake. Later he began to take lessons from Ken Smith, the legendary Texas-style contest fiddler, who lived nearby in Kinder. Ken's influence led him to love Texas fiddling and the sounds of Benny Thomasson, Lewis and Major Franklin, Orville Burns, and Vernon and Norman Solomon. He stated, "I wore out all the Texas fiddle records moving the needle back and forth." Brenda once said, "He would stay in his room for hours. All we ever heard around here was Benny Thomasson."

By 1985 he had become a formidable foe at local contests and began to attend events around and beyond Louisiana. Curry began playing all over the country, attending contests and jamming with some of the great swing and contest fiddlers of our time, such as the Solomons, Franklins, Morrises, Hartz, Hopkins, and Westmorelands. By 1988 Curry was the Junior Louisiana State Champion and well on his way to being a fiddler to be reckoned with. He

Curry and Brittany Perkins on Perkins front porch, Reeves, July 2007. Photo by author.

won the Louisiana State Championship three times (1989, 1992, and 1999). In 1999, he also won second at the World's Championship in Crockett, Texas; the Grand Masters in Nashville; and the SPGMA Bluegrass Championship at Mountain View. He has won countless contests all over the country.

In the mid-1990s, he turned his focus from contests to Irish, Scottish, and Cape Breton fiddling, studying the music of Kevin Burke, Sean McGuire, Alasdaer Fraser, and Jerry Holland. He played and learned the Irish style with the same fervor as he learned Texas style. His Irish studies have added a new set of tunes to his already vast repertoire of Texas and old-time music. He now has command of hundreds of airs, hornpipes, jigs, polkas, slides, and reels. He attended Scottish and Irish festivals when he could and offered lessons to students in both Irish and Texas styles of fiddling when time permitted.

The past few years have been devoted to playing old-time music and studying everyone from Rayna and Dan Gellert to Doc Roberts. For a while, he performed and jammed with local old-time fiddler and guitarist, Jim Spitzkeit. They appeared at the Folklife Festival in Natchitoches on two occasions. Their show was one of diversity, trading instruments, playing Irish and old-time fiddle tunes, and twin fiddling. Curry not only learned fiddle but also loved the music so much he learned all the backup instruments so he could enjoy the whole spectrum of sounds. He plays clawhammer banjo, thirty-button accordion, guitar, tenor guitar, bouzouki, pennywhistle, bodhran, mandolin, and would just love to get his hands on a set of uilleann pipes.

He has recorded two tapes and has a CD project in the mill.

Although the toils of country life have overshadowed his fiddling performance in the last few years, he continues to pick with friends when he can. Much of his time is now spent teaching the instruments of old-time music to his children, both of whom have shown a major interest in the musical heritage of their father. Daughter Brittany has begun learning mountain dulcimer, joining in duets playing at home. In April 2007 she won third place at the Rebel State Historic Site Museum mountain dulcimer contest. In July 2008 she performed with her father at the NSU/Natchitoches Folklife Festival.

Current projects include studies with Ron Yule on the fiddlers of the Louisiana Pineywoods, who provided the basis for their fiddling today. He continues to informally jam with Yule, Clifford and Sue Blackmon, Emily Young, and David Sonnier when he can. In the summer of 2008 he was inducted into the Hall of Master Folk Artists at the NSU/Natchitoches Folk Festival. Curry has come full circle, and is back in the country doing what he does best, being a country boy fiddler.

Interviews by Ron Yule: Curry Perkins (3-3-2003 and 6-7-2007).

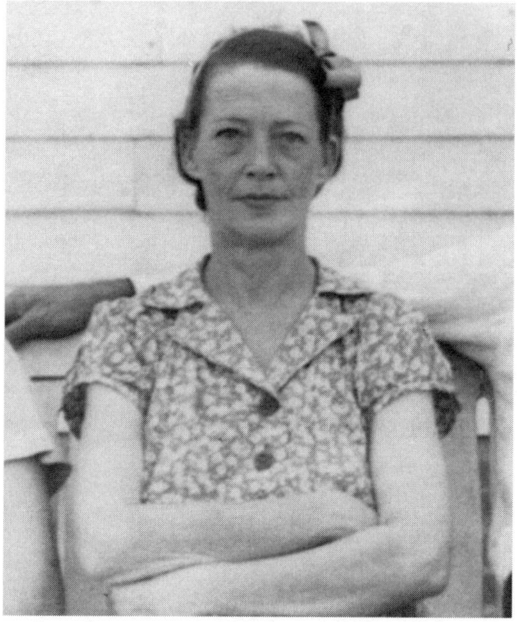

Photo courtesy of Thomas Philyaw Collection/Ron Yule.

FLEECY CASTON PHILYAW

(1898–1976) Red Oak

Fleecy Caston Philyaw was the premier lady fiddler on the north Louisiana fiddle scene in the early 1900s. Born on December 10, 1898, in Red Oak, a few miles north of Coushatta, she was taught by her father, W. E. Caston, who was a champion fiddler. From being around her father and other great northwest Louisiana fiddlers, she learned the sound and technique it takes to be an award-winning fiddler herself—during an era that did not solicit or cater to women fiddlers.

Her son, Tom, describes her unusual style of playing the fiddle. He writes in a letter, "Her unusual method of playing was to sit the fiddle in her lap in an upright position and drag the bow across the strings horizontally. This habit was formed early in life because she was too small to hold the fiddle under her chin when her father was teaching her to play. Someone once told me she was three years old when he began to teach her." Murray Richardson recalls her playing the fiddle much in the manner of playing the cello with the fiddle propped on her knee. She never changed her way of playing. Murray Richardson recalls, "She was a crackerjack fiddler." Bill Kirkpatrick notes, "I'll tell you what. She'd beat them [the men] up. Most of the fiddlers around here couldn't stay with her." He also recalls that her fiddle had such a good sound that she was offered a thousand dollars for it several times.

After a move to Shreveport in the 1920s to work, she began playing with the Old Fiddlers Club of North Louisiana, probably introduced to them by her father, who had been playing in Shreveport since the early part of the century. She was known to play with them on KWKH and KRMD and at fiddle sessions at the Majestic Building in downtown Shreveport. She played at square dances and barn dances with them as late as 1947. She played all the reels and waltzes and is remembered playing "Chicken Reel," "Grey Eagle," "Sweet Georgia Brown," and "Tennessee Waltz." Bill Kirkpatrick also recalls that she especially loved swing music. He said her "Grey Eagle" was second to none.

Fleecy married Thomas Philyaw, a local guitar and piano player, in the 1920s; they began playing together at country dances and jam sessions around Shreveport and as far north as Haynesville. Tom does not recall whether they played together before that, but suspects they may have met at one of these gatherings. They played with an unnamed bass fiddler who had polydactyly: Thomas remembers he had "six fingers on each hand and a three-quarters-inch callous on his picking finger." She also played with Gene Austin, the popular singer of "My Blue Heaven," when he was in the area.

Like her father before her, Fleecy was an award-winning contest fiddler. She entered many contests in the twenties, thirties, and forties. The results for a few were recorded in the media. In November 1928, only weeks after her father's death, she won second in the Four State Fiddle Contest in Haynesville, finishing behind noted fiddler Reamey Patterson. Mrs. Philyaw entered the 1941 Louisiana State Fair Contest, the first woman to participate since its origin in 1912. Previous attempts by Mrs. L. E. Mattern, in 1912 and 1913, had led to a boycott by the old fiddlers. Fleecy won second in 1941 and first in 1942 in the young division. In November 1948 she won first at the Claiborne Parish Fair.

During World War II, while working in a window factory, she cut off the little finger of her left hand with a saw. Undaunted, she continued her fiddling, teaching, and playing throughout northwestern Louisiana.

Fleecy never played music on a continual basis for a living; she was known to work as an usher at the Majestic Theatre in downtown Shreveport, and at various hotels as an elevator operator. She lived for a while in the Homer/Haynesville area and was a neighbor of Bill Kirkpatrick, who notes that several of the Caston clan lived there.

Fleecy taught fiddle and guitar to numerous people around Shreveport, teaching "upscale chords" to country musicians. Her son remembers one musician was Mel Tillis, who came to jam sessions at their home. Also during the mid-to-late 1940s, she played a stint with Jimmie Davis and his band. Playing with numerous Shreveport musicians, she played on local radio and shows. She was known to play with many of the musicians who played on the Saturday Night Roundup and the Louisiana Hayride, although she was never known to play on the Hayride.

Early on, she had a reputation as a fiddler and guitarist. She played guitar in a swing style and jammed with local groups at her home off Sheridan Street in Shreveport with Bill Kirkpatrick, Dr. J. E. Richardson, H. C. Wilkerson, Bill Harper, and Willie Gough. She played in many of the local clubs and was known to play with Slim Whitman, Gene Austin, and Bob and Joe Shelton and the Sunshine Boys. Bill Kirkpatrick notes that Whitman wanted her to travel and play with him but she turned him down.

In the early 1950s she retired from professional fiddling and moved to Florida, to live with her son until her death in 1976.

Interviews by Ron Yule: Bill Kirkpatrick (10-8-2006), Thomas Philyaw (4-17-2004), and Murray Richardson (3-3-2005).

References

Haynesville News. "Old Fiddler's Contest Attracts Interest Here Last Thurs." November 28, 1928.

———. "Winners at the Claiborne Parish Fair." September 20, 1948.

Philyaw, Thomas Jr. Letter accompanying photographs of Caston family fiddlers, April 25, 2004.

Shreveport Journal. "Champion Old Fiddlers at State Fair." October 24, 1941.

———. "Old Fiddlers Hold Contest." October 29, 1942.

Shreveport Times. "Tender Melodies from Fiddle Bows." November 5, 1912.

———. "Old Fiddlers Have Good Time." November 10, 1914.

———. "Shreveport Fiddlers Win Fair Events." October 30, 1942.

Smith, Christine. "Fiddlin' Champ." *Shreveport Times*, July 20, 1979.

Southwest Louisiana Fiddlers and Bluegrass Club Newsletters. Ron and Georgia Yule, editors. DeRidder, Louisiana, 1974–76.

Wilson, J. L. "She's Fit to Fiddle." *Shreveport Times*, December 7, 1975.

Yule, Ron. *When the Fiddle Was King*. Fiddle Country Publishing, DeRidder, Louisiana, 2006.

Photo courtesy of Mary Evans.

EDDIE RAXSDALE

(1922–1992) Alexandria
by Mary Raxsdale Evans

Editor's Note: This article was written by Mary Evans, Eddie's daughter. When I told her I wanted to interview her, she said she would make a few notes. I decided to use her notes as she wrote them.

Eddie Raxsdale was born on November 13, 1922, in Turkey Creek, to the union of George Albert Raxsdale, who I am told was a fine fiddler, and Caroline Corrine Elizabeth O'Neal, who played the accordion. His father was killed in a hunting accident when Eddie was only six weeks old. He went to live with his father's two brothers and one sister, all of whom never married and were "educated musicians," as Daddy would say when referring to them.

Living with his uncles and aunt and their music ability sparked a drive in Eddie at an early age to also play an instrument, and to no one's surprise he

Mary Evans, Eddie Raxsdale, and Albert Carnahan. Sweetheart Banquet at Homewood Baptist Church, Alexandria, early 1980s. Photo courtesy of Mary Evans.

chose the violin, which later, after much heated discussion, became the fiddle. The elder of his uncles, Uncle Ed, was a violinist and played cornet. He played in the orchestras on the big riverboats. Uncle Sid played upright bass and piano, and Aunt Mary was an accomplished pianist.

Uncle Ed always kept his violin on top of the upright piano and no one was to touch it, especially a seven-year-old boy. When Uncle Ed would go to work, daddy would take it out of the case, and taught himself to play "Twinkle, Twinkle Little Star" with one finger. "Boy it sounded horrible, but I really thought I was doing something," he would say. One day, when Daddy least expected anyone to walk in on him, Uncle Ed appeared in the door. "I don't know how long he had been standing there," he said, "but I quickly realized that he had been there long enough to hear the mess I was making." He turned to face his uncle, expecting to get a tongue lashing, when he saw a little smile come on Uncle Ed's face, and he asked him "Do you want to learn to play the violin?" "Yes sir, I do," Daddy answered. "Well then, I think we better go down and get one that fits you, and get you started with some lessons."

You wouldn't have known it if you knew my dad, but he was raised with a silver spoon in his mouth, and came from the then-called "upper crust" of Alexandria. To have wanted to change from violin to fiddle was a disgrace to the family, especially his aunt, but the story continues. In those days, on Saturday nights he would turn on the old battery-operated radio and try to tune in to the Grand Ole Opry, on WSM. Aunt Mary would make him pull down the blinds and windows in the house, so the neighbors would not hear what he was listening to. "What she didn't know," Daddy said, "the neighbors were listening to the same thing, and didn't want her to know." It was on one of these Saturday nights that Daddy heard the Crook Brothers on the radio, and at that time he knew what he wanted to do. He wanted to play the fiddle, not the violin. I believe, even though Daddy was too small to really know his father, his father's mannerisms may have kicked in, because if you remember, his father, too, played the fiddle, not the violin.

An elderly man who lived in the neighborhood had some records of old-time fiddlers, and Daddy would go down and listen to those early recordings and play along with them. His uncles would take him to the fair to listen to the fiddling contest. He recalled, "We would stay for hours and listen to some of the finest fiddlers around. I would watch and listen, trying to pick up on some of their style and form."

Some of his earliest playing was at country dances at someone's house. Cake and coffee would be served for your pay. There may be three or four fiddlers there. "At that time none of us knew more that ten or fifteen tunes," Daddy would say, "So we each took a turn playing. When one would finish the other would start, and you would listen to them so you could learn other tunes."

As time went on, Daddy got where he was playing pretty good, and at one of these house playings, back in 1947, he luckily met two young boys from Forest Hill, Louisiana, Wiley and Guy Barkdull. Wiley and his family are still today some of my dearest friends. Guy went to be with the Lord in 1989, but he was a man that I greatly respected and loved dearly. From this friendship Eddie Raxsdale and the Melody Playboys were formed. From 1947 until 1951, they were on KVOB radio every Saturday morning for two shows, and played nearly all the country dances and stage shows in this area. They took a survey of the radio stations at that time and only the Alexandria Aces ballgame beat out the Playboys. During one of these Saturday morning shows, another friendship was formed, one that lasted until Daddy passed away in 1992.

One morning after the radio program was over, Daddy walked out of the program room and a man was standing there by the name of Sheb Wooley. He told daddy that he was in Alexandria promoting Calumet Baking Powder, and had turned the radio on in his motel room and heard their program. He had brought his band with him from Nashville, but was in need of a fiddle player while he was here and wanted to know if Daddy was interested in helping him out. Daddy agreed, and for three weeks, every night of the week, he played with Sheb Wooley and the Calumet Indians. When Sheb left this area, he was then going to Hollywood. "He was going to star in movies," as Daddy put it. He begged Daddy to go with him. "I know we can make it," he would say, but Daddy was afraid. He knew he had a wife and two little boys looking at him for support. "I was making a pretty good living here in Alexandria, and was afraid of losing what I had, so I turned him down. I thought, if I give up everything I have here and get out there and they don't like me, what am I going to do then? They may send me home with an egg sandwich and a one-way ticket. Sheb called me over an over after he got out there, but I still wouldn't go." He said that he often wondered what would have happened if he had moved his family out there. Sheb was right, they could have made it, because he did.

It was about this time Daddy felt that he was holding the boys back who played with him because they wanted more out of the music business than he did, so he dissolved the band. Ambrose Williamson who played with Daddy told me that for the longest time he wondered why Daddy quit playing when everything was going so well for him, but now he knows. "Eddie was a family man who never liked the bars or liquor." He said, "I know he quit to spend more time at home, because we were on the road a lot."

Around 1953, Jelly Elliott talked Daddy into playing again. He needed someone to play piano and hoedown fiddle for him. This is when Daddy met fiddle player Bobby Henderson, and a long friendship was once again established. Because of things that Daddy didn't really believe in, I don't think he stayed with Jelly too long, but his friendship with Bobby lasted. In 1983, while attending a ballgame in Gonzales, Louisiana, Daddy and Bobby got back together and played to the early morning hours. It was something they both enjoyed.

I think, after Daddy's short stay with Jelly, he thought he was going to get out of the music business, and did for many years. I was born in 1951, and it wasn't until around 1960 that I even knew my daddy played the fiddle. There was a piano in our home, and Daddy played it almost every night, when we as a family would gather round and sing those good old gospel hymns. It was a great surprise to me when one day, while digging through the closet, I came upon a fiddle. "Who does this belong to?" I asked my mother. "Your father," she replied. "Can he play this?" I asked. "Yes," she said. Because I loved music so much, I could hardly wait until Daddy came home to ask the most important question I would ever ask: "Can you really play this thing?" Well, as you guessed, the answer was yes. "Play it for me," I begged. I watched as he rosined up his bow and slowly pulled it across the strings, strings that were much in need of being replaced. It had been many years since he had played, but to me it was the most beautiful music I had ever heard. This closet digging brought country music back into our home.

It wasn't long before the Melody Playboys were back together, but only for home playings. The word quickly got around that Daddy was back playing, and Don Wiley called him about doing some television and stage shows with him. Daddy played with Don Wiley and the Catahoula Playboys for about two years.

In 1971, Troy DeRamus called Daddy and asked him if he would be interested in helping him get the Old Barn Dance started again. Because of the atmosphere, and no liquor being sold, Daddy agreed to play there. He played the first fiddle tune at the Old Barn, and when it closed in 1984, he played the last. I remember well the last song he played to close the Old Barn forever, "Sweet Bunch of Daises."

Daddy continued playing at a spot called Mountain View, Arkansas, and is remembered there today. He loved to go there. Two or three times a year he would walk over to my house and say, "Don't you think it's time we made a trip to Mountain View to fiddle on the square?" There were no electric instruments, and no drinking. They would start playing at 8:00 a.m., would stop only to eat and rest a little while, and then they were back at it. He recorded some with Ronnie Bryant, and played with Ronnie when he opened J.R.'s Nightclub, but that was very short-lived. He only agreed to play there for a dance contest.

Daddy passed away on June 28, 1992, from cancer. He played his last tune at Christmas when I asked him to try and play some carols on the fiddle. His arm was broken from the cancer and had a rod in it, but he was a trouper. He did the best he could for me. The last song I asked Daddy to play for me on Christmas Eve of 1991, was "The Story of the Fiddle," or as some other fiddlers may know it "The Joys of Quebec." I will treasure that night forever, and always know that I had the pleasure and honor of being able to tell anyone that Eddie Raxsdale was not just a great fiddler, he was the greatest Daddy a girl could ask for.

Mary Evans
March 7, 2005

Photo courtesy of Chris Strachwitz. Photo © Chris Strachwitz. Courtesy Arhoolie Records, El Cerrito, Ca.

WALLACE "CHEESE" READ

(1924–1981) Prairie Rhonde

Wallace "Cheese" Read was born on August 12, 1924, in Eunice, Louisiana. His ancestors were immigrants from France and Germany who settled in the Prairie Rhonde region north of Eunice. His father practiced medicine in the region and learned the Cajun French language from his association with the local people.

As a youngster Cheese tuned his ear to the music around him and began a journey to play the music he heard. One of his main influences was the musicians he heard at house dances he would attend with his father. Several included dances featuring black musicians like accordionist Adam Fontenot, Canray Fontenot's father.

In 1936 Cheese began learning the harmonica, but eventually turned to the fiddle, which would be his main instrument. By the age of fifteen he had

Cajun House Party LP/CD 414, 1979. Photo courtesy of Chris Strachwitz. Courtesy Arhoolie Records, El Cerrito, Ca.

formed a string band that included banjo, fiddle, and guitar, and was listening to the sounds of other great fiddlers, including Cajun musicians like Leo Soileau and J. B. Fuselier, as well as the country/Cajun sounds of Luderin Darbone's Hackberry Ramblers. Several other Cajun musicians who influenced him were the Robins, Mayeus Lafleur, Harry Choates, and the Breaux family.

He was also a fan of the music of Bob Wills and the Texas Playboys, and always played these tunes at jam sessions. One highlight for him occurred during his service in the military, when he played with some of Bob Wills's musicians while stationed in Amarillo, Texas.

Unlike many other fiddlers, Cheese did not continually play in the atmosphere of a dance hall, but opted for the more intimate setting of house parties, house dances, and jam sessions. He loved playing in these settings, and was an

Cheese Read and Ken Smith. Mamou fiddle contest, 1980. Courtesy of Calvin Ardoin.

entertainer even in a small jam session at someone's home, keeping the session going with a constant patter of fun and music. He especially became noted for this in the fifties, sixties, and seventies, when he played with musicians including Marc Savoy, Ken and Buford Smith, and Harry Lafleur, to name a few.

Cheese's claim to fame would probably come from these many house parties. Dr. Harry Oster, a folklorist at LSU, was documenting the folk tradition of the area in the late 1950s and taped numerous house parties. Several of Cheese's tunes appeared on Harry's LP *Folksongs of the Louisiana Acadians*. Well-known Arhoolie record producer Chris Strachwitz heard the tapes, sought out the talented Read, and recorded a complete LP featuring Marc Savoy and others on twelve cuts from Cheese's vast catalog of Cajun tunes. *Cajun House Party* gave the world access to the sounds of one of the prairie region's most respected fiddlers.

Read is featured on several other projects recording a couple of songs for La Louisianne Records. Currently, renditions of some of Cheese's performances recorded by Revon Reed in the early 1960s at the Mamou Social Club can be heard at the "Hadacol It Something" website, npmusic.org. Musicians include fiddlers Aubrey Deville, Chuck Guillory, and Cheese with guitarist Preston Manuel.

Cheese was one of the earlier musicians influenced by diverse styles of music whether it was the phonograph, jukebox, or personal appearances. Using the many fiddlers who influenced him as well as the vocals of Oliver Edwards, a singer and left-handed fiddler, Cheese took almost any kind of music he liked and brought it into his repertoire. Consequently, any jam session may include an array of styles where you may hear Bob Wills's "Faded Love" or "Maiden's Prayer," blues numbers like "Milk Cow Blues" or "St. Louis Blues," hoedowns like "Tennessee Wagoner" or "Ole Joe Clark," non-Cajun waltzes like "Wednesday Night Waltz" or "Over the Waves," as well as his vast cache of Cajun waltzes and two-steps. And, he sang them with the same enthusiasm he portrayed when he played them on fiddle.

Ken Smith recalls that Cheese's fiddle, a gift from his grandfather, was a copy of an Amati complete with a carved man's head that replaced the scroll. It was always a wonderful sight at any jam session or house party. With this amazing-sounding instrument, Cheese influenced the fiddling of many of the area's next generation of fiddlers. Anyone who came in contact with him appreciated his talent and learned something.

Interview: Ken Smith (4-28-2007) and Cheese Read from undated informal conversations at jam sessions in Kinder in the 1970s.

References

Doucet, Sharon Arms. "If You Remember My Song You'll Remember Me." *Fiddler Magazine* (Fall 1995).

Savoy, Ann. Liner notes. *Wallace "Cheese" Read: Cajun House Party*. Arhoolie LP 5021, 1979.

Strachwitz, Chris. Producer notes. *Wallace "Cheese" Read: Cajun House Party*. Arhoolie CD 414, 1994.

Photo courtesy of Richardson family.

DR. J. E. RICHARDSON

(1875–1963) Shreveport

Dr. Joseph Emmett Richardson was from Highland Home, Crenshaw County, Alabama, fifty miles south of Montgomery, and migrated to Shreveport around 1900. After graduating from high school he attended Highland Home College, where he obtained his Bachelor of Science degree. He then moved to Shreveport and joined the Draughon's Business College staff, where he taught mathematics, Greek, Latin, and penmanship. In 1911 he left Shreveport with his family, to attend Vanderbilt University Dental School in Nashville. He graduated in 1915 and returned to Shreveport, setting up a practice downtown at the Majestic Building (corner of Edwards and Milam). After a move to the Medical Arts Building in a few years, he practiced dentistry for forty-nine years until his retirement in 1964.

During his time in Shreveport, he was an advocate for better dental health. He was the first dentist to own a dental x-ray machine, was instrumental in the organization of the Dental Assistant's Society, and served as president of the Shreveport Dental Society.

He met his wife, Lydia, through his teaching and managing position at Draughon's College. Lydia moved from Centerville, Mississippi, to attend the school and after graduation became his secretary. They eventually married and had nine children: Rawlin, Bill, Irene, Allen, Phillip, Murray, Elbert, Elsie, and Ralph.

He was known as "the fiddling dentist" in and around Shreveport. His family believes he learned on his own, since they cannot recall any fiddlers in the family. He began playing musical instruments as a child and especially liked the violin. His son, Ralph, notes that his father played as a group with two of his sisters, Lois and Bertha, but cannot recall the instruments they played. In his early days in Shreveport, he played tuba in the Shreveport Philharmonic Orchestra and one other unnamed band. With his ability to read and write music, it is thought he had some type of formal training. Elbert relates he played many instruments and was "known to play any of them." They recall him playing fiddle, five-string banjo, mandolin, and guitar. Not only could he read and write music, he also played by ear. Lydia played violin in her youth, but did not play after the first part of their marriage.

Dr. Richardson was known to love fiddle music, or as Murray notes, "He was primarily interested in old-time fiddling." He loved it so much he kept an old fiddle (one of seventeen he owned) around his dental office so he could strike a tune when business was slow. Murray said he even had a five-string banjo standing beside his bed. He was an important figure in old-time music circles in northwest Louisiana, known in the community for bringing square dancing to Shreveport. He was a driving force in the continuance and organization of the Louisiana State Fair Fiddle Contest from 1925 to 1942, and the motivating force behind the Old Fiddlers Club of North Louisiana who sponsored the contest for those years. Besides square dances, he was instrumental in bringing old-time music to the public with radio programs on WGAQ, KWKH, KTBS, and KRMD during the twenties and thirties.

There were constant jam sessions at the Richardson home, sometimes on Wednesday and other times on the weekend. Local fiddlers from all around would attend, accompanied by guitar, banjo, mandolin, and bass fiddle. The music was mainly instrumental, featuring the fiddle playing hoedowns, hornpipes, waltzes, jigs, reels, and polkas. A few who attended off and on over the years include Baron Hollingsworth, H. C. Wilkerson, Bill Gough, John W. Daniel, S. R. Patterson, Reginald Ward, Bill Harper, I. B. Rambin, plus nearly

J. E. Richardson, 1904. Photo courtesy of Richardson family.

all of the fiddlers who lived around Shreveport. They also played at the exhibit building at the fairgrounds many times, and the public would come to watch and listen. In the mid-thirties the group began to perform concerts at schools like the elementary school on Claiborne Avenue. They played old-time music, put on skits and contests, and did comedy.

Elbert and Ralph recall that, in the twenties, thirties, and forties, their dad would go out with a group of musicians and play for square dances. Members of this band included Bill Harper (fiddle and guitar), Baron Hollingsworth (fiddle and guitar), Bill Gough (fiddle), Jack Burns (banjo), I. L. Rambin (fiddle), Bob Bains (guitar), and Dr. Richardson (five-string banjo and fiddle). Hoss Harper was the caller.

Two of Dr. Richardson's sons played fiddle, starting when they were teenagers. Bill took lessons from a local teacher, learned classical violin, and played both classical and old-time fiddle music. He entered the 1928 state fair contest and won first place in the younger division. On two occasions he teamed with S. R. Patterson and won the doubles competition. Murray notes, "Bill played

Dr. Richardson in his office in the Majestic Building, 1916. Photo courtesy of Richardson family.

the lead while Mr. Patterson played the harmony." After learning from Bill, Murray also took violin lessons, but played mainly country music instead of classical. He entered the state fair contest in 1937 and 1940, when he won second place. Murray recalls he had a small band, the Dixie Blueboys (not to be confused with Bill Nettles's band), that played at clubs, dancehalls, and a few house dances around nearby Shreveport in the late thirties. They also played a regular show on KRMD for a while. They played country dance tunes, waltzes, and a little swing. He played with an accordionist, Edwin Martin, who had played with his brothers at the Salvation Army, and another man who played violin. Murray played fiddle, French harp, mandolin, banjo, and guitar. He recalls several other instruments in the band including banjo and bass violin.

Dr. Richardson's influence on fiddling in prewar Shreveport was monumental. His comments in the *Journal* and *Times* indicate his love for fiddle music and his knowledge that this musical form was being cast aside for more modern forms of music. He struggled to keep fiddle contests going and to promote the music he enjoyed. An April 6, 1968, *Shreveport Journal* article expounds on Dr. Richardson's contributions to the old-time fiddling community in Northwest Louisiana:

> *Dr. J. E. Richardson, who practiced both as a dentist and an old-time fiddler for more than a half-century in Shreveport will celebrate his 91st birthday today. . . . The fiddle playing dentist was considered an authority on old-time breakdown or hoedown fiddle music and waltzes, schottisches, hornpipes, and polkas. Other fiddle*

players would go play with "Doc" when they wanted to learn an old tune the right way. He held many old-time fiddler championships in the area, but in later years, confined his playing to sessions at home with friends. His influence was far reaching.

In a letter to Lincoln Parish fiddler Seab Hood (July 24, 1936), Dr. Richardson requests that Seab and all the Hoods attend a fiddle contest to be held in Atlanta, Texas, in the latter part of July 1936. He continually promoted the art of fiddling by establishing clubs in various towns and parishes as well as contests throughout north Louisiana.

Dr. Richardson was an innovator, creating many new events and changes for the state fair contests including age divisions for younger contestants, the acceptance of women contestants, square-dancing competitions, judge authorization by the contestants, old-time dance demonstrations, instrument demonstrations, and hog- and chicken-calling competitions. He also judged at other contests like the Haynesville contest, in 1928, and was continually promoting fiddling and fiddle clubs in other towns. He was from a rural Alabama background and wanted to continue and preserve the country tradition.

He passed away in 1968.

Interviews by Ron Yule: Elsie Ferguson (9-3-2004 and 2-5-2005), Elbert Richardson (9-2-2004), Murray Richardson (9-3-2004 and 2-5-2005), and Ralph Richardson (9-3-2004).

References

City Directory. Shreveport, Louisiana. Selected years, R. L. Polk and Company, Dallas, Texas.

Haynesville News. "Old Fiddler's Contest attracts Interest Here Last Thurs." November 28, 1928.

Richardson, J. E. Letter to Seab Hood, Hilly, Louisiana, dated July 24, 1936. From the personal collection of Lillian Hood Fallin.

Shreveport Journal. "Thirty-Seven Old Fiddlers Enter Annual Contest at La. State Fair." November 4, 1925.

———. "37 Old Fiddlers Stage Fine Show at the 1926 Fair." November 5, 1926.

———. "Heavy Rain Fails to Dampen Ardor of Fiddlers Entered in State Fair Contest Thursday." November 2, 1928.

———. "Old Fiddlers at Fair Draw Large Crowd Thursday." November 7, 1929.

———. "Local Man Wins in Old Fiddlers' Contest at Fair." October 31, 1930.

———. "S. R. Patterson is Winner of Old Fiddler's Meet." October 25, 1934.

———. "Winners of Fiddle Contests." October 31, 1936.

———. "Winners in Fiddle Contest at State Fair." October 28, 1938.

———." Many Fiddlers Compete at Fair." October 24, 1940.

———. "C. J. Morris and C. B. Hood Chosen as Champion Fiddlers at Fair." October 25, 1940.

———. "Old Fiddlers Give Concert / Old Fiddlers Compete at Fair." October 23, 1941.
———. "Old Fiddlers Hold Contest." October 29, 1942.
———. "Dr. Joseph E. Richardson." April 6, 1968.
Shreveport Times. Radio Program, March 8, 1925.
———. "Old Fiddlers to Play Today." November 7, 1929.
———. "Shreveport Old Fiddlers Winners in Two Classes in Annual Contest at State Fair Grounds on Thursday." November 8, 1929.
———. "Old Fiddlers Contest at Fair Has 35 Entries." October 29, 1930.
———. "Old Fiddlers Hold Contest." October 30, 1930.
———. "Winners in State Fair Contest." October 30, 1931.
———. "S. R. Patterson, H. C. Wilkerson, Best Fiddlers." October 26, 1934.
———. "Champion Fiddlers in Contest Thursday / Tom Sawyer Best Fiddler at Fair Here." October 25, 1935.
———. "Fiddlers Have Their Day at State's Fair." October 29, 1937.
———. "Haynesville Man is Named Best Fiddler." October 1940.
———. "Shreveport Fiddlers Win Fair Events." October 30, 1942.
Yule, Ron. *When the Fiddle Was King*. Fiddle Country Publishing, DeRidder, Louisiana, 2006.

Photo courtesy of Ralph Richardson.

RALPH RICHARDSON

(1923–) Choupique

One of the foremost exponents of western swing fiddle in the "Highway 90 Swing Belt" that runs from Lake Charles to Houston, Ralph Richardson personifies the hot swing era that burst onto the early country scene in southwest Louisiana and southeast Texas in the thirties, forties, and fifties. A list of his musical heroes dots the panorama of swing players throughout the country. One of the original innovators of swing fiddle, Cliff Bruner, is his fiddling hero and mentor. The list of fiddle personalities Ralph has been on the stage with is overwhelming.

To Ralph, the making of music goes down many paths and wears many coats. Music is a hobby to him, but is important. "Music comes from the soul," he says. He feels his audience should sense this in his playing. To hear him play is to hear him give everything he has and to get a look into his musical genius. Music is a family affair and is enjoyed by all the Richardson clan. Ralph notes,

Front row: Deacon Anderson, Leon Payne, and Floyd Tillman. Middle row: Lew Frisby, Ellis Wheeler, Biff Collie, Cotton Thompson, Gordon Baxter, and Leo Raley. Back row: Buck Henson, J. D. Standlee, Lennie Benoit, Shang Kennedy (obscured by microphone), Ralph Richardson, and Ben Mullins. Lighthouse Club, Port Arthur, 1949. Photo courtesy of Ralph Richardson.

"I had offers to go on the road with many bands but didn't. My family was too important to me." He continues, "Bob Wills used to call me out of the audience to play a couple and one time offered me a job with the Texas Playboys, but I turned it down because of my family." He believes that a person should not squander his talent, but he should use it. Ralph has more than done that.

Although Ralph's family was from Louisiana, Ralph was born in Orange, Texas. The family moved back to Choupique, south of Sulphur, when Ralph was small. It was there that Ralph first heard the strains of the old country fiddle in the voice of his father Steve's old Strad copy. Ralph said, "He played all those old tunes. What's the one those contest fiddlers all play? 'Sally Goodin.' He played that. He also played in cross key and played tunes like 'Pick a Buzzard.'"

The first fiddler he heard that piqued his interest in playing was Sulphur fiddler Mason Sweeny, when Ralph was seven years old. He told his mother he wanted to learn, so he was sent out in the backyard with the chickens, guineas,

Bill Dunn, Deacon Anderson, B. D. Williams, Ralph Richardson, Bob Dunn, Abe Manuel, and Bobby _____. The Oaks, Lake Charles, 1948. Photo courtesy of Ralph Richardson.

turkeys, and geese. He said his family was tired of the squeaking sounds of a beginner. He relates that after he learned, the family invited him to come in and play. "I told them no and continued to go out and play among the hens and guineas and turkeys."

This led to playing at house parties and country dances, which he did with his family and local musicians like his uncles Lennie, Turk, and Bill Benoit, as well as his father. Ralph says they would pull the furniture out of the room and have a dance.

In the late 1930s he began to really listen to the sounds of Cliff Bruner and other swing fiddlers, and his playing became more focused on the dance band and swing style of fiddling. He recalls playing at the High Bound Club south of Sulphur with his Uncle Lennie. He notes, "We drove an old Model A. Uncle Lennie and I have been playing music ever since." They continue playing today at the Vinton VFW once a month and at various celebrations and benefits.

By the early 1940s he had begun playing with the Manuels, Joe and Abe, and then he joined the navy. Crawford Vincent recalls that one night Leo Soileau and his Rhythm Boys were playing at the Showboat, on the Sabine River in East Orange, Louisiana. Ralph showed up in uniform and sat in with them. The Showboat had a reputation as a rough place, and Crawford said the bouncer wanted him to leave because the club was off limits to service personnel at the time. The band talked him into letting Ralph stay a little longer.

After his discharge from the service, Ralph moved to Orange and began to work for the state of Louisiana as a bridge inspector. Ralph never gave up his

Pee Wee Lyons, Ralph Richardson, W. M. Floyd, Amos Comeaux, and unidentified. Silver Star, Sulphur, ca. 1950. Photo courtesy of Ralph Richardson.

day job and played music only as a hobby on the weekends. Throughout the 1940s, Ralph played every chance he could with everyone he could, including his hero, Cliff Bruner and his Boys.

Ralph played with many other notables including Earl Caruthers, Abe and Joe Manuel, Leon Payne, Benny Barnes, Floyd Tillman, and Harry Choates, to name a few. He asked, "Did you know Harry Choates liked to play guitar better than the fiddle? I remember him coming in and picking the guitar up and just going all over it." Others include Sleepy Tompkins, Sleepy Johnson, Curly Fox, and "Tiny" Moore with Dean Rasberry and the Streamliners.

He has played at all the clubs along the strip: the Sparkle Club, Lighthouse, Club 87, Moulin Rouge, Plantation Club, Green Frog, Showboat, Club 88, Oaks, Silver Spur, and Yvonne's Club. He has sat in with many bands for one night or played with them when they were in the area. Besides playing with his own group, he played with acts such as Bob Wills and the Texas Playboys, Tex Ritter, Hank Thompson and the Brazos Valley Boys, Pete Fountain, and Ray Price and the Cherokee Cowboys.

Like nearly all country musicians of the time, he played on local radio stations. He appeared on KGOT (Orange) with Don and Jesse Tyler, KFDM

Kings of Swing, July 1948: Earl Caruthers, Ralph Richardson, unidentified drummer, Sue Romero, Murphy McDowell, and Doc Lewis. Photo courtesy of Ralph Richardson.

(Beaumont) and KPLC (Lake Charles) with W. M. (Bill) Floyd and Brooks Hamilton.

Ralph has recorded with several musicians over the years, in Gulfport, Mississippi, as well as New Orleans and locally. The first recording he can recall was a 1953 recording he and the Gulf Coast Top Hands made at the KGOT studio with a local singer and guitar player, "Pee Wee" Pitre, a Louisiana singer and Lake Charles barber who played around Lake Charles and had heard Ralph playing on KPLC. Tunes included "7 Come 11" and "C. C. Rider Blues,"; Ralph believes the musicians included Ivy Gaspard, R. C. Martin, Brooks Hamilton, and Lennie Benoit. Ralph recalls Pitre as a character: "I've seen him set a glass of beer on his head and do some dancing."

Another was "I Gave Her the Ring and She Gave Me the Finger" with Ramblin' Jack, cut in New Orleans. Ralph recently did some session work with Ronnie Leavoy Jr. in Lake Charles. He recalls recording with Lake Charles country singer Skip Dowers and the La-Tex Swamplanders at Goldband several years ago. Four songs were recorded: "Whiskey (Wash the Pain from My Heart)," "Walk Through My Mind," "Old Memories," and "Say You Don't Mind." "'Walk Through My Mind' made a hit," he says, adding, "If it made a hit, somebody else capitalized on it, ole Ralph didn't."

A Jador recording cut at Eddie Shuler's Goldband Studios produced "Time Changes Everything" and "Swampland Special." Musicians included Guy Barkdull (guitar), Randy Richardson (sax), and Carl Melancon (drums). Ralph used his special ten-string fiddle on this recording session, an old Strad copy that Mr. Perkins, an Orange fiddle maker, had adapted with a longer scroll, so it could accommodate ten strings. Using a regular five-string tuning, Ralph doubled each string to create the instrument. Ralph says he overdubbed the other parts with the same fiddle.

During the nineties he attended many western swing benefits, celebrations, and Bob Wills reunions and festivals. Several occasions included gigs at the Astrodome, in Houston. Most of these bands were put together especially for the events and featured different musicians. Ralph called them the Cruisin' Cajuns. Another yearly trek has been to Athens on the last weekend in May for the old fiddlers' contest. Until recently Ralph helped to judge this major Texas fiddle contest with the likes of Cliff Bruner, Johnny Gimble, "Little Red" Hayes, and Ernie Hunter. To top it off, the group would play for the street dance that night.

In a September 23, 2001, article in the *Lake Charles American Press* by Brenda Merchant, Ralph states, "I think my fan appeal came from the fact music is a genuine love for me. I love to share my music, and feel that it's important to live your life with a loving and cheerful heart. I don't play music for a living and never have. If it became a job, I don't think it would have appealed to me so much."

Ralph loves the fiddle. He can play swing or country; he may cross tune the fiddle and play "Pick Buzzard"; he may tear into "Jole Blon" or some other Cajun tune; or he may loosen the hair on the bow, drape the hair over the fiddle and play "Lieberstraum" in the key of F, playing four parts. After sixty years in the business, he still talks with anticipation and enthusiasm about playing a dance on Saturday night. He is very talented and is thankful for it.

Ralph is currently putting another band together, the Tex-La Country Cousins, to entertain patrons in southeast Texas and southwestern Louisiana. Playing at the Vinton VFW Hall, the band includes old friends Nelson Collum, Jerome Stubbs, and Deacon Anderson.

Interviews by Ron Yule: Ralph Richardson (4-16-2005 and 6-15-2005) and Crawford Vincent (undated conversations at the Basile Nursing Home).

Reference

Merchant, Brenda. "Ralph Richardson." *Lake Charles American Press*, September 23, 2001.

Winston Salard and Buzz Salard. Photo by author.

H. P. "BUZZ" SALARD

(1937–) Natchitoches

WINSTON SALARD

(1935–) Baton Rouge

The Salard family was from the Janie Community near Cloutierville. Growing up in the hill country of south Natchitoches Parish allowed Winston and H. P. (Buzz) to hear some of the best country fiddlers in Central Louisiana. They were first inspired to play from hearing their brother-in-law, Carl Watson, and the fiddlers on the Grand Ole Opry. Listening to the Opry was a family affair. Winston recalls those Saturday nights of his youth: "When I was about seven, we'd listen to WSM on a battery-operated radio, hoping to hear Arthur Smith. Sometimes they'd use the fiddle for an intro or at the end of the set and they'd cut the songs short and that made my daddy mad."

Another influence each remembers vividly are the 1940s house dances around the hill country community. Fiddlers at these dances included Julian and Grover Vallery, the Carnahans (Cliff and Eldren), Uncle Adrian Vercher, and Ray Beebe, to name a few. They played the old-time waltzes and breakdowns that influenced the Salards.

In 1946, after much begging, Winston and Buzz began making music on a Silvertone Gene Autry guitar their parents bought for them. By 1948 Winston became interested in fiddle and began trying to emulate the fiddlers he heard at country dances and on the radio. He recalls his learning experience: "On a stump on a hill across the creek. Mama wouldn't let me play in the house."

In the early 1950s Winston joined the staff at the Old Barn Dance in Alexandria, playing square dance music with Hermon Lasyone, Eddie Friday, and others. He appeared on KSYL during his short stint there. After playing dances and a three-year stint in the U.S. Navy, he moved to Baton Rouge in 1958, going to work for the state police and eventually the local district attorney.

Winston did not immediately play the fiddle in Baton Rouge, but eventually met a neighbor, Alton Day, with whom he began to play at country jam sessions in the area. His first introduction to bluegrass came around 1965 when he met a policeman, Jimmy Slocum, who played mandolin. Slocum had been an early influence on bluegrass in the Baton Rouge area and had formed a group with guitarist Jimmy Brecheen, Jimmy and Jimmy. Adding Winston on fiddle, Jimmy Edwards on banjo, and Lum York on bass fiddle, they played on an early-morning bluegrass show on WLBI, Denham Springs, called Bluegrass Breakfast Time. Jimmy Edwards notes the group also played under the name Bluegrass Ramblers.

As one of the pioneering bluegrass fiddlers of the Florida parishes, Winston played with every group that was available in the area. A list of the musicians he played with over the next thirty years is an honor roll of Florida parishes bluegrass pickers and includes Jimmy McKeen, Jimmy Stewart, Lum York, Jimmy Edwards, Chuck White, Bucky Woods, Kathy Woods, John Hart, Dallie Simeon, the Meyers Brothers, Luke Thompson, Kennie Lamb, Travis Stewart, and Buck White and the Downhomers. He also played with numerous bands at the Old South Jamboree at Walker, Pineywoods Opry at Abita Springs, and every bluegrass festival throughout southeastern Louisiana and southern Mississippi. He has recorded on several albums with local bluegrass groups.

In 1985 Kennie Lamb and Jim Nation, along with other Florida parishes bluegrass musicians, formed the Louisiana Bluegrass Association and presented monthly shows in a building in Denham Springs. National acts were booked and Winston was a member of the house band.

Bluegrass Buddies, 1983: Dave Graham, Bobbie Harris, J. D. Harris, Buzz Salard, Bruce Lichti, Ann Graham, and Andy Lord. Photo courtesy of Ann Graham.

Although he is retired, he still plays occasionally when someone needs him, and the crowd welcomes his traditional style of fiddling. Winston's favorite fiddlers are Arthur Smith and Kenny Baker. His favorite fiddle tune is "Sally Goodin," although he states, "I like them all."

Buzz took up the fiddle around 1950 and recalls that, besides listening to Julian and Grover Vallery, Uncle Adrian Vercher, Ray Beebe, and the Carnahans, a local bluesy dance band fiddler, Duma LaCour, was a very early influence. He recalls him playing at the Brown Derby on Cane River for dances.

Buzz recalls that, although they had a fiddle, he seldom played on it because Winston had it most of the time. He wanted his own fiddle but could not afford one. Around 1952 Buzz and Winston attended a house dance at Jesse Bynog's, an eight-mile walk to the Derry community. After playing up into the night they began the long trek home and on the way a cousin, Artis Kerry, told Buzz he had a fiddle that he did not play and he would sell it to him for six dollars. Buzz did not have any money, but he got it on credit and paid for it when he could.

Following the years of his youth, Buzz served four years in the navy. After his return to the area he did not play professionally, but worked for

Luke Thompson and the Green Valley Cut Ups, 1968: Johnny Rushing, Winston Salard, Dennie Blount, Travis Stewart. Photo courtesy of Winston Salard.

the Louisiana Department of Public Safety as a state trooper. He played only sporadically until the late 1960s.

In 1967 Byron Berline left Bill Monroe's Bluegrass Boys when he was drafted into the army. Byron was in the Special Services unit at Fort Polk, near Natchitoches, for two years, and was able to pick with the Southern Bluegrass Boys, the Stone Mountain Boys (Dallas, Texas), Luke Thompson, Jim Smoak, and other groups throughout the region. Buzz listened to his championship fiddle style and became excited, renewing his interest in fiddling. He began to seek out local bluegrass musicians, jamming and picking with Louisiana bluegrass pioneers Travis Stewart, Dennis Lucas, Al Jordan, Joe Spence, and Gene Alford. They traveled throughout the state nearly every weekend to attend country shows in Jonesville, Monroe, and Walker.

In the early 1970s the Southland Bluegrass Boys (Jimmy, Raymond, Bruce, and Donald Nugent) were returning late one Saturday night from a church singing in north Louisiana, and Buzz happened to be patrolling that stretch of road. They were speeding, so Buzz pulled them over to investigate. Upon looking in the back of the station wagon he discovered their instruments (the bass fiddle was tied to the top of the car). After finding out the situation, he let them go. He says, "They were bluegrass musicians and I figured they didn't have any money anyway." A week or so later they invited him to a practice session at Jimmy Nugent's house in Deville. He was hired that night and played his first stage show on Clyde Baum's inaugural bluegrass festival at Shady Dell Acres near Pollock. He stayed with them for several years, cutting one LP, *The Southland Arises.*

His job as a trooper kept him so involved with work that he was unable to play regularly for long periods of time with any one group. He continued to attend festivals and played with many groups including the Southland Bluegrass, Cox Family, Twice as Nice, Bluegrass Buddies, Don Wiley and the Louisiana Grass, Driskill Mountain Boys, and All Points South, as well as playing on KALB television with Don Wiley.

Professional recordings include albums with the Southland Bluegrass, the Bluegrass Buddies, the Cox Family, and Vivian mandolinist, J. W. Alexander.

Besides the many Hill Country fiddlers of his youth, Buzz is drawn to the strains of bluegrass/old-time fiddlers like Howdy Forrester, Chubby Wise, Kenny Baker and Byron Berline. His large repertoire of fiddle tunes contains songs from all styles of country music and includes favorites "Virginia Darlin'," "Bill Cheatam," "Panhandle Country," and "Uncle Joe."

As an advocate of folklife preservation, Buzz has made a conscious effort to keep the fiddling of the early part of the century alive, playing many of the numbers of his youth found only in the south Natchitoches Hill Country area. Tunes such as "Bayou Derbonne" and "Mitchell's Waltz" survive through Buzz's playing.

Noteworthy is the fact that both Winston and Buzz play the same tunes and can back up a singer on a stage show or recording, but each has a completely different style. Winston's fiddling is more bluegrass-sounding, whereas Buzz's is more old-timey.

Buzz relates that over the years they have played very little together. He does recall one time when they were both in the navy and stationed on the USS *Seckler,* patrolling in the Red Sea. Every couple of weeks they would come in for refueling and restocking the ship's supplies. As they entered the port each time the receiving ship would usually have a military band playing patriotic music to greet them. Since the *Seckler* did not have a ship band, the captain requested that some of the musicians from the ship form a "morale band" to play at these functions. At the next port stop, the newly formed band—Winston on banjo, Buzz on fiddle, and an unnamed guitar player—stepped out from behind a stack on the second deck and began to play over the PA just as the other band was readying to play. Buzz recalls he played "Ragtime Annie" and they stole the show. They were so well liked they continued their morale band status throughout their tour on the *Seckler*.

Both continue to attend festivals and play when they can. Each has retired from playing regularly with a band but loves attending jam sessions.

Anytime you are at a festival and you hear a fiddle sounding off in the woods or behind a camper, it might be the Salards with a nephew, Jimmy Edwards, on the banjo, as only he can play it. It's worth a listen.

The influence of these two brothers is far-reaching. Each has made great contributions to the pioneering sound of bluegrass fiddling in Louisiana, Winston in the Florida parishes and Buzz in the north and central part of the state. They are some of the last surviving fiddlers who both play bluegrass and also continue to play hundreds of the old-time hoedowns and waltzes.

Interviews by Ron Yule: Buzz Salard (2-10-2003 and 7-21-2007) and Winston Salard (4-4-2004, 11-12-2006, and 7-27-2008).

Photo courtesy of David Simpson, LSU-E.

KEN SMITH

(1961–) Kinder

Ken's ancestors played fiddle, and he grew up listening to traditional sounds of Louisiana fiddling. His uncle Martin and grandfather Kirby had played fiddle music since the 1930s. Martin began to play fiddle in his youth and was accompanied by Kirby, who played rhythm guitar. Martin was a country fiddler who liked breakdowns and waltzes, and his son, Robert Lee, followed in his father's footsteps. He became a very good fiddler, placing in the finals at the Texas Fiddler's Frolics on one occasion.

Buford, Ken's father, began to learn the fiddle at age eleven, inspired by the music of his father and Uncle Martin, who constantly played around the house. Although he loved breakdowns and seconded on the guitar behind them, his passion was playing waltzes. His favorite tune is "Wednesday Night Waltz" or, as he puts it, "any beautiful waltz."

Ken took up mandolin at age nine and fiddle at eleven, learning from his father. Ken's original Cajun influence was Wallace "Cheese" Read, from Eunice, who was a constant figure in jam sessions at the Smiths' home. Another influence was Merlin Fontenot, who at the time was playing at Etley's Lounge in Eunice.

In the early 1970s Ken became enamored of the Texas style of fiddling and studied under A. R. Westmoreland, from Houston, for the major part of the summer of 1974. The next couple of years led to a tour around the country with legendary Texas fiddler Dick Barrett, from Pottsboro, Texas. They attended contests all over the western half of the country, finally lighting at the National Oldtime Fiddle Contest in Weiser, Idaho, where Ken won fifth place behind super–contest fiddlers Mark O'Connor and John Francis.

Ken was a major fiddling force tearing onto the contest scene in the early 1970s. He introduced Texas (contest) style fiddlin' to south and central Louisiana, and his impact is still felt today. Old-timers still talk about "the kid from Kinder" and his many contest performances. His talent was so overwhelming that many fiddlers changed their style in order to compete with him. Many added to their repertoire contest-style tunes and licks they heard Ken play at contests and jams. Ken's LP, *Louisiana State Champion,* also influenced many local fiddlers. Ken won many contests, the major ones being the Louisiana State Fiddle Championship (five times), DeRidder VFW (1974 and 1975), World Championship (second place, 1976) and Crowley Rice Festival (six times).

The Smith family (Buford, Ken, and mother, Juanita) was instrumental in the promotion of fiddle music via contests such as those in the Kinder area (K.C. Hall and Sauce Piquante Festival). They have spent numerous hours promoting and hosting jam sessions, sometimes lasting all night, with some of the best fiddlers from Louisiana, Georgia, Alabama, and Texas.

His influence even affected his own family when his grandfather, Kirby, who had been around fiddlin' all of his life, at age fifty-five, decided to pursue the instrument. He liked pretty waltzes and the eastern fiddling style of groups like Gid Tanner and the Skillet Lickers. In the 1970s Kirby entered and placed in numerous contests. His favorite tunes were "Carroll County Blues" and "Goodnight Waltz," two of Ken's masterpieces.

In 1976 Ken was honored as a part of the southern group of fiddlers who played at the National Folklife Festival at the Smithsonian in Washington, D.C. for the Bicentennial celebration. This troupe, organized by John Callahan of Birmingham, Alabama, included master fiddlers J. T. Perkins, Roy Crawford,

Ken and Buford Smith at B&K Music in Kinder, 2004. Photo by author.

and Frazier Moss, plus their accompanists Claudie Holt, Algie Surratt, and John Salley, all from Tennessee and Alabama.

Ken presently plays everything from country and swing to Cajun fiddle while operating B&K Music in Kinder. Their trade specializes in violins and violin accessories as well as instrument repair. A large stock of fiddles is always available, as well as other instruments.

Ken had always played some Cajun music, and in 1981 he started playing with Tim and Marty Broussard, and toured with D. L. Menard and Eddie Lejeune. Two LPs were recorded with Menard (*No Matter Where You At, There You Are*) and Lejeune (*Cajun Soul*). A third, *Le Trio Acadien*, on Rounder Records, featured all three. During the 1980s Ken played with Paul Daigle, of Church Point, and they recorded two projects. He has also worked with Bruce Daigrepoint, from New Orleans, on several projects. Marc and Ann Savoy, the noted accordion maker and Cajun historian/vocalist, joined Smith on an album of Cajun songs they performed while they toured and traveled throughout the world. It was titled, *Savoy-Smith Band: Now and Then*. He was nominated for a Grammy several years ago for *the Le Trio Acadien* CD with Lejeune and Menard.

Ken still plays with Paul Daigle, Jason Frey, and Marc and Ann Savoy when they need him. For years, he traveled with these groups, playing for festivals, colleges, art centers, and clubs all over the United States and Europe. He has not traveled much in recent years because his music shop takes up most of his time.

His influence as a teacher has reached far and wide and now is in its second generation. Ken's influence can be seen in the fiddlers of today who learned from both Ken and his students. These include Curry Perkins, Lauren Hodges, Wilson Savoy, Casey Sanchez, Emily Young, Ron Yule, Delmar Sonnier, Miranda Wells, Clint Ward, Greg Edwards, and many more. He has influenced their playing of both Cajun and oldtime fiddle music.

Ken says he has always been lucky to enjoy his music and not be forced to play to make a living. He loves Cajun music and says he loves to play with a good accordion player that has good technical ability. "When you listen to a good accordion player, it sounds like it has some reels and hornpipes in it the way they pop those notes and the patterns they use. I like the exchange, and applying the fiddle to it." He says that they sound like they are playing hornpipes the way they approach it. He adds, "I still find the most enjoyment is to sit down and play with my dad. I've enjoyed my life in music, but I find no more enjoyment than to sit and play fiddle tunes with Dad."

In the pineywoods of western Louisiana the mention of fiddle contests will bring up the name of "the kid from Kinder." He was a "Legend in His Own Youth."

Interviews by Ron Yule: Ken Smith (4-17-2005), numerous undated informal conversations with Ken Smith, Buford Smith, Delmar Sonnier, Kirby Smith, Curry Perkins, and numerous others at contests, shows, and jam sessions over the years.

KEN SMITH

By Shawn Martin

The following article by Shawn Martin appeared in the American Press on May 21, 1993. It is reprinted by permission of Shawn Martin.

He's known as the state's best fiddler and is considered in many musical circles as a rising star among the nation's top folk music fiddlers. This musical virtuoso calls Kinder home, not exactly a place known to be on the cutting edge of the musical world; but, that's where Ken Smith spends much of his time, that is when he's not off fiddlin'.

Smith, 32, began his musical evolution over 20 years ago, sparked by weekend family "Jam sessions." "Everybody would get together at our house or at my grandparents house and begin playing music, mostly old French tunes," Smith said. "And I guess my first attempt at making music was when I was nine and the family musicians would take a break from playing to go eat a bowl of gumbo. I'd grab a fiddle and sneak away to a back room and begin trying to make sounds. That's really when I got started."

Smith said it wasn't until he was about 11 that he really began an organized effort to learn to play the fiddle. And fiddle is Smith's preferred term, rather than violin. "I get asked that a lot . . . if am I a violinist or fiddler, and I always answer that I'm a fiddler because violinist sounds too formal and stiff and really what I do is fiddle."

He said his first formal musical experience came shortly after his father, Buford, an off-shore worker, bought a fiddle when Ken was 11 and brought it home. "When Daddy would leave I would get the fiddle out and begin playing what I had heard at the family jam sessions the weekend before," Smith said. "I think Daddy knew I was playing with his fiddle because when he'd come home from off-shore some of the strings would be broken, so I think he knew something was going on.

"He came in from work and I had been practicing and I played him the 'Wednesday Night Waltz' and I haven't looked back since." When asked how long it took him to learn the old waltz tune, his narrow, thin face turned a bright red, and he responded, "Really and truly, about one day. I guess you could say I have the ability to hear something once and play it."

Smith, who has no formal musical training, manages the family music store in Kinder when his father is working. He plays the fiddle every day to "keep sharp" since his musical repertoire is so large and vast and continues to grow. "I play a large variety of music," Smith said. "I play blues, French-Cajun, old-time breakdown, waltzes, ragtime, polka, bluegrass, and now I think my favorite, Irish folk tunes."

Because of his abilities and love of music, Smith has been touring nationally and internationally for several years.

"I won my first fiddling contest at the Beauregard Parish Fair in DeRidder when I was 13," Smith said. "The fair's fiddlers' contest used to be big but it's not anymore. But the year I won was special because one of the world's greatest fiddlers, Chubby Wise, was judging the contest and I was chosen as the best."

Last month Smith won the Louisiana State Fiddlers Championship at Rebel State Park in Marthaville. It was his fifth state championship.

"I had competed for several years and so I guess I go back every once in a while to make sure I can still do it," Smith said. "There are a lot of good fiddlers out there and I'm glad to see that."

Smith, a third-generation musician, not only plays fiddle (a 200-year-old Amati copy), but he also plays mandolin, guitar, and accordion. "I like knowing that I can play music on several different instruments, but my first love is the fiddle," he said. "I went from the fiddle to the mandolin and then on to the other instruments . . . I suppose it was just a natural progression that I play lot of different instruments and types of music."

Smith has been on seven albums in just over 15 years and recorded his only solo album when he was 14 in Ville Platte at Floyd Soileau's famous recording studio. His latest effort, *Le Trio Cadien*, recorded with accordion player Eddie Lejeune and Erath's famous resident, Cajun crooner D. L. Menard. "I got a chance to play with those legends and it has been a very successful venture," Smith said smiling. "We have toured several European countries and will begin another four-week European tour in October."

When Smith wraps his long, thin fingers around the neck of his favorite fiddle and begins sliding the bow over the instrument's four strings and the music begins to flow, the atmosphere is charged and a metamorphosis occurs.

"I never play a tune the same way twice," Smith said. "I feel the instrument is a window into the soul of the person playing it. We can hide our feelings on the outside but we can't on the inside, and the music is a tap, which allows those feelings to flow out. If I'm happy, then that's reflected in what I play. But on the other hand, if I'm sad, then that too is reflected and it can't be covered up or controlled."

He said many times at concerts, elderly people, especially women, will say his music brought back memories so thick they had to be swatted away from their faces like flies. "When I'm told that I know what I'm doing is good and right. I know that I reach people and that's the real payoff."

Smith said if there is a single message he could send it would be that "music is the greatest thing and to be involved in music that touches people's lives means a great deal."

Smith is fulfilling a dream to teach music. He was awarded a state grant to teach music to 20 children in rural schools. Smith's teaching project is a pilot for the state. He teaches at schools in Kinder, Reeves and Oberlin.

"I would like to say that music means everything to me," Smith said. "It also has meant a great deal to my family and I will continue to work to keep all types of folk music from being lost."

Photo courtesy of Crawford Vincent Collection/Andrew Brown.

LEO SOILEAU

Cajun Fusionist

by Kevin S. Fontenot

Kevin Fontenot is a professor at Tulane University in New Orleans who is completing his work on a Ph.D. in history with a focus on the life of Jimmie Davis. He has written many articles on country music and is a reviewer of numerous articles and recorded projects. He is the co-editor with Ryan Brasseaux of Accordions, Fiddles, Two-Steps, and Swing: A Cajun Music Reader, *Center for Louisiana Studies, 2006.*

During the late Depression and World War II, Leo Soileau and his bands dominated the dancehalls of southwestern Louisiana. True, he experienced competition from a wide range of bands, including those fronted by western swing giants Cliff Bruner and Moon Mullican and fellow Cajuns, the Hackberry Ramblers. But Soileau's reputation kept him in demand and dominant in the

Bill _____, George Duhon, Leo Soileau, Crawford Vincent, Bollie Thibodeaux, Rufus Laverne, Johnny _____, and "Papa Cairo" Lamparez (steel guitar). Pleasure Club, 1940's. Photo courtesy of Lamparez family and the Center for Louisiana Studies, Lafayette, Louisiana.

region, and though the Hackberry Ramblers are better remembered, their style of Cajun Swing drew upon the formula first articulated by Leo Soileau.

Leo Soileau was born in 1904 in Evangeline Parish. His father played the fiddle and worked as a farmer. "My papa and his brother would plough all day and come in and make music every night. My papa used to take his fiddle out after supper. I can see him now," Soileau told reporter Joe Darby, " . . . and he could play, brother. Ooooh, my daddy had a sound on that fiddle." None of the other nine children played music, though Leo recalled a sister who "banged a little bit on the piano," but she didn't follow through with her study of music. Leo spent his early years in the fields around Evangeline Parish and attended school through the sixth grade. He also began to play the fiddle, first around the house but by the age of twelve in 1916, he was playing house dances. Those early gigs paid between four and five dollars a night and he usually performed with the rising Creole accordionist Amédé Ardoin. Leo recalled that there were few musicians in the area between Ville Platte and Eunice, and he and Ardoin soon learned of each and started playing together, first in Chataignier. The dancehall in Chataignier could accommodate several hundred people and the two musicians developed a broad repertoire to keep the couples on the dance floor. Ardoin's strong, emotional voice and his powerful playing style was much in demand in the early 1920s, and the Creole cultivated a fan base among the Cajun clientele of the dancehalls.

Soileau played with other accordionists as well. His favorite accompanist was Mayeus Lefleur with whom he started playing about 1920. Lafleur was an excellent singer and an expressive accordionist. The two young men quickly reached simpatico in their playing. In 1928, Joe Falcon and his fiancé, Cleoma Breaux, cut the first Cajun records in New Orleans. They barely beat Soileau and Lafleur to the studio. On October 19, 1928, in Atlanta, Soileau and Lafleur cut four sides, classics in the fiddle-accordion style—"Basile Waltz," "Mama, Where You At?" "The Criminal Waltz," and "Your Father Put Me Out." Lafleur's playing was brighter and more enthusiastic than Falcon's more traditional style. Nine days later, the two played a house dance in Basile. On the way home, they stopped at a "blind tiger" (illegal drinking establishment) run by Alexander Bellon. A violent fight broke out between gamblers shortly after the duo arrived, and Lafleur was killed in the melee. Soileau cradled his dying friend's head on the blood soaked bar floor. It haunted him the rest of his life.

Lafleur's death left a hole in Leo's music that no other accordionist ever filled. Soileau began a year long partnership with Moise Robin, but the two failed to click. Soileau aggressively pursued music as a career and arranged recording dates in New Orleans, Memphis, and Richmond, Indiana. The Soileau-Robin recordings are interesting for their tension filled playing, particularly Soileau's "special," the "Easy Rider Blues", which indicated a debt to the Texas bluesman Blind Lemon Jefferson. But the tension stemmed from artistic differences. Soileau was starting to chaff under the limitations of the accordion. In French music, he told Ralph Rinzler, "you stay right there. It's the same D, G, C (standard accordion-based musical keys)." "There's no chorus in that son of a gun (Cajun music) . . . accordion and fiddle, its just you got to pap. You just can't stop." Robin recalled the tension as well, "Leo always wanted to take the lead when we played. He kept the lead and I had to follow him. It's bothersome to always follow a violin, you see. It's difficult. I had to play below his violin's volume. We didn't play too long together, about one year."

Soileau spent the next six years playing the area around Crowley and searching for a new sound. He and Joe Falcon dominated the scene, both earning a living from playing professionally. "When I was in Crowley in 1932, I was playing in 14 different dancehalls. I was every two weeks to each place. I did that for about eight years." Soileau gained a reputation as a fair boss, and his band was very stable through the years. He also moved away from accordion based music. "I got me two guitars, and a drum, and fiddle." This new string band was based on the hot dance band music coming from Texas.

Soileau listened to radio broadcasts out of Dallas, Fort Worth, and southeastern Texas, by groups such as the Light Crust Doughboys, Milton Brown and his Music Brownies, and Floyd Tillman.

It was this hot string band style that Soileau and his Three Aces first recorded in 1935. That first session for Bluebird included "La Valse de Gueydan," an early fiddle driven version of "Jole Blon." Over the next three years, Soileau and his Aces (of varying number) laid the framework for Cajun swing, introducing drums into Cajun music and opening the door for groups like the Hackberry Ramblers and the Alley Boys of Abbeville. Soileau's band included the talented singer Floyd Shreve (who performed English only vocals), Tony Gonzales and Crawford Vincent (1940s) on drums, Dewey Landry on guitar, and the young Harry Choates (1940s) on fiddle. Choates learned much from Soileau, as a comparison of his "Jole Blon" with Soileau's "La Valse de Gueydan" reveals.

Soileau's repertoire reflected his and his audience's catholic taste. He recorded French language versions of Jimmie Davis' "Nobody's Darlin' but Mine" and "Columbus Stockade Blues," and English language songs such as "Love Letters in the Sand." "My band could really mix 'em up. We could play French, English, or Mexican songs. I don't remember any requests we couldn't do." The string band format allowed Soileau and his band members the freedom to explore musical ideas, "take off" on themes not possible with the limited range of the accordion. He successfully negotiated the waters between country and Cajun music, mainly recording for Decca in the mid-1930s.

During the late 1930s, Soileau formed a new group, the Rhythm Boys and moved his base of operations to Lake Charles. For eight years his home was the Silver Star Club and his band included Happy Fats Leblanc. The band regularly broadcast from the club for KPLC and they cut transcriptions for the Community Coffee Company. The war years were a heyday for the dancehall scene and Soileau extended his gig-range into east Texas. After the war he played for two years at the Showboat Club in Orange, Texas, and often engaged in "battle of the bands" contest with Cliff Bruner.

The years following the war saw a slow decline in Soileau's career. He did not participate in the accordion revival of the late 1940s, though he recalled that Iry Lejeune did occasionally sit in with his band. Nor did he enter a recording studio after the war, so his stellar lineup of the war years remains one of the great unrecorded bands. By 1953 he retired from music. He worked in an oil refinery near Lake Charles for six years and then as a janitor in Ville Platte. He retired in 1968. All through the Cajun revival of the postwar years,

Rufus Laverne, George Duhon, Leo Soileau, Crawford Vincent, Liz _____, Bollie Thibodeaux, "Papa Cairo" Lamparez (steel guitar). Silver Star, Sulphur, 1946. Photo courtesy of Crawford Vincent Collection/Andrew Brown.

Leo Soileau quietly lived his life away from the music he did so much to define. He died on August 2, 1980, in Ville Platte.

Interview by Ralph Rinzler: Leo Soileau, October 20, 1965, Center for Louisiana Studies, University of Louisiana at Lafayette.

interview by Kevin S. Fontenot: Crawford Vincent, November 1993.

References

Darby, Joe. "Leo Soileau Remembers Little Boy Who Snuck His Papa's Fiddle." *Times-Picayune*, August 25, 1975.

Fontenot, Kevin S. "Cajun Musician, Cajun Mystic: The Improbable Legacy of Moise Robin." Annual address presented to the Phi Alpha Theta, Lafayette, Louisiana, May 2005.

Nelson, Donald Lee. "Mama Where You At? The Chronicle of Maius Lafleur." *JEMF Quarterly,* XIX (Summer 1983): 76–80.

Russell, Tony. "Leo Soileau." *Old Time Music* 27 (1977).

Photo courtesy of Jean Strickland.

ORVILLE "HANK" STRICKLAND

(1917–1995) Winnfield

Orville "Hank" Strickland was born in Many, Louisiana, on February 7, 1917, and by the age of four his musical talent was beginning to emerge. His mother played accordion, his father, Jesse Monroe, played fiddle, and a host of uncles all played country music of some kind. He wanted to play piano, but his mother insisted on him playing fiddle, so his eyes and ears became focused on the fiddle.

His father was an old-time fiddler in the area and Hank would help him when he played the fiddle as best he could by holding the straws (fiddlesticks), but he was listening to the sounds of the fiddle because he liked them. His father kept the fiddle under the bed and at the age of four, when his father was gone, Hank dragged the fiddle out from under the bed and tried playing a tune or two. His father noticed that the fiddle was misplaced when he went to get it and asked Hank if he had played with it. He admitted that he had. His father asked him to play a tune on it and he did. He played two tunes as best he could and his father was impressed enough to let him become more involved in the instrument.

By the age of six Hank was playing at dances in the area. Jean Strickland, Hank's wife, told the *Winn Parish Enterprise* in an April 28, 1999, article a story Hank related to her:

> *When his family realized how good little Hank was with a fiddle, they began to take him to country dances and school fairs. Hank's Dad would set out a little teacup and people at the dances, in appreciation for Hank's playing, would drop coins into the teacup. The money accumulated rapidly and Hank's Dad was able to make a crop using Hank's fiddle playing earnings.*

In a more recent interview she noted that, in time, Hank began to wonder where the money was going, so he asked his father and he told him they were using it to make a crop.

At the age of seven, Hank began taking lessons from a local music teacher, Mae Beville, who had played and studied in Germany, England, and around Europe. For his first week's lessons she would have him play for her, whatever he wanted. After the first week she told him, "Forget everything you know." He then spent the next week learning the bow. Each week she continued to try to teach him classical violin technique. After one year of lessons, he became disinterested in learning violin music and technique and quit. When Mrs. Beville got wind of this, she approached the family and told them, "I've never seen a child with so much talent. I'll teach him free." He never went back to lessons. Hank also learned mandolin and guitar.

Hank had a first cousin, Aud Lewing, a noted hoedown fiddler from Many, who became his mentor at an early age. They played together and Hank learned many old-time tunes and much of the drive in his fiddling from Aud. They played at jam sessions and some country dances around Many.

Much of the non-working time at the Strickland home was spent playing music. Besides Jesse and Hank, the whole family played: Elmer (fiddle), Bill (guitar), Eddie (bass fiddle and jug), and Rayburn (guitar). A. G. and Ruby each played, but no one can recall their instruments. They played at family gatherings and a few dances.

The family moved to Vidalia in Hank's early teens to work on a farm for a doctor. They worked by day, played music by night, and had country dances on the weekend. One night tragedy struck the family, when Jesse was run over by a car while directing and parking cars at one of the Saturday night country dances. The driver did not see him.

This led to a move to Winnfield, where they continued to work farms. Hank worked on a dairy farm owned by Dr. Fritz and played music when he found the time. During the 1930s he began to play with Linton Henderson, who owned the local cab company, and they played everywhere they could. In the late 1940s, he played with John Finney at jam sessions around Winnfield. Over the rest of Hank's life, John would play rhythm guitar for Hank at most of the reunions, family gatherings, and fiddle contests he would attend.

In early 1948 the Mercer Brothers, a Georgia-based country group, placed an ad in the Shreveport paper stating that they needed a fiddler. Hank answered the ad, auditioned, got the job, moved to Shreveport, and began playing on KWKH during their fifteen-minute time slot each day.

The Mercers, Wallace and Charlie, had moved to the area and had previously played on the Big D Jamboree in Dallas. Hank, known as Doyle Strickland on billings for the show, did comedy as well as playing the fiddle. His comedy routines were done under the name of "Oscar Tanglefoot." He'd don overalls and an old straw hat, blacken his teeth and tell jokes and do country comedy routines. He continued this ability to communicate with an audience throughout his career.

On April 3, 1948, the Louisiana Hayride was born and Hank played with the Mercer Brothers on the first night of the show. While he was at the Hayride, he took every opportunity to play and perform with many bands. Hank Williams came to the Hayride in the latter part of the summer and carried a guitar player named Bob McNalty, who had recently quit Patsy Montana. Hank became friends with McNalty and, because Williams would use a pickup band, Hank got to play with him on numerous occasions. Stints with country stars like Hank Locklin, Webb Pierce, and Red Sovine also dotted his stay in Shreveport, as well as playing in impromptu jam sessions with Paul Warren and others backstage on the Hayride. The Mercers stayed in Shreveport and played for about seven months before they moved on to Oklahoma, Monroe (KNOE), and finally back to their hometown of Macon, Georgia. Hank went with them.

During his stay in Shreveport came an offer to play with Hank Williams as a permanent member of his band. Williams was headed to the Grand Ole Opry and he wanted Hank to be his fiddler, but prior commitments preempted this offer. He also had a chance to go on the road with Bill Monroe and the Bluegrass Boys.

Mercer Brothers, 1948: Hank Strickland, Charlie Mercer, Wallace Mercer, and Wayne Raney. Photo courtesy of Jean Strickland.

In an undated article from the *Macon Telegraph* in the possession of Jean Strickland, the Mercer Brothers described the road and the live performances they needed to play to stay financially afloat:

> *The live performances were another matter. There was nothing glamorous about them even if they did give the brothers enough stories to write several books. They played at every backwater stop along the way—on what was called the kerosene circuit.*
>
> *"You didn't have paved roads then. You couldn't make any speed driving," Wallace said. "We'd play in places that didn't have any electricity. A six-volt (car) battery ran the sound system. You better have a good battery or you wouldn't get home. You never knew what you'd encounter."*

They played in buildings with saw-milled slab walls lit by Coleman lanterns (hence the kerosene circuit) and heated by potbellied stoves.

While in Georgia, the Mercer Brothers played shows in the area around their hometown. Hank was unhappy with their business practices and became disgruntled with the band. The Mercers would not take all the bookings they could get and for some reason, unknown to Hank, they turned down good bookings. He came home.

He returned home to raise his family and worked as a dairyman and water well driller. He continued to enter fiddle contests when he could and usually placed high or won. About 1950, Hank joined Eddie Friday, Hermon Lasyone, Charlie Walding, Gene Wilson, Winston Salard, and Jewel Lasyone playing at the Old Barn Dance, in Alexandria. This was a square dance show produced by Mel Hinkley, the square dance caller. Hank had a part on the Saturday afternoon appearances on KSYL, which advertised the show. He won fiddle contests throughout the area including one at Northwestern State University in 1952.

He continued to play the old tunes that had made him a regional standout. Several of his favorite tunes were "Sally Goodin," "Run Nigger Run," and "Black Mountain Rag," which he loved to play in cross tuning even though he could play them in regular tuning. Other favorites and contest tunes included "Devil's Dream" and "Sugar in the Gourd." His showpiece "Over the Waves" could have been a holdover from some of the classical training he received as a child. He would play the waltz with a guitar accompaniment in a country style for a couple of rounds, and then would have the guitar drop out and would play the song utilizing many classically oriented moves. It was something to hear, and he always brought down the house with it.

His crowning achievement was his victory in the Louisiana State Fiddle Championship in 1973. He won and continued to win contests at Fish Creek, Pollock, Natchitoches, and throughout northern and central Louisiana during the 1970s.

In the 1980s and early 1990s, Hank played around the area with John Finney and began repairing violins. In his later years, he made a couple of violins.

Hank passed away in 1995.

Interviews by Ron Yule: Ruby Allen (11-14-2003), John Finney (11-12-2003), Buford Jordan (8-12-2003), Ann Strickland (11-14-2003), Jean Strickland (11-14-2003), and undated informal conversations with G. W. Conlay, Hermon Lasyone, and Gene Wilson.

References

Macon Telegraph. "Mercer Brothers Passed Up Chance at the Big Time." Undated article in possession of Jean Strickland.

Winn Parish Enterprise. "Storytelling, Fiddle Playing See First Time Appearance." Winnfield, Louisiana, April 28, 1999.

Yule, Ron. *When the Fiddle Was King*. Fiddle Country Publishing, DeRidder, Louisiana, 2006.

Photo courtesy of CFMA Hall of Fame Collection, Lake Charles.

RUFUS THIBODEAUX

(1934–2006) Ridge

One of the most influential fiddlers of the second half of the twentieth century, Rufus Thibodeaux was born January 5, 1934, in Ridge, Louisiana, to Olympe and Ellias Thibodeaux. He moved to Hayes, Louisiana, at the age of three and started his musical career at six playing guitar, learning from his father, who played accordion. Ellias bought Rufus a fiddle at the age of twelve and began what Rufus termed "A long career of over fifty years." He noted his fiddling has been inspired and influenced by the fiddling of Harry Choates and Johnny Gimble.

His overwhelming talent emerged early on. He began his career playing at the famous Bucket of Blood in Lake Arthur. At the age of thirteen, he was playing dance jobs on a regular basis with the Rayne Playboys. They traveled the club circuit and performed on Happy Fats's Saturday morning radio show on KSLO, Opelousas. Larry Benicewicz, a blues writer, notes, "Eddie Shuler, a record pioneer with Goldband in Lake Charles, recalls a young Rufus stealing the show from his own band, the Reveliers, at a festival, in 1946." Another fiddler recalls hearing him twin fiddling with the late Doc Guidry in an awesome display of harmony playing. In 1948, while playing throughout southwest Louisiana, he joined the house band playing at the Silver Star, on Highway 90 west of Lake Charles. Carrol Broussard, who played the steel guitar with Harry Choates, recalls Rufus sitting in with Harry Choates's band at the Green Lantern in Lawtell in 1949. Harry was leaving the bandstand to take a break and did an about-face when he heard Thibodeaux playing. Harry's reaction was one of the biggest thrills of Rufus's life. Carrol believes he played "Jole Blon" and notes that he was playing on Harry's fiddle. Carrol also recalls that Rufus could play it just like Choates or he could put his own unique style to the piece. Choates did comment later to Broussard that he thought he was playing and was hearing himself play. Luderin Darbone recalls playing at the Silver Star every Saturday night in the late 1940s and Rufus would sometimes sit in and play twin fiddle.

By 1949 he started playing for Papa Cairo, and in 1950 began his long association as a sideman with Jimmy C. Newman, where he was a stellar performer. One single show might showcase Rufus playing improvisational, smooth country on one of Jimmy's hits, with a quick move to an instrumental swing standard like "In the Mood," and follow with a rousing rendition of "Diggy Liggy Lo," which brought down the house many nights. Their travels throughout the world—to the Wembley Festival in London, the Smithsonian Festival in Washington, D.C., as well as others—introduced the sounds of Cajun music to a new audience. By 1954 they played on the Louisiana Hayride, eventually landing on the Grand Ole Opry. Rufus's fine Cajun fiddling sparked many fiddlers to begin playing Cajun music in their bands and in dancehalls and clubs outside Louisiana. His improvisational skills on breaks and instrumentals influenced fiddlers throughout the country.

Recordings kept Rufus in touch with his audience and also showcased his versatility. Rufus recorded "Cry, Darling" and "Diggy Liggy Lo" in the early fifties with Jimmy C. Newman, demonstrating both his superb country and Cajun fiddling skills. One single recorded by Rufus in 1957 for Starday recalls Rufus's love for his homeland, which had incurred the wrath of Hurricane Audrey. The two tunes, "Cameron Memorial Waltz" and "Mean Audrey," bring to mind the major loss of life and the raging cyclone that devastated the Gulf Coast of Louisiana.

House band at the Silver Star, 1948: Amos Comeaux, Rufus Thibodeaux, unidentified, Tibby Edwards with guitar, others unidentified. Photo courtesy of Luderin Darbone.

His amazing versatility is apparent in that he played with both Bob Wills, in the late 1950s, and Neil Young in the mid-1980s. Rufus notes "I was living in Lake Charles and went to see him [Wills] at a club.... He hired me right there. Playing with him was a dream come true ... I played harmony and Bob played lead." Concerning his playing with Neil Young, he says, "He came to Nashville to record and Ben Keith was playing with him and we had worked the road together before.... He asked me if I wanted to do a record session and I said 'yeah. With who?' Ben replied, 'Neil Young.'" Rufus continued, "'Who's that?' That was rock and roll." He played on five of Young's albums.

When not on the road with Newman in the sixties and seventies, Rufus returned to his home and worked in clubs around Lake Charles, Lafayette, and southwest Louisiana, working with Abe and Dottie Manuel, Jo-El Sonnier, Joe Douglas, and many others. Country acts with whom he has played and recorded include Lefty Frizzell, Hank Williams Jr., Porter Wagoner, Jim Reeves, George Jones, Everly Brothers, Cal Smith, Carol Channing, Rusty Draper, and Lynn Anderson. He has also worked with many south Louisiana musicians, including Rod Bernard, Johnnie Allan, Zachary Richard, Jim Olivier, Slim Harpo, Al Terry, Tony Thibodeaux, and Rodney Miller and the Cajun Born Band. In addition, Rufus played at the 1984 World's Fair in New Orleans and was also featured on the 1984 Festival Acadien poster.

Rufus, Jimmy C. Newman, Tom T. Hall on drums, Ivy Vanicor, Hermon Lasyone, and Abe Manuel. Bamboo Club, Lake Charles, 1965. Photo courtesy of Hermon Lasyone Collection.

Rufus worked at J. D. Miller's Crowley studio in the sixties, playing various stringed instruments. Many south Louisiana records feature him playing everything from swamp pop to Cajun music and every instrument from bass guitar to fiddle. Pee Wee Whitewing, who played steel guitar with Hank Thompson in the 1950s and recorded numerous sides with Thompson, played with Rufus in the mid-1960s. He notes that Rufus would return to south Louisiana between tours with Jimmy Newman to try to earn a living. He recalls, "Rufus and I must have cut a thousand sides for J. D. Miller." Pee Wee played steel guitar on Rufus's fiddle album for Carol Rachou at La Louisianne. In 1964 and 1965 they formed a band, the Country Boys, and played on KSIG, Crowley. Other members included Al Foreman and Pee Wee Trahan.

In 1970 Rufus recorded with Newman on the first song in Cajun French to become a gold record, "Lache Pas la Patate." Rufus also recorded several solo albums on the Plantation and La Louisianne labels, *Cajun Fiddle* and *The Cajun Country Fiddle of Rufus Thibodeaux,* which are many fiddlers' favorite Cajun and swing recordings. His 1962 recording for Miller, *A Tribute to Harry Choates and His Cajun Fiddle*, is one of the most sought-after albums by Cajun fiddlers wanting to learn the many voices of the Cajun fiddle, as only Rufus could play them. Accompanying him on the landmark album were former Choates band members Abe Manuel and Carrol Broussard. Carrol comments that if you listen closely to the recording, you can hear him grunting while he played. He is also featured on *Phyddle* and *Folk Songs of the Bayou Country*. In 1998 he teamed up with longtime friend Tony Thibodeaux to record a CD titled *Rufus and Tony Thibodeaux: Fiddlin' with Friends*. It garnered numerous awards and received accolades from the Cajun French Music Association and Cajun community. This album features some of the finest vocalists in south Louisiana, including Johnnie Allan and Ivy Dugas, as well as some awesome twin fiddling as only two great talents like Tony and Rufus could play.

He wrote twelve songs, including "Forever in Your Eyes" and "Teala's Waltz," the latter named for his daughter.

He received numerous awards, including induction into the Louisiana Hall of Fame and Cajun French Music Association Hall of Fame, Fiddler of the Year from the CFMA, and the Award of Excellence at the LeCajun Festival and Awards Program in 1998.

His fiddling was a blend of Cajun, country, swing, and, as he explained it, "My own style." He even played bluegrass on a few occasions, playing with Bill Monroe and the Bluegrass Boys on the Grand Ole Opry when they needed him. Carrol Broussard played with Rufus on many of the one-night stands at local clubs when stars like Carl Smith and Jimmy C. Newman came through Lake Charles on tour. He notes, "Rufus, he could play anything. Bluegrass, country. He played with Bob Wills for a long time . . ."

Rufus is revered by fiddlers and musicians alike and has influenced the fiddling of Ken Smith, Val Lindsey, Laten Miller, Ivy Dugas, Murphy Sensat, Duffy Sensat, Jamie Bearb, Adrian Brack, Cliff Hoffpauir, Wilbert Benoit, and many others. The impact of his fiddling is heard in many country, swing and Cajun bands playing today.

Rufus passed away in August 12, 2005.

Interviews by Ron Yule: Luderin Darbone (5-10-2004 and 6-8-2004), Ivy Dugas (11-7-2003), Rufus Thibodeaux (8-27-2004), Pee Wee Whitewing (6-18-2005), and undated informal conversations with Hermon Lasyone and Gary Newman.

References

Bastin, Bruce. Liner notes. *A Tribute to Harry Choates and His Cajun Fiddle*. Flyright LP 572, 1981.

Benicewicz, Larry. "Rufus Thibodeaux: Blues Violin?" *Baltimore Blues Society Newsletter*, March 1991.

Olivier, Jim. Liner notes. *Cajun Fiddle*. La Louisianne LP 137, 1973.

Yule, Ron, et al. *Cajun French Music Association Hall of Fame, Lake Charles Chapter*. Fiddle Country Publishing, DeRidder, Louisiana, 2004.

Photo courtesy of CFMA Hall of Fame Collection, Lake Charles.

TONY THIBODEAUX

(1938–) Scott

Tony Thibodeaux, like many master fiddlers plays with a package of impeccably clean intonation drawn with an equally smooth bow, creating some of the prettiest tones heard in his Cajun/country/swing style. He has never been an out-front star per se, but has been one of the most capable sidemen in south Louisiana, both as a performer and a recording artist.

He was born on June 2, 1938, to Mary G. Thibodeaux and Nestor Thibodeaux, and the family of twelve lived south of Rayne. Nestor was a construction worker and part-time farmer who played the harmonica very well and also played "a little" accordion. In 1948 Nestor bought a fiddle with the hope that Tony's brother, Leon, would learn to play. After listening to his brother, Tony realized he liked the sound and wanted to play. He notes in a January 29, 2007, interview:

My brother drug it all over the yard. Finally one day I picked it up and dusted it, cleaned it up, and started scratchin' on it . . . it had a string missing. A friend of the family played the fiddle and he brought me a set of strings a few weeks later and strung it up for me. I'd hear mama and daddy's radio, old battery operated radio, and I'd listen to Joe Falcon and all these old timers. And I'd listen to Bob Wills, he's the one who really inspired me . . . then there was the old fiddle players from here, around Lafayette and Rayne. I started rubbin' and finally picked up a tune and took it from there.

He acknowledges that local fiddlers who influenced him were Hector Duhon, Aldus "Popeye" Broussard, and Clopha Dugas.

By 1949 Tony began playing in his first band, with David Roy on accordion and his son on guitar. Tony recalls, "Back then I couldn't afford to get my bow rehaired so my daddy would rehair my bow with sewing thread. It would last three or four jobs, that was it. Then he'd rehair it again."

Soon he began playing in a three-piece band with a Scott native, Adam Maitre, and followed that by playing with Walter Mouton on some of his early work.

In 1955 he joined Aldus Roger and the Lafayette Playboys and stayed with him for over thirteen years. At times their schedule was grueling, playing as much as seven nights a week. Tony recalls, "I was driving a concrete truck back then. I'd come home from a job at two or three in the morning, go to bed for an hour or so, get in my work clothes, and go to work. And, that went on for about a year or year and a half."

During this period, the Lafayette Playboys became household names throughout south Louisiana with their weekly appearances on Lafayette television station KLFY. Throughout his tenure, although many fiddlers went through the ranks, Louis Foreman played lead fiddle and Tony played the harmony on their breaks, while they usually "bassed" during the rest of the songs. Doc Guidry also played in this band for a while in the 1960s. Tony says he thinks three or four LPs resulted during this time with the Playboys. Tony notes, "Aldus was a good guy, but when you played with him you didn't play with anyone else. . . . It just so happens if you tuned your fiddle just before you started he'd ask you, 'Who did you play with last night?'"

By the mid-sixties Tony was becoming more popular and in demand as a sideman. He began a series of stints with many noted accordion players, sometimes playing single fiddle, but many times twin and even triple fiddles. This allowed him the opportunity to play harmony, something he loves to do.

Louisiana Ramblers: Carrol Broussard, Hilrae Mott, Ronnie Anderson, Jo-El Sonnier, Tony Thibodeaux, and Robert Bertrand. Shamrock Club, 1965. Photo courtesy of CFMA Hall of Fame Collection, Lake Charles.

His career, which has spanned over fifty years, includes playing at nearly every major festival and venue in the southern part of Louisiana.

Tony, like many other musicians, juggled his schedule to play in numerous bands. In the late 1960s he joined Belton Richard, recording three albums during this fifteen-year period. He joined his cousins, Paul Daigle and Cajun Gold and Doris Matte and the Lake Charles Ramblers, in their bands. Several LPs resulted, including at least two with Paul and Cajun Gold.

Around 1971 Jo-El Sonnier called and invited Tony to join him at a local festival where he was playing. This resulted in a six-year stint, playing mainly in the area around south Louisiana from Lake Charles to New Orleans. He had played briefly with Sonnier and Robert Bertrand in the mid-1960s on several jobs with the Louisiana Ramblers at the Shamrock in Lake Charles, but no recordings resulted with Tony playing the fiddle. In recent years, he has continued to play with Jo-El when the opportunity has arisen. Tony was also continually present in the bands of many other Cajun performers, including Rodney Miller and Vin Bruce.

Over the years one of his prime associations was with his friend Rufus Thibodeaux, a fiddling legend who played with Jimmy C. Newman, Bob Wills, Neil Young, and others for over forty years. Anytime Rufus was in the area and the opportunity was available, Tony and Rufus would join to play twin

Rufus and Tony Thibodeaux. Harry's Club, Cade, 1980. Photo courtesy of Tony Thibodeaux.

fiddles. This resulted in numerous recordings culminating in their award-winning 1997 CD, *Fiddlin' with Friends*. This classic album features many famous south Louisiana vocalists and musicians. One of the highlights of the album is a twin-fiddle rendition of the beautiful "Fiddler's Waltz," a tune Tony wrote while he was with Paul Daigle and Cajun Gold. He recalls:

> *I was playing with Paul Daigle back then at Lewisburg and Mrs. Borque's Club and my late brother, Bill Thibodeaux heard me play the tune and told me, "Why don't you make something out of it?" . . . I kept working at it and one night the bass player and I got together. He picked it up and we played it the same night. It was rough but it was there. I recorded it on one of Paul Daigle's albums.*

Currently in semi-retirement, he fronts a new band, Tony Thibodeaux and the Cajun Five, featuring Reggie Matte, David Guidry, Joe Simon, and Leon Thibodeaux. They appear at local festivals and restaurants, pleasing crowds wherever they play.

The Thibodeaux family has been blessed with several other family members who play. Joe played drums and Leon currently plays drums in the Cajun Five.

Tony's impact on younger fiddlers is a major part of his legacy. Several of his students have already affected the Cajun music scene, creating highly regarded recordings and performances. One, Travis Matte, was chosen as CFMA Fiddler of the Year in 1997, while Jamie Bearb and Travis Benoit have each been nominated for the prestigious award. Other noted students include Hunter Hayes, Arthur J. Simon, Louis Dronet, Beau Thomas, Elodie St. Martin, and Pat Savant.

With over twenty-four LP/cassette/CD projects under his belt, he is one of the most sought-after and recorded fiddlers around Lafayette. These projects encompass a long list of Hall of Fame musicians, including Aldus Roger, Belton Richard, Paul Daigle, Jo-El Sonnier, Vin Bruce, Pat Savant, Jason Frey, Johnnie Allan, and Rufus Thibodeaux, to name a few.

Not only has Tony been cited by fiddlers for his excellence, he has been honored by fans of Cajun and country music of south Louisiana and southeast Texas. A partial list of these awards includes the Texas Longhorn Club Fiddler of the Year in 1988, Fred's Lounge Wall of Fame, Cajun French Music Association Fiddler of the Year in 2002, Louisiana Hall of Fame, and he was the recipient of the Cajun French Music Association Award of Excellence in 1998. Induction into the Cajun French Music Association Hall of Fame in both Eunice and Lake Charles has been icing on the cake of a brilliant career.

Interviews by Ron Yule: Tony Thibodeaux (1-29-2007 and 2-26-2007).

Photo courtesy of Eloise Stack.

HENRY DAN WELCH

(1888–1938) Dodson

There are a large number of unique people who have played the fiddle. Many of these fiddlers were short on talent, but loved it so much that they practiced, listened, and persevered until they became decent instrumentalists. They were driven because they loved the instrument and the sounds it made. Many were natural musicians but squandered their talent by not honing their skills. And many had great talent and developed it no matter what difficulties—letting nothing stand in their way. Such a talent was Henry Dan Welch.

Dan learned the fiddle as a boy in the late 1800s and reportedly was a good fiddle player. Like most boys his age in Forest Hills, Louisiana, he loved to hunt and meander through the woods pursuing and enjoying the outdoor environment. At age eleven, his fiddling days were abruptly put on hold when he dropped his gun, and it discharged while he was crossing over Little Spring

Creek on a log. He shot his right arm off four inches below the elbow. His daughter, Eloise Stack, from Haughton, Louisiana, relates the story that Dan was not down over the loss of his arm as much as he was mad. He was determined to play again. For several years he lay the fiddle down, but of all things, his love of sugar cane would birth an idea that would bring him back into the fiddle world. After noticing the sugar cane peeling, he came upon the idea that he could tie the bow to his nub with it, and he might be able to play again. It worked, and he was back in the fiddle business. He eventually used other types of materials to attach the bow, and he never slowed down.

In fact, he never slowed down or let his one-handed status be a handicap. He worked on the railroad and eventually became a schoolteacher in several of the old one-room schoolhouses in north central Louisiana. He played baseball, shot marbles, was an artist, and rolled his cigarettes by laying the paper in the crook of his right arm. Eloise says she can remember many of the old fiddle tunes he would play. "He could play the fire out of them." He played "Soldiers Joy" and "Ole Joe Clark" plus many more tunes she cannot recall.

He was a champion fiddle player and loved to enter fiddle contests. She remembers all the red, white, and blue ribbons hanging from his fiddle when he would play. She notes, "He won nearly every parish fair in north Louisiana." She recalls his winning the Winn and LaSalle Parish Fairs, plus many more. Several newspaper articles attest to this. She also believed that he came to contests in west central Louisiana, but is not sure which parish fairs he attended.

He entered the Louisiana State Fair Contest on three occasions: 1934 and 1935 (both second place), and 1936(first place). The *Shreveport Journal* states, concerning the 1936 contest: "H. D. Welch, the bow secured to the stump of his right arm was an easy winner over opponents in the 'under 50 years' bracket of the old fiddlers event." In 1934 the *Shreveport Times* reports: "A feature of the contest was an outstanding performance by H. D. Welch, one-armed fiddler of Winnfield. Mr. Welch, besides playing his required three pieces for the contest, staged a brief one-man show before the largest audience ever assembled in this city for a similar contest."

His musical skills were not limited to the fiddle. His father took a cow horn, honed it down, and made Dan a pick with a hole in it that he tied to his nub so he could pick guitar. Eloise recalls hearing him play the "Steel Guitar Rag" and "Down Yonder" and not missing a run in either song. Many times, in the evening, he would lead the Welch family singings by leading them on guitar. He also played mandolin, bass fiddle, and piano, but his main talent lay in the fiddle.

In 1939 he was to attend a fiddle contest in Monroe, but needed to get a battery for his car. On his way to Ruston his car quit on him, and in an attempt to flag someone down a vehicle hit him. Mrs. Stack believes it was a log truck because of the massive injuries and condition of his body.

He was only fifty at the time of his death, but his determination, discipline, and love for his God-given talent will live forever in the minds of those who knew him. His life is a testament to the can-do," "where there's a will, there's a way" attitude that successful men have, making it look so easy.

Interview by Ron Yule: Eloise Welch Stack (10-21-2002).

References

Shows, Joan Weeks. "One Room Schoolhouse." *Pine Country Backroads*, May 1997.
Shreveport Journal "One-Armed Fiddler." October 25, 1934.
———. "S. R. Patterson Is Winner of Old Fiddler's Meet." October 25, 1934.
———. "Tom Sawyer Wins Fiddlers' Contest at Fair Thursday." October 25, 1935.
———. "23 Fiddlers Are Registered for Contest at Fair." October 28, 1936.
———. "One-Armed Fiddler Wins Contest at Louisiana Fair." October 30, 1936.
———. "Winners of Fiddle Contests." October 31, 1936.
Shreveport Times. "S. R. Patterson, H. C. Wilkerson, Best Fiddlers." October 26, 1934.
———. "Champion Fiddlers in Contest Thursday / Tom Sawyer Best Fiddler at Fair Here." October 25, 1935.
Winn Parish Enterprise, undated articles in possession of Eloise Stack.

Photo courtesy of Paul Woodard.

PAUL WOODARD

(1943–) Arcadia

The Woodards, who lived in the Alabama community north of Arcadia, were fiddlers at country dances of the early part of the 1900s. James and Harold, along with Payton, played at most of these house dances. Paul Woodard came from this background, having music in his blood and wanting to play. At the age of seven he took up the guitar, playing tunes like "Crying Heart Blues" and "Mockingbird Hill" with his brother Buddy. They would join their sister, Helen, and play on top of the concession stand at the Country Maid Drive-In in Arcadia. He recalls fiddlers like "Mutt" Hood playing fiddle at these shows, And says, "We'd have to climb up a ladder to get up there. We'd stand up there and play and all the cars—there'd be cars for a block it looked like. And for the applause, they'd blow their horns." He soon "moved to the big time," as he calls it, and appeared on the Hill Country Hoedown at the Dixie Theater in Ruston.

Paul describes the scene in "My First Guitar," written for the *North Louisiana Bluegrass Club Newsletter* in April 1999:

> *I'll never forget the 1st night there. I sang Red Foley's "Ole Shep" (that was Elvis' first song too). When did we part ways? The only problem with my song was that due to my playing at home, standard pitch was an unknown. Before I went on stage a nice young man from the Louisiana Hayride tuned my guitar with the staff band. I had the guitar tuned very high and got used to it that way. This guy brought the guitar down a couple of steps and when I tried to sing with it all I could do was produce a growling sound. Probably like Ole Shep himself would have sounded toward the end of the song. Many years later I was playing in a band with Ed Dettenheim from Homer. One night I learned that he was the nice young man who had tuned my guitar. I never let him live that down.*

Paul began to learn the fiddle at age twelve, from his father, Payton. By the late fifties he was playing on the Jonesboro radio station, KTOC, with Leslie Raborn as a part of the Country Raiders. Lexon Duty, Cotton Quarles, Benson Smith, Dorothy Duty, and Nettie May Cotton rounded out the band. One time they went to El Dorado, Arkansas, to play on the Big Ten Jamboree that had been started and promoted by country star Carl Belew. When Paul was about thirteen, he recalls reappearing on the Hill Country Hoedown at the Dixie Theater, in Ruston.

At the age of seventeen Paul took a job in south Louisiana, working on the pipeline with his cousin, Homer Woodard. He played honky tonks and lounges in the New Orleans area, playing at Scotty's Lounge with Jim Vanderpuddy, a.k.a. Jimmy Joy, a western-style accordion player who had been associated with Roy Rogers and Dale Robertson. By the time Paul moved to work in New Iberia, he was beginning to pick up the Cajun style of music. Their final job was in Singer where Paul played very little music.

After returning to north Louisiana, he learned to butcher, a trade not conducive to a fiddler's fingers. During this period, he began to play on another local country show, the Homer Hayride, and began an association with fiddler Fred Beavers, whom Paul lured back into the music business. On the Homer Hayride he played with Dub Thomas, Louie Gant, Fred Beavers, Eugene Kendrick, and Ed Dettenheim. He also jammed with another group south of Arcadia that included Byron "Bun" Hiser, a member of Foster Taylor's Louisiana Melodymakers who had recorded in Memphis in 1929. "Bun" played

Amanda Dark, Don Belton, Paul Woodard, Leslie Raborn, Fred Beavers, and Sam Raborn. Rebel State Park, 1999. Photo courtesy of Susan Roach.

a "The Gibson" mandola, Allen Caskey and Paul were on fiddles, and Doug Stone was on electric guitar.

He continued to play with Beavers, and in 1966 began attending Louisiana Tech to pursue a degree in music with a specialty in violin. Paul had played the fiddle by ear until this time and knew he needed to learn to read music. He notes, "If they'd sing it to me I could play it, but I couldn't read the music." To prepare for his studies he took violin lessons from Hugh Price, a classical guitarist, in Haynesville. Although Hugh and his family were country guitar pickers, he had majored in guitar at the Sherwood School of Music in Chicago. After getting off work every Wednesday night at the Log Cabin Grocery in Ruston, he would drive to Haynesville for his lesson. By the time he started his studies at Louisiana Tech, he was already reading music.

While at Louisiana Tech, he was concertmaster of the Ruston Civic Symphony Orchestra and played in the Monroe Symphony Orchestra and the South Arkansas Symphony Orchestra. (He presently plays in the Monroe Symphony Orchestra.) In the late 1960s he played on the Twin Cities Jamboree, a regional country show based in Monroe.

Paul entered several fiddle contests, and recalls one he attended with Penton Thornton and Virgil Smith in Dubach. Hiter Colvin, who had re-

Bill Kirkpatrick and Paul Woodard. Louisiana State Championship, NSU Folklife Festival, 2004. Photo courtesy of Peter Jones.

corded six sides for Victor in 1929, was the local favorite and favored to win. He recalls winning second place with Hiter in third and not happy with the results.

After graduation he taught strings in various public school programs, and in 1979 became the band director at Ruston High School. He seldom played the fiddle during this time, but he did judge and attend a few contests. He recalls entering a contest in Columbia, as a part of an art show. "It was the first one they ever had down there. I won it . . . The way I won it was old Elmus [Brandin] or Ray Beebe, one was playing and they had a parade goin' on up the street and these muzzle loaders were on this flat bed truck and got right behind the stand when Elmus, it was Elmus or Ray Beebe, was playing. . . . When they shot those things he started turning around real slow and he lost. He got so mixed up he didn't know where he was."

During his days as a teacher he played fiddle very little, because directing the band left him no time for fiddling except for an occasional gig. He recalls playing on a show with Troy DeRamus and the North Louisiana Stringband at Ruston High School in the early 1980s. In the mid-1980s, he played with Don Belton and the Piney Hills Swing Band as well as other local groups. Members included Tom Head (keyboard), Don (guitar), Larry Stanley (electric bass), and Paul (fiddle).

After retiring from the public school system in 1989, he began to tune and repair pianos in north Louisiana and continued to play music with a few groups, including Don Belton, Fred Beaver's Grey Eagle Fiddle Band, and Homer Bailes. He has played at numerous festivals including the NSU/Natchitoches Folklife Festival, the Red River Revel, and the Louisiana Folklife Festival in Monroe. He is adept at the country, breakdown, and swing styles of fiddling, and is currently one of the top waltz players in the state of Louisiana. Fred Beavers recently remarked that Paul was one of the best harmony players he had ever played with in north Louisiana.

He has entered numerous contests, winning and placing in the Louisiana State Fair and Monroe events. In 1997, he was the Louisiana State Division III Champion and in 2004, he won 2nd place in the Open Division in the Louisiana State Fiddle Contest at the NSU/Natchitoches Folklife Festival.

Paul continues to fiddle with various groups, usually informally, and plays every Sunday at the Antioch Methodist Church near Simsboro, playing old hymns accompanied by piano and guitar.

Interviews by Ron Yule: Fred Beavers (undated informal conversation) and Paul Woodard (6-12-2005 and 7-28-2008).

Reference

Woodard, Paul. "My First Guitar." *North Louisiana Bluegrass Club Newsletter*, April 1999.

REFERENCES

AF Plant 66 Newsletter. "From Folk Tunes to Rockets." Thiokol Chemical Company, 1957.

Allan, Johnnie. *Memories, Volumes I and II*. Johnnie Allan Publishing, Lafayette, Louisiana, 1995.

Alexandria Town Talk. Alexandria, Louisiana, selected articles.

Ancelet, Barry. "Dewey Balfa: A Cultural Ambassador." *Accordions, Fiddles, Two-Step, and Swing*. Ryan A. Brasseaux and Kevin S. Fontenot, editors. Center for Louisiana Studies, Lafayette, 2006.

———. "The Cajun Music Festival: Genesis and Legacy." *Accordions, Fiddles, Two-Step, and Swing: A Cajun Reader*. Ryan A Brasseaux and Kevin S. Fontenot, editors. Center for Louisiana Studies, Lafayette, 2006.

———. *Cajun Music: Its Origins and Development*. The Center For Louisiana Studies, Lafayette, 1989.

Ancelet, Barry, and Elemore Morgan Jr. *The Makers of Cajun Music*. University of Texas Press, Austin, 1984.

Ancelet, Barry, Jay D. Edwards, and Glen Pitre. *Cajun Country*. University Press of Mississippi, Jackson, 1991.

Ancelet, Barry, Michael Doucet, and David Greely. Liner notes. *Louisiana Folk Masters: Varise Conner*. Louisiana Crossroads Records, Lafayette, 2004.

———. *Fiddlin' Cajun*. La Louisianne LL-142, ca. 1977.

Bastin, Bruce. Liner notes. *A Tribute to Harry Choates and His Cajun Fiddle*. Flyright LP 572, 1981.

Beauregard Daily News. DeRidder, Louisiana, selected articles.

Benicewicz, Larry. "Rufus Thibodeaux: Blues Violin?" *Baltimore Blues Society Newsletter*, March 1991.

Bernard, Shane K. Interview of Doc Guidry, February 11, 1991. Tape in possession of Oran Guidry Jr.

Binge, Dagmar Anita. *The Shelton Brothers, Down on the Farm*. Liner notes, Cattle Compact CCD 241, 2001.

———. Liner notes. *The Shelton Brothers, Joe and Bob*. Cattle Compact CCD 258, 2002.

Boyd, Jean A. *The Jazz of the Southwest: An Oral History of Western Swing*. University of Texas Press, Austin, 1998.

Bradshaw, Jim. "Canray Learned from His Father." *Daily Advertiser*, December 29, 1998.

Brasseaux, Ryan. *Bayou Boogie: The Americanization of Cajun Music*. Thesis, Louisiana State University, Baton Rouge, 2004.

Brasseaux, Ryan A., and Kevin S. Fontenot, editors. *Accordions, Fiddles, Two-Step and Swing: A Cajun Reader*. Center for Louisiana Studies, Lafayette, 2006.

Broussard, Alton. "Skilled Hand Carves Violin from Native Wood." *Advertiser,* Lafayette, Louisiana, March 11, 1973.

Brown, Andrew. "Devil in the Bayou" (liner notes). Bear Family CD, BCD 16355 BH, 2002.

———. E-mails dated August 4, 2008, and August 6, 2008, about Lonnie Hall's recordings.

———. E-mail dated August 5, 2008, re: Henderson recordings with Lefty Frizzell and private recordings on the Louisiana label.

———. E-mail dated September 21, 2008, re: history of Oklahoma Tornadoes and Floyd Leblanc's recordings.

Broven, John. *South to Louisiana*. Pelican Publishing Company, Gretna, Louisiana, 1983.

Burge, Bill. E-mail dated October 10, 2005, re: certain generations.

Burman-Hall, Linda. *Southern American Folk Fiddling: Contest and Style*. Dissertation, Princeton University, Princeton, New Jersey, 1974.

Burton, Larry. "Fiddlin' Around, Shreveport." *Times*, Shreveport, Louisiana, 1991.

Busbice, Wayne F., and Patricia Busbice. *Uncovering the Secrets of a Southern Family.* Author-House, Bloomington, Indiana, 2007.

Caddo Citizen. "Harkness Inducted Into Hall of Fame." May 29, 2003.

City Directory, Shreveport, Louisiana. Selected years. R. L. Polk and Company Dallas, Texas.

Coffey, Kevin. Liner notes. *Leon Chappel, Automatic Mama*. Bear Family Records, 16254AH, 1999.

Colvin, Ethel, and Baker Colvin. *Colvin and Allied Families*. Hurley Printing, 1965.

Corrigan, Candace. Interview with Gatemouth Brown on *The Nashville Nobody Knows*, June 12, 2005.

Crowley Signal. "Angelas Lejeune Wins Accordion Contest." October 1, 1929.

Daigle, Pierre. *Love, Tears, and Laughter: The Story of the Acadians*. Acadian Publishing, Church Point, Louisiana, 1972.

Darby, Joe. "Leo Soileau Remembers Little Boy Who Snuck His Papa's Fiddle." *Times-Picayune*, August 25, 1975.

DeRamus, Troy. *Louisiana I Love*. Unpublished account in possession of author, 2004.

DeRidder Enterprise. DeRidder, Louisiana, selected articles.

Devil's Box, The. Steve Davis, editor, Madison, Alabama, and Columbia, Missouri, selected articles.

Dobber Johnson—Hayride Fiddler. LP liner notes, ca. 1990.

Doucet, Michael. Canray Fontenot eulogy. Unpublished.

———. Liner notes. *Louisiana Hot Sauce, Creole Style*. Arhoolie CD 381, 1992.

Doucet, Sharon Arms. "If You Remember My Song You'll Remember Me." *Fiddler Magazine*, Fall 1995.

Ferbrache, Lyle. "History of the Pine Grove Boys." Unpublished manuscript in possession of author, 2007.

———. "Musical 4 + 1." *Blues and Rhythm* 206 (February 2006).

Fontenot, Kevin S. "Cajun Musician, Cajun Mystic: The Improbable Legacy of Moise Robin." Annual address presented to Phi Alpha Theta, Lafayette, Louisiana, May 2005.

Forrester, H. H., Jr. *Bluegrass Music and Feliciana Grass*. Unpublished work in possession of Jim Rushing.

Fox, Nikolai. *Music in the Sky.* DVD, 60 minutes. Vermont Music and Library Shop, 2008.

Francois, Raymond E. *Ye Yaille Chere.* Swallow Publications, Ville Platte, Louisiana, 2000.

Franks, Tillman. *I Was There When It Happened.* Sweet Dreams Publishing, Many, Louisiana, 2000.

Gardner, Charles. "The Origins of the Texas Style of Traditional Old-Time Fiddling." *2001: A Texas Folklore Odyssey.* F. E. Abernethy, editor. University of North Texas Press, Denton, 2001.

Gardner, Joel R. *Folklife in the Florida Parishes: Introduction.* Louisiana Division of the Arts, Baton Rouge, 1989.

Gentry, Robert. *The Louisiana Hayride, Volumes I and II.* Robert Gentry, Many, Louisiana, 1998.

Gimble, Johnny, and Paul F. Wells. "Texas Fiddling and Texas Fiddlers: A Short History" (liner notes). *The Texas Fiddle Collection*, CMH-LP 9027, 1981.

Ginell, Cary. Liner notes. *Leon Chappelear: Western Swing Chronicles, Volume 2.* Origin Jazz Library, OJL-1001, 2002.

Gonzalez Weekly. "A Tribute to Robert E. 'Bob' Henderson." Gonzalez, Louisiana, November 1, 1996.

Grisham, Dinah. "Mary Grimsley's Students Love Fiddling Around." *Shreveport Journal*, June 9, 1984.

Gruhn, George. "An Interview with Kennie Lamb." *Bluegrass Unlimited*, April 1989.

Hartford, John. "Indian War Whoop." Tune transcription. *The Devil's Box*, 25, no. 4 (Winter 1991).

Hatley, Don. "Two Notes Higher Than a Gin Whistle: The Sound of the Louisiana Hayride." Louisiana Folklife Archives, Northwestern State University, Natchitoches, July 1, 1981.

Haynesville News, Haynesville, Louisiana, selected articles.

Hevey, Kimberly. "The Music Box Legacy." *Advocate*, Baton Rouge, Louisiana, January 10, 1997.

Humphrey, Mark. "Doug Kershaw." *Frets Magazine* vol. 3, no. 10 (October 1981).

Kershaw, Doug. *Cajun Sweet Home Louisiana.* International Music Series, CD, 2001.

———. *Louisiana Man: The Doug Kershaw Songbook.* Collier Books, New York, 1971.

Kitsinger, Otto, and Richard Weize. Liner notes and discography. *Webb Pierce, The Wondering Boy (1951–1958).* Bear Family Records, 1990.

Knight, Tim. Interview with Dewey Balfa. July 18, 1980, Port Neches, Texas.

———. Liner notes. *Harry Choates: His Original Recordings, 1946–1949.* Arhoolie Records 5027, 1982.

Lafayette Daily Advertiser. Lafayette, Louisiana, selected articles.

Laird, Tracey E. W. *Shreveport's KWKH: A City and Its Radio Station in the Evolution of Country Music and Rock-and-Roll.* Dissertation, University of Michigan, Ann Arbor, 2000.

———. *Louisiana Hayride: Radio and Roots Music Along the Red River.* Oxford University Press, New York, 2005.

———. "Country Chameleons: Cajuns on the Louisiana Hayride." www.louisianafolklife.org.

Lake Arthur News. "Mr. And Mrs. Euzebe Trahan Celebrate Their Sixtieth Wedding Anniversary." Lake Arthur, Louisiana, May 4, 1934.

Lake Charles American Press. Lake Charles, Louisiana, selected articles.

Leesville Leader, Leesville, Louisiana, selected articles..

Life Tabernacle Newsletter. "Popular Musician Won to Christ." November 1957.

Louisiana State Archives. Death Certificate of John W. Daniel. December 11, 1931.

Luster, Mike. "Remembering Hiter Colvin, the Fiddle King of Oilfield and Gumstump." *Shreveport Sounds in Black and White*. Kip Lornell and Tracey E. W. Laird, editors. University Press of Mississippi, Jackson, 2007.

Macon Telegraph. "Mercer Brothers Passed Up Chance at the Big Time." Undated article in possession of Jean Strickland.

Maples, Ernie. Liner notes. *Travelin On, Jewel Lasyone*. Southern Star Records, SS337, 1982.

Martin, Shawn. "Ken Smith." *Lake Charles American Press*, Lake Charles Louisiana, May 21, 1993.

———. "Canray Fontenot." *Lake Charles American Press*, Lake Charles, Louisiana, July 30, 1995.

Merchant, Brenda. "Ralph Richardson." *Lake Charles American Press*, Lake Charles, Louisiana, September 23, 2001.

Muleskinner News. Special edition, Elon College, North Carolina, 1975.

Nation, Chuck. Liner notes. *One Man Band*. Murrayville, Georgia, 2006.

Nation, Jim. *A History of the Louisiana Bluegrass Association*. Unpublished manuscript in possession of the author, 1987.

Nelson, Donald Lee. "Mama Where You At? The Chronicle of Maius Lafleur." *JEMF Quarterly* XIX (Summer 1983).

Olivier, Jim. Liner notes. *Cajun Fiddle*. La Louisianne LP137, 1973.

O'Neal, Donna. "Tex Grimsley and Friends—Let's Saw a Spell." *Shreveport Journal*, October 16, 1981.

Pick and Bow, the Newsletter of the Southeast Texas Bluegrass Music Association. Edited by Edy Mathews. Beaumont, Texas.

Pierce, Webb. Letter from Webb Pierce to Tex Grimsley dated October 10, 1952. Louisiana Folklife Center Archives, Northwestern State University, Natchitoches, Louisiana.

Pilione, Tina. E-mail, March 1, 2007, re: Wade Frugé.

Pittman, Nick. "Remembering the Balfa Brothers." *Times of Acadiana*, Lafayette, Louisiana, April 18, 2006.

Post, Lauren. Liner notes. *Joe Falcon: Cajun Pioneer*. Arhoolie CD 459, 1997.

Prime, John Andrew. "Hayride Alumni Gather for Taping." *Times*, Shreveport, Louisiana, April 7, 1984.

———. "Hayride Veterans Lead Hometown Delegation to D.C." *Shreveport Times*, Shreveport, Louisiana, June 23, 1985.

Ray, Gayleen. "Dennis McGee, Dean of Cajun Music." *Daily Reveille*, Baton Rouge, Louisiana, February 12, 1987.

Roach, Susan. Liner notes. *The North Louisiana Stringband*. LP 37882. Louisiana Folklife Center, Northwestern University, Natchitoches, 1981.

Russell, Tony. *Country Music Records: A Discography, 1921–1942*. Oxford University Press, New York, 2004.

———. "Leo Soileau." *Old Time Music* 27.

Sabine Index. Many, Louisiana, selected articles.

Savoy, Ann Allen. *Cajun Music: A Reflection of a People, Vol. I*. Bluebird Press, Eunice, Louisiana, 1984.

———. Liner notes. *The Savoy-Doucet Cajun Band: Home Music With Spirits.* Arhoolie CD 389, 1992.

———. Liner notes. *The Complete Early Recordings of Dennis McGee: 1929–1930.* Yazoo 2012, 1994.

———. Liner notes. *Wallace "Cheese" Read: Cajun House Party.* Arhoolie LP 5021, 1979.

———. Liner notes. *Wade Frugé: Old Style Cajun Fiddler.* Arhoolie CD 476, 1998.

Schwarz, Tracy. Liner notes. *Cajun Legend Dewey and Friends.* Swallow Records, 1986.

Seelinger, Terry A. "Don't Give Up Your Day Job: Country Music." *Folklife in the Florida Parishes.* Louisiana Division of the Arts, 1989.

Shows, Joan Weeks. *Pine Country Backroads,* May 1997.

Shreveport, Louisiana, City Directory, 1925. R. L. Polk and Company, Dallas, Texas.

Shreveport Times. Shreveport, Louisiana, selected articles.

Shreveport Journal. Shreveport, Louisiana, selected articles.

Simmons, Michael. "Michael Doucet: A Fiddler's Education." *Fiddler Magazine* 8, no. 1 (Spring 2001).

———. "Michael Doucet On Beausoleil." *Fiddler Magazine* 8, no. 1 (Spring 2001).

———. "Doug Kershaw: The Real Deal in Cajun Fiddle." *Fiddler Magazine* 10, no. 10 (Spring 2003).

Smith, Christine. "Fiddlin' Champ." *Shreveport Times,* July 20, 1979.

Southwest Louisiana Fiddle and Bluegrass Club Newsletter. Ron and Georgia Yule, editors. DeRidder, Louisiana, 1975–76.

Strachwitz, Chris. Producer notes. *Wallace "Cheese" Read: Cajun House Party.* Arhoolie CD 414, 1994.

———. Liner notes. *Joe Falcon: Cajun Pioneer.* Arhoolie CD 459, 1997.

Strickland, Rhonda. "Buzz Busby: A Lonesome Road." *Bluegrass Unlimited,* November 1986.

Sweetman, Ron. "Recording Activity in New Orleans in the 1920s." www.bluesworld.com/NODiscog.html.

Tarleton, Sam. Papers, McNeese State University Archives, McNeese State Library, Lake Charles, Louisiana.

Thompson, Luke. *50 Years of Bluegrass Music with Luke Thompson and the Green Valley Cutups.* CD, Luke Thompson, Baton Rouge, Louisiana, 2004.

Tucker, Stephen R. *Louisiana Saturday Night: The History of Louisiana Country Music.* Dissertation, Tulane University, New Orleans, Louisiana, 1995.

Uhr, Tom. Liner notes. *Jewel Lasyone: Cajun Grass.* Southern Star Records, SS-3361980, 1980.

United States Census Records. Alexandria Historical Library, Alexandria, Louisiana.

Weill, Gus. Interview with Gatemouth Brown on *Louisiana Legends.* PBS, 2000.

Wenberg, Thomas. *The Violin Makers of the United States.* Mt. Hood Publishing, Mt. Hood, Oregon, 1986.

Whipple, Dan. *Daily New Journal,* Murfreesboro, Tennessee. Undated article in possession of Dorothy Manuel.

Willey, Robert. Transcript of interview with Michael Doucet. Music Industry Lecture Series, September 25, 2002.

Wilson, Joe. Liner notes. *Masters of the Folk Violin.* Arhoolie CD 434, 1995.

Windham, Ellis. Liner notes. *Hey Diddle Diddle the Cat and the Fiddle.* Winner LP 103, 1982.

Winn Parish Enterprise. "Storytelling, Fiddle Playing See First Time Appearance." Winnfield, Louisiana, April 28, 1999.

Wolfe, Charles K. *The Devil's Box: Masters of Southern Fiddling*. The Country Music Foundation Press and Vanderbilt University Press, Nashville and London, 1997.

Woodard, Paul. "My First Guitar." *North Louisiana Bluegrass Club Newsletter*, April 1999.

Yule, Ron. *Iry Lejeune: Wailin' the Blues Cajun Style*. Fiddle Country Publishing, DeRidder, Louisiana, 2006.

———. *My Fiddlin' Grounds*. Center for Louisiana Studies, University of Louisiana Lafayette, 2007.

———. "Robert Bertrand, Louisiana Rambler." Unpublished article and discography.

———. *When the Fiddle Was King*. Fiddle Country Publishing, DeRidder, Louisiana, 2006.

———. "The Louisiana State Championship—1974." *Louisiana Folklife*, Louisiana Folklife Center, Natchitoches, Louisiana, Volumes 26–27.

Yule, Ron, and Georgia Yule. *Southwest Louisiana Fiddlers and Bluegrass Club Newsletters*. DeRidder, Louisiana, 1974–77.

———, et al. Cajun French Music Association Hall of Fame (Lake Charles Chapter) Biographies. Fiddle Country Publishing, DeRidder, Louisiana, 2004.

INDEX